BUT MOST OF ALL, I REMEMBER THE LONG ROAD TO TOWN, OF WHICH THERE WERE TWO. AND DECIDING WHI_____ TRAVEL HOME, FOR BOTH WERE OF EQUAL D_____ ONE CONTAINING MORE LAND, THE OTHER, MORE _____.

AND SEEING AS WE HAD THE OLD CHEVY WAGON, THAT ALWAYS STUCK IN 2ND GEAR, IF YOU WERE NOT CAUTIOUS, WE WERE BEST TO AVOID DOWNSHIFTING AT ALL, AND TOOK THE LONG ROAD.

IT WAS WINTER AND EVENING AT FIVE. A NAVY BLUE SKY, AND THE WHITE OF THAT SNOW, BRILLIANT AND ABUNDANT THAT YEAR, LINING THE LAND, DEFINING ITS SHAPE, LIGHT BOUNCING OFF THE SNOW, AND DRIFTS BLOWN ACROSS THE ROAD.

WE REACHED FOR THE SMALL TRANSISTOR FROM BENEATH THE SEAT, (PAST THE BLUEBERRY BARRENS, ALL THAT VAST SPACE)..., **AND TURNED TO HEAR YOU.**

FIRST THAT THEME SONG THAT RANG IN ITS VOLUME OVER THE LOUD, CLANKING ENGINE, THEN THE VOICES:

Hello, I'M SUSAN STAMBURG, AND I'M BOB EDWARDS WITH "All THINGS CONSIDERED."

AND IT WAS NOT TEN, BUT TWO, Almost 3 YEARS AGO. NO SPECIFIC REPORTS, EVENTS, JUST THE STILL AND WINTER OF THAT NIGHT, AND THOSE VOICES, TAKING US HOME.

DIANNE BALLON. STOCKTON SPRINGS, MAINE.

HAPPY BIRTHDAY "All THINGS CONSIDERED."
(It's NOT THAT I COULDN'T THINK OF ANY "MEMORABLE REPORTS," It's JUST THAT <u>THIS</u> KEPT COMING BACK TO ME...)

EVERY NIGHT AT FIVE

Susan Stamberg's All Things Considered Book

with a foreword by Charles Kuralt

Pantheon, New York

Library of Congress Cataloging in Publication Data
Main entry under title:

Every night at five.

A collection of the best of ten years' worth of transcripts from the radio program, All things considered.

Contents: A day in the life of All things considered / Susan Stamberg—Listening for America—Telling the news—[etc.]

I. Stamberg, Susan, 1938–   . II. All things considered (Radio program)
AC5.E78   081   81–18861
ISBN 0-394-70652-8

Manufactured in the United States of America

First Edition

Cover and Part Title Photographs by Edward Rysinski

Design by Stephanie Tevonian of Works

Illustration Credits

Michael Alexander: p. 211. Copyright © Michael Alexander, 1981. Stan Barouh: pp. 3, 6, 11, 14, 86 (top left), 87 (top left, top right), 187. Katherine Bouton: p. 194. Dennis Brack: p. 8 (center). Tom Dodge: pp. 125, 126. Metropolitan Edison Company: pp. 93, 94, 95, 96. Courtesy of Janet Murrow, CBS: p. 88. Paul Ollswang: pp. 46, 47, 123, 124. Copyright © Paul Ollswang, October, 1981. Cornelia Piper: p. 2. D. Stevens: p. 86 (top right). T. Swayze: pp. 13, 15, 108, 109, 110, 179. Courtesy of the Thomas Merton Studies Center, Bellarmine College: p. 159. Vietor: p. 53. Copyright © 1978 The New Yorker Magazine, Inc. Manoli Wetherell: p. 57. Leroy Woodson: pp. 8 (bottom), 86 (top center, bottom center, bottom right), 87 (top center).

For my family.

For our listeners.

For Bill Siemering.

CONTENTS

SOME PRELIMINARIES AND ACKNOWLEDGMENTS

This book began with a carton of letters. For *All Things Considered's* tenth birthday in 1981, I asked listeners and the staff of National Public Radio and its member stations to send me lists of favorite pieces they'd heard over the years. Those collective memories shape this book. Just as the staff and listeners have helped make the radio program, so too have they helped put the program in print.

The book is a handful of minutes from thousands of hours of broadcasts. The pieces leap over years and events. No attempt has been made to create a history or chronology. There are major omissions. *All Things Considered* is a news program (with daily emphasis on political and foreign affairs), yet you'll find few straight news reports here. They date quickly, as good reporting must.

This is a chance to read radio. All of the pieces have been edited for print. But converting radio into print has its limitations. You lose the laughs, for one thing. And there have been lots of them. You lose the silences, too—the long, revealing pauses for thought or mutual understanding or embarrassment that build tension against the expectation of constant sound. The music of the voices can't be read, nor the music of bands, kazoos, synthesizers. By definition, the purest radio pieces don't translate into type. But you can tune in every night to hear them.

Because this book grows from a radio program, many radio people must be thanked. The first is Bill Siemering, who conceived *All Things Considered*.

I came to National Public Radio a month before *All Things Considered* went on the air. The studios were still being built, the offices makeshift, with few desks or chairs. Each day we would sit on the floor and listen to tapes. Bill told us what to listen for—where the tapes were effective, where they were stentorian or dull. He taught us to listen, so we could speak.

Hundreds have worked for *All Things Considered,* at National Public Radio, member stations, and at the Corporation for Public Broadcasting. Many of their names and contributions appear on these pages. Others who played key roles in the life of the program: Don Quayle, Cleve Mathews, Jim Russell. Jack Mitchell, our first producer, gave us the structure and format we follow today. Jack is also the one who decided *All Things Considered* should have co-hosts—a man and a woman—and that I should be the woman.

National Public Radio and its president, Frank Mankiewicz, supported the idea of this book and gave me the seven months to write it. Frank also smiled the right way in the halls, on days when the task seemed impossible.

Felicity Swayze smiled from the desk near my office. A tireless editorial assistant and researcher, she checked facts and remained a friend.

Very little of what appears here was ever committed to a page until my indefatigable typist, Joanne Kent, transcribed it from tapes. We did what we could to check spellings for hundreds of names, but some were uncheckable—people have moved, disappeared, or unplugged their phones. Their names are spelled according to our ears' best guess. Any other mistakes are the work of gremlins.

Valuable help for the book also came from Leonor Chaves, Anne and Sam Rosenfeld, Robert Siegel, Jay Kernis, Steven Reiner, Stephanie Tevonian, Sally Janin,

Lorraine Alexander Veach, Tom Dunne, Marc Rosenbaum, Bob and Sharon Edwards, and Larry Massett, who actually enjoys reading fifteen versions of the same paragraph.

My editor, Sara Bershtel, a true collaborator, is a similarly avid reader, wise in her judgments, supportive and organized.

My husband, Louis, and our son, Joshua, made room for the eternal presence of a book at our dining table, just as they have, for so many years, generously set an extra place for the program.

And Diana Michaelis got me into radio. I wanted to say that. And thank her.

*Susan Steinberg
Washington, D.C.
June, 1981*

FOREWORD

by Charles Kuralt

Day in and day out, *All Things Considered* is the most interesting program on the air. Notice I didn't say on the radio. *All Things Considered* beats anything else on radio, television, shortwave, CB, or ship-to-shore.

I can't remember exactly when I discovered this wonderful program, but it must have been pretty soon after it went on the air in 1971. I had a traveling job at the time. A camera crew—Izzy, Larry, and Charlie—and I drove around the country in an old bus, and as we drove we'd listen to the radio. The ignition system of the bus was faulty and made the AM radio buzz loudly, and we could never fix it, so it was always FM we listened to. There is plenty of good music on FM but not much good talk. We used to take what we could get on the radio until late afternoon, and then we'd turn the dial minutely, looking for *All Things Considered*. When we found it, we knew we were in for a rich hour and a half. There would be a story about what was really going on in the Senate Foreign Relations Committee, and then an interview with a bagel baker. Izzy and Larry and Charlie and I were informed and amused by this program, and, being more or less in the same line of work, we admired it. We made it a habit.

One time, we were driving along in the hills above the Shenandoah Valley listening to somebody explain Lebanon on *All Things Considered*. It was raining, I remember that, and we still had a long way to go before we could have our supper, and so we stopped outside Clifton Forge, Virginia, and I ducked into a gas station/country store to buy some cheese and apples to tide us over. The man who ran the store and his teenaged daughter were sitting in there in rocking chairs listening to a radio on the shelf. They were listening to *All Things Considered*, too, hearing all about Lebanon while the rain fell on the tin roof of their store on a back road in the Appalachian Mountains. After I had picked out my cheese and apples, the man got up to take my money and then went back to rocking and listening. I had the impression that this man and his daughter made a habit of listening to *All Things Considered* together in the afternoon, just as Izzy and Larry and Charlie and I always did.

It started me thinking about all the people listening every day to *All Things Considered*, in buses wandering down back roads, in country stores in Virginia, in California sports cars and New Mexico bunkhouses, and in the cuddy cabins of lobster boats off the coast of Maine—so many Americans who otherwise have so little in common sharing this one experience.

This struck me then, and strikes me now, as very fine. *All Things Considered*, while it doesn't really consider *all* things, comes a lot closer to it than most newspapers, and goes deeper than the popular magazines, and covers more ground than the television news programs. These ninety minutes every day are curious and thoughtful and humane, and link up people in Clifton Forge and San Bernardino and Portales and Presque Isle, telling them things about one another.

E.B. White said good writing elevates people and bad writing depresses them. This is probably one of the reasons I find *All Things Considered* so elevating. Its words are well chosen and the voices that speak them are calm. The program has an air of reason and good humor about it, and hopefulness. It's obvious that it is not put together by jaded old geezers looking backward at humanity's wrecks and disasters, but by energetic young men and women looking ahead. I bet that man and his daughter in the store where I bought the cheese and apples listen to *All Things Considered* not only because it informs them but also because it makes them feel better. It makes me feel better, too.

It makes me feel better about the world by confirming, from time to time, that there is cause for cautious optimism or even for celebration. It also makes me feel better about this craft of broadcast journalism. The big commercial networks, with their much greater resources, could have put together a daily news program with the length and scope and intelligence of *All Things Considered*—but it took National Public Radio to go ahead and do it. *All Things Considered* will serve as a standard, now, for news on the air. It has demonstrated that news programs don't have to be short and shallow. They can be long and deep, and as nourishing as apples and cheese.

EVERY NIGHT AT FIVE

A Day In the Life

10:00

MORNING MEETING

ALL THINGS CONSIDERED

CUTAWAY

"Did it land yet?"

It's two in the afternoon, and I am making my daily joke. No one ever laughs. They're right. It's not much of a joke. I'm simply trying to break the tension. Two o'clock is the most difficult hour of the day.

The staff is clustered in the middle of the room, staring at the wall. To me, it always looks like that scene in *Close Encounters of the Third Kind*—where everyone crowds around, waiting for the spaceship to land.

In our case, the spaceship is *All Things Considered*. The program will go on the radio at five o'clock. But first it has to materialize, at two, on a huge, wall-mounted board.

"What's the lead?"

"Taxes. Wertheimer's piece."

"How long?"

"Don't know. We'll see what comes out of the news conference."

"Well, let's figure three."

That's three out of ninety minutes. It's a start. Now we just have to figure out where to put everything else. On a typical day: reports from Lebanon, Poland, the BBC, Capitol Hill, Iowa, Oregon; an essay on the demise of *Harper's* magazine; notes on what to do with tobacco when you've quit smoking ("spread it around the floor instead of shag carpeting"); interviews with novelist John Irving and a woman who makes magic wands; and maybe, for the grand finale, a profile of bluegrass superstar Ricky Skaggs. For all this to happen every night at five, a number of encounters take place throughout the day.

The most decisive is at two o'clock, when everyone gathers around the big board, staring. Closest to the board stands the producer, stubby felt marker in hand.

Road-map meeting

With that marker, he outlines the "road map" of the evening's program—the order in which pieces will be broadcast. Some landmarks never change. My co-host and I will introduce *All Things Considered*. First comes the bouncy, electronic opening theme, followed by the billboards (our highlights of what's coming up) and a short newscast. The program is divided into three half-hour segments. Each will begin with a "hard" news story and get progressively softer. But everything else is up for grabs. If it were simply up to the producer and his marker, mapping out the program would take about fifteen minutes. Instead, it takes an hour, sometimes longer. Everybody gets into the act. It's a time of fierce lobbying.

"Where's Johannesburg?" That's foreign affairs editor Marc Rosenbaum. He's not talking geography. He's talking placement. He has a piece on Afrikaner liberals, just in from a freelance reporter in South Africa. He doesn't see it on the road map.

"It's too long. It won't fit. I'm holding it for tomorrow." That's the producer. Maury Schlesinger. He's just decided that several million listeners won't hear about South Africa tonight. A lot has happened in the world today, and the producer has to balance today's news with the more reflective pieces. The South Africa report is a background piece. It can be held for a day when the news runs more slowly.

Maury at Road map

"But if you hold it, that means my interview with the South African editor won't go tonight. Then I only have one piece on the program." That's Sanford Ungar, my co-host. We hosts are continually reminding the producer that we do more than introduce other people's stories. We have stories of our own that need to get on.

"Listen, what about the White House briefing?"

"We have to get the Supreme Court story in."

"Don't forget the sidebar on taxes. Remember? We talked about it at the morning meeting?"

"Oh, god." That's the producer. Maury Schlesinger.

We're fighting for time, you see. There are only ninety minutes. Today there are more items than can possibly fit. Tomorrow, we'll scrounge to fill the hour and a half.

"Eight isn't enough for Molpus. He's been working on that Klan piece for weeks. It's full of sound, terrific actuality. His writing is good. We've been cutting it all day and can't get it in under ten." That's Steven Reiner, the senior editor. He supervises the nineteen reporters in Washington and at NPR bureaus in New York, Chicago, and London, assigns them to stories, edits their work, and argues for them at two o'clock.

"Oh, god." That's the producer. Maury Schlesinger.

GLOSSARY

...because every book should have one

NPR *National Public Radio. A network of some 260 non-commercial, mostly FM, radio stations.*

ATC *All Things Considered. A radio program (ninety minutes on weekdays, sixty minutes on weekends), broadcast from Washington, D.C., every night at five, Eastern time. George Geesey, NPR's first operations manager, came up with the program's title.*

NBC *Another network, not mentioned in this book.*

Nipper *A loving way to refer to NPR. "The Nipper" refers to times, at the end of each half hour of ATC, when the host says, "This is NPR, National Public Radio."*

Nipper net *See above. "Net" is short for network.*

Dinks *A non-technical term, referring to the short electronic beeps (or bleeps) that announce the opening of ATC and also signal the end of the ATC newscasts.*

Fade *A technical term, referring to a gradual change in the volume of sound, e.g., "Fade the dinks."*

Voice-over *Another technical term, referring to the superimposing of a narrator's voice over background sound. If you fade the dinks for the host Nipper, that's a voice-over.*

"Where's Buzenberg?" Marc Rosenbaum, the foreign affairs editor, again. Still not talking geography. Bill Buzenberg is the State Department correspondent and has spent the week investigating U.S. policy in El Salvador. No mention of El Salvador on the road map.

"Buzenberg will lead the third third." Translation: Bill Buzenberg's report will be the first item after the second newscast in the third half hour of *ATC* after the dinks.

"Four is too much for Susan's Poland interview. It's three right now, and I'm not finished cutting it." Neenah Ellis, one of four production assistants who edit the program's tapes.

"You realize you don't have a single thing from stations on that map? What is this? We've got to get *outside* of Washington and El Salvador!" John McChesney is head of the Acquisitions Unit. He and his staff pull in reports from places like Wilberforce, Ohio; LaCrosse, Wisconsin; Greeley, Colorado. Places where NPR has member stations. McChesney thinks an entire nation exists beyond the boundaries of greater Washington, D.C.!

"Oh, god." Sure. Maury. Funny, how he gets religion every afternoon at two.

And on it goes. Lobbying, squeezing pieces together, pulling time from one to give more time to another, arranging stories in order, re-arranging them twice, three times, trying to make it all fit together with some kind of logic. We stand like this for at least an hour, arguing, agreeing, getting our feelings hurt, laughing, wrestling *All Things Considered* onto the big board.

What gets marked up at two was thought up at ten at the morning editorial meeting. Morning meetings begin promptly at ten.

"It is now twenty-seven minutes *past* ten. Will the *ATC* staff kindly assemble in the conference room? The morning meeting is about to begin." The voice of producer Schlesinger, god-like but impatient, over the public-address system.

The conference room is rectangular, windowless, equipped with a long wooden table and chairs. There's nothing on the walls but white paint. There's nothing on the table either. For about eight months, a salt shaker sat there. Finally our director, Jo Miglino, grew tired of staring at it every morning and threw it away. The room is anonymous, antiseptic. Every day *All Things Considered* begins here.

We straggle in, juggling Styrofoam coffee cups, half-eaten doughnuts, newspapers, clippings, notes. A tousled crew. Blue-jeaned, mostly. And T-shirted. It's inside work (and no heavy lifting), and clothes are for comfort, not impressions. Besides, salaries are low enough to keep most of us under-dressed.

Fifteen people ease into chairs around the table: producers; editors, who make assignments and check content and accuracy; the director, who gets the program on and off the air on time; the technical supervisor, who makes arrangements that let us talk by satellite from Washington to Los Angeles and sound as if we're all in the same room; and production assistants, who handle the program's tapes. Also here this morning: the desk assistants, who track down people for the hosts to interview. And the hosts: Sandy Ungar and me. The average age at the morning meeting,

Our TENTH Anniversary Class Picture - May, 1981

with a few close, personal exceptions, is twenty-six and a half. This is the basic *All Things Considered* staff, the corps that puts the program together each day.

We meet like this day after day, year after year. Only the cast of characters has changed since May 1971, when *All Things Considered* began broadcasting.*

In the beginning, there were far fewer of us, but we were just as opinionated. National Public Radio was a new network and *All Things Considered* was its first program. The network and the program created themselves as they went along.

Commercial radio, when *All Things Considered* started, was mostly a matter of disc-jockey shows, five-minute newscasts, and interminable call-in programs where listeners got the chance to sound off and be mistreated by the talk-show host.

Public radio, on the other hand, consisted of hundreds of small, low-budget stations, mainly on university campuses, that broadcast classical music and educational programs—language lessons, lectures, speeches, readings from books. If a station had the money, it got a wire-service machine that chugged out news written for broadcast by the reporters of the Associated Press or United Press International. Every now and then, someone came in to rip the wire copy off the machine and read it on the air.**

All Things Considered was designed to bring more comprehensive news cover-

---

* In fact, it's surely changing as you read this. There's much job mobility at NPR. For instance, in the first ten years, *All Things Considered* had eighteen different producers!

** A notable exception was Pacifica—exclusively listener-supported radio stations in Berkeley, Los Angeles, New York, and Houston. Controversial, imaginative, and willing to take risks, Pacifica stations are still places to turn to for creative broadcasting and the freest of speech.

age to radio each and every day. Reporters would have time to tell their stories properly. If it only took two minutes to get the story right, they got two minutes. If the story needed thirty or forty-five minutes, that was fine, too.

But this was not to be *only* a news program. We would also pay attention to the arts, humanities, science, and everyday life. All Things Considered would take its name seriously. "Celebrate the human experience" is how our first director of programming, Bill Siemering put it. Ten years later producer Rick Lewis said the same thing: "All Things Considered is the first program to recognize that people interested in news also play tennis and fix their cars and raise children and listen to music. People interested in news go to concerts, as surely as Pinchas Zuckerman reads newspapers."

Since we were National *Public* Radio, we wanted the public to become part of the program. We broadcast listeners' ideas, their voices, read from their letters. Murfreesboro, Tennessee spoke to New York City, and Buffalo, Missouri heard from Kankakee, Illinois. Many listeners said they'd never thought of writing to a radio program before, but there was something about *this* radio program that turned them into pen pals. Partly, it was the way we spoke: simply and directly. And we liked to laugh. We showed we were as intelligent and bewildered and ordinary and special as our listeners. There were a million puzzlements a day in the world. We would try to sort some of them out as best we could, and we welcomed listeners to join us.

We also wanted to experiment with the possibilities of the medium. Radio serials like "The Shadow" or "The Lone Ranger" had mesmerized listeners with sound effects—creaking doors and horses' hooves. We would go further and use the sounds of life to tell real stories. With our microphones we would take listeners to stock car races, duck blinds, Nazi rallies, and into a room where a child was being born. Listeners could imagine the events from the sounds we played. That, too, was a new kind of participation.

Those, then, were the early aspirations. Missionary zeal? Oh, yes. The sense that we were, if not re-inventing the wheel, at least re-inventing radio? Certainly. And some "let's save the world through the airwaves" thrown in for good measure. All things considered, not a bad set of premises on which to build a new program.

An ATC
In-Joke

Question: *When was the Golden Age of All Things Considered?*

Answer: *The Golden Age of All Things Considered was always six months before you came to work here.*

MY CO-HOSTS

Mike

Mike Waters *and I shared the studio table and microphones for two years. Someone wrote that Mike has a cathedral in his head. A perfect description of the magnificent instrument that is his voice. He once cast himself as the Angel Gabriel, directing a sunset. A classic production, it ran on* ATC *three times in our first year. Mike taught me about phrasing and where to pause. He knows just how to use a microphone—leaning in to whisper, rearing back to let out a yelp. Once he even put a microphone into a barrel and threw it over Niagara Falls. Just to hear how it sounded. He left* ATC *to produce other programs, all laced with rich sounds.*

Bob Edwards *took over in 1974, and stayed until 1979. Bob's first job at NPR was as the* ATC *newscaster. Before that, he'd presented news at various commercial stations, perfecting a skill I still find awesome: the ability to take twelve yards of wire-service copy and compress it into twelve typed lines. Bob's other qualities: a commitment to stories about the people of Appalachia (he's from Louisville, Kentucky), a first name for his first and last name; the driest sense of humor in the place; the temperament to put up with the marked differences in our personalities, backgrounds, and attitudes toward desk tops (his, impeccable; mine, chaotic). In our five years together we developed a relationship on the air that often sounded like the desk tops. His coolness let me be hotter—take more risks, laugh, be silly. My style made him more authoritatively relaxed. It was a good combination and brought out new dimensions in each of us. When Bob left to host NPR's* Morning Edition, *I missed him more than I told him at the time.*

Sandy

Enter **Sanford Ungar.** *Sandy, to his friends. Since 1980 he's been making my desk look like the Siberian plains. Twenty years' worth of newspapers, magazines, books, memos and letters obliterate Sandy's desk and his floor, the walls, the radiator. If Mike Waters has a cathedral in his head, Sandy Ungar has an encyclopedia; and what he hasn't been able to fit inside his head takes up residence in every available space of his office. Sandy came to us from Wilkes-Barre, Harvard, and the printed page —he was a reporter for UPI and the Washington Post; wrote books about the FBI, the Pentagon Papers; was managing editor of Foreign Policy magazine. The move from print to radio lets him share his interest and expertise in international affairs and politics with a wider audience.*

Bob

August 24, 1979

Dear Ms. Stamberg and Mr. Edwards,

We feel you should be informed that two imposters claiming to be Susan Stamberg and Bob Edwards are pictured in the current issue of Time magazine.

As regular listeners of "All Things Considered" we know perfectly well that the calm, soothing, resonant voices which utter the mature wit and wisdom we enjoy so much do not emanate from such obviously youthful -- indeed teenage-looking -- frauds.

We, of course, don't know what dire plot is behind this transparent deception, but felt you should be advised.

Yours truly,

Robert Paul Jones
Kay Jones

Robert Paul Jones
Kay Jones
Kenosha, Wisconsin

Dear Susan:

March 12 , 1979

For the last six years I've been listening faithfully to ALL THINGS CONSIDERED. I have probably spent more time listening to your voice than any other person I know.

Now, suddenly, Newsweek magazine discovers National Public Radio (March 12 issue). Where, may I ask, have they been? What really ticks me off, though, is the nerve they have publishing that picture of Roseann Roseannadana and Chevy Chase and claiming that they are the people who own my two favorite voices in all the world. Talk about GALL!

Never mind, Susan - I STILL BELIEVE in you! I'm not so sure about Edwards.

Sincerely,

Dan Weddell

Portland, Oregon

I grew up with voices speaking to me from the magic box that sat on the kitchen table, telling me stories, making me laugh, informing me about war and peace and the death of President Roosevelt. Radio was the authoritative source, and, when the chance came to work in it, I felt I was joining a world that had fascinated me since childhood.

The chance came in 1963, at a public radio station in Washington. The greenest member of a full-time staff of three, I learned to edit tape, lug around fifty-pound recorders, produce programs . . . and, eventually, I heard my voice through a headset, telling listeners that a president had died in Dallas.

National Public Radio hired me in 1971 to edit tapes for the new program it was about to put on the air. After a few weeks, I was reporting. After ten months, I became host of All Things Considered.

My oldest friend remembers that, at the High School of Music and Art in New York, I always said I wanted to have a salon some day — a place where interesting people came to talk. All Things Considered is a good place for talking.

I was an art major in high school and studied English Literature at Barnard College. I have spent hours learning to sing every note of Dave Brubeck's nine-minute piano solo on "Balcony Rock" and to recite, in Middle English, the first page of The Canterbury Tales. But I do not know, without looking them up, the provisions of the Ninth Amendment to the Constitution or the terms of the Camp David Agreement.

I tend to look for novels in news events — for conflicts, relationships, and feelings. Usually I find them. When I sat in the Oval Office with President Carter, moderating a call-in program, I watched the changes in his eyes as closely as I listened to the words he spoke. Power attracts but does not intrigue me. I want to know how events affect ordinary people, and I would rather talk to them than to officials.

Every night at five I do talk to them — on radio, that most intimate medium. Shortly before five, I perform two rituals. I put on lipstick. And I worry. The lipstick is a kind of preparation — recognition that I'm company coming into their kitchens. The worry is preparation, too. Soon I will be greeting listeners and asking for ninety minutes of their attention. I want to be sure that their time is well spent. I want to be sure that the box remains magical.

"All right, crew. It is now close to ten-thirty. Let's figure out what we've got for today."

Program editor Jim Angle runs the morning meeting. He's the newest member of the staff, new enough to show up at ten wide awake. He'll learn. The rest of us are grunting and gulping coffee.

"Molpus has his Klan piece. Buzenberg says some kind of announcement is expected on El Salvador today, so he'll hang out at State and use whatever he gets to top that long Salvadoran background thing he's been working on."

Everyone is listening to Angle, but no one is looking at him. Our eyes are scanning the newspapers now spread across the conference table. We sift through our papers, searching for ideas, unanswered questions that _All Things Considered_ might answer by tonight.

"Did you see what ABC did on El Salvador last night?"

"Yeah. Good film, but they didn't tell you anything."

"Linda Wertheimer's on the Hill She'll do something on the tax bill "

"All right, but I'd rather talk with some people who'll be affected if the plan goes through. Why don't we? . . ."

"We could get something quick and dirty from San Diego. Send a reporter out to a shopping center for some man-on-the-mall reactions."

"Okay, that's good."

Foreign affairs editor Marc Rosenbaum arrives, yellow legal pad flapping. He's just gotten off the phone with a reporter in Peking. Before that, he was talking to Israel.

"Jerusalem says the Begin interview will be six minutes. I asked for five."

"That means we'll end up with seven. Okay. What else?"

In this room each morning at ten o'clock the world is compressed onto a long sheet of white paper on the table in front of the producer. This is not the time for philosophical or academic discussion. It is the time for good ideas that will work on the air. We at this table are facilitators. Pragmatists. Dealers in information. Sometimes I long for more dreamers. But dreams rarely drift into this discussion.

The faces are serious. Concentration varies. I doodle on a note pad. Production assistant Neenah Ellis plays with her hair. Much drumming of fingers against chair arms, capping and uncapping of pens. Very few smokers in this room. Surprising, given the pressures.

"What else?"

"There's a national headache conference in Washington."

Everyone perks up. Relief at last. So far, the list is full of disasters: El Salvador, taxes, the Middle East, the Klan. By comparison, a headache conference sounds like fun.

More ideas are tossed out, debated, discarded. "Good, but we can't do it right by tonight, so let's hold it." "No, we did that last year." "Forget it; it's a magazine story, not radio." "Why don't we try it this way?" "Because it would be boring."

"How come you're so full of good ideas today?"

Morning Meeting

npr

National Public Radio
Washington, D.C.

memorandum

Date: February 9, 1979
To: ATC staff
From: Rick *Rick*
Subject:

Attendance at the 10:00 daily story conference seems to have dropped sharply, to the point where sometimes no one comes at all.

This is a reminder, therefore, that the 10:00 meeting is NOT optional, and that it should not be allowed to start later and later. All production staff are expected:

a) to show up, on time

b) to come prepared with ideas for the program, and to discuss the ideas of others.

The responsibility of every staff member begins with the contribution of ideas that later become stories. In a very real sense, the production of ATC is only the mechanical completion of ideas that came earlier. All staff should be at the 10:00 meeting, unless assigned to other duties.

Let us not get involved in calling the roll every morning.

"I didn't sleep all night."

Mondays are the worst days in this room, just as they are in many rooms. Monday radio programs are rarely worth listening to. Like cars on the assembly line, news programs get better by Wednesday. Thursday tends to be the best broadcast day of the week. Words flow well; originality spills from typewriters and microphones. Friday's a toss-up. Either we get sloppy, or something exciting happens because the momentum has been building all week.

"This is not a terrific radio program we have here."

"Wait! You forgot about the Velcro orchestra." I'm getting ready to pitch.

"What's that?"

"Jay Allison takes different lengths of Velcro, rips 'em open and then closes them—they're the percussion section of the orchestra." I'm pitching. "And I phone the guy who invented Velcro. He's an engineer in Switzerland. Plus a man from the army says they use it for dog booties."

It must be Thursday.

"And my voice man could run today." Now Sandy's pitching. "The one who gives me voice lessons, makes me keep saying *EEEEEEEEOOOOO, AAAAAAEEEEE.* . . . We really should run it. You've held it for a week now. Not only is my voice changing, but the tape's getting brittle!"

The list is growing. It's definitely Thursday.

"Listen, we've got enough for four programs. We may as well stop."

There are forty-two story ideas on the long sheet of white paper. About twenty of them will get on the air tonight. The rest either drop out (the guest was inarticulate . . . there wasn't a story there after all . . . the tape didn't arrive in time) or get held over because something new and unpredictable will happen in the next few hours that must be reported tonight.

The meeting is over. The room empties. It's eleven-thirty. The next five and a half hours will be spent making tonight's program. At least three-quarters of the pieces on _All Things Considered_ are taped and edited before the five-o'clock broadcast. Everything the staff does now is aimed at getting the tapes ready for airing.

The reporters at NPR and member stations are already out on stories—finding sources, asking questions, taping for pieces they will file later today. For some reporters, the day is a hurry-up-and-wait affair. Linda Wertheimer sits for hours in a paneled room on Capitol Hill listening to senators debate the tax bill, chases down the hall after one senator, tapes his statement, returns for more debate, waits through delays and arguments, and races to a news conference to record final statements for her report tonight at five.

The desk assistants grab phones and spin Rolodexes, tracking down guests for the hosts to interview today. It's often detective work. Once a desk assistant had playwright Arthur Kopit paged at the Pittsburgh airport so that I could interview him by phone about Buffalo Bill. Another dragged comedian Henny Youngman to a phone in the lobby of a Las Vegas hotel, one steamy July, so he could tell us "hot" jokes. Sometimes desk assistants are bearers of bad news. In 1978, anthropologist Colin Turnbull learned of Margaret Mead's death when someone on the desk called to ask for his help with the _All Things Considered_ obituary. The assistants phone, inveigle, cajole, fill the studio sign-up sheet with small, jotted victories.

The hosts go to their offices to prepare for the day's interviews. At this point I feel like a graduate student cramming for finals. I read files, clippings, make notes and phone calls.

Studio Five opens to _All Things Considered_ at noon, and, from then on, Sandy and I dart in and out for fifteen-minute stretches, taping interviews with guests in person, by phone, or via satellite.

"Susan, my guest is late. Can I bump you to one-thirty?"

"No. The senator is going to the NPR booth on Capitol Hill promptly at one-fifteen. I can't change it."

"Senators never show up on time."

"This one will. He's running for re-election. Why don't you see if you can get into Studio Six?"

Here's what it's like on the worst days: Cartoonist Gahan Wilson and his wife, novelist Nancy Winters, are with me in Studio Five, describing their trip to Transylvania. As we record, an editor tells me in my headset that the senator has arrived at the booth early and must do the interview right away or he'll miss a quorum call. I stop taping with Wilson and Winters and start taping with the senator. As we record, foreign affairs editor Marc Rosenbaum tells me in my headset that the call we've

been waiting for from Teheran has finally come through and I must do that interview right away or we'll lose the line. Wilson and Winters smilingly agree to wait (I think they're finding this all rather exciting). I thank the senator. Teheran is punched up into my headset, and a reporter gives me the latest news on the hostages. We tape for five minutes, then I turn back to Wilson and Winters. I inform Marc Rosenbaum that if the Pope calls, he should be put on hold.

Here's what it's like on the best days: all of the above, and the Pope doesn't call.

While waiting for the day's tapes to come in, the production assistants start cutting tapes already in house that may run tonight: interviews Sandy and I did yesterday or last week; stories that were held over; or a personal opinion from our pool of *All Things Considered* commentators—perhaps someone of national reputation (former New York Senator James Buckley, writer Marya Mannes, or journalists such as Pauline Frederick and Daniel Schorr), but, just as likely, some local folks spotted by member stations for their outspokenness, their way with words and ideas.

As the day progresses, we'll accumulate enough tape for a forty-hour radio program. But *ATC* listeners will only hear the best ninety minutes; the liveliest three of my fifteen with Wilson and Winters, the most important five minutes of the half-hour news conference on the tax bill. Deciding which minutes *are* the best is a process that takes place hundreds of times throughout any given day at meetings, on the telephone, at typewriters, in edit booths, and in front of the big board.

Two o'clock. Standing and staring.
   "There is nothing on that road map that I want to listen to."
   "Oh Susan!"
   "Too damn much politics."
   "Not enough foreign news."
   "Too many light pieces. Where's the *substance?*"
   "WHERE ARE THE STATIONS?"

Three-thirty. Everyone is screaming for decisions. The map must be finished. It's getting close to air time.

Three forty-five. No one is at a desk. We're in the studio mixing sounds; or in small booths, editing tape.
   "THEIMPERIALWIZARDREFUSEDTOBEPINNEDDOWNTOTHEPRECISEMEM-BERSHIP. . . ." Chipmunk bleats from David Molpus's edit booth. He's playing his Klan tape at double speed, trying to cut it.

   CLACKETY-CLACK-CLACK-CLACK-hold-R-I-I-I-I-I-I-NG. Typewriters clatter as scripts are typed.
   Coded conversations interrupt: "We'll end the second with Velcro and take the orchestra up to the Nipper." "Stand by with the dinks."

R-I-I-I-I-I-I-NG. Linda Wertheimer phones to say the tax news conference won't start until four o'clock. You can hear she's frustrated.

The public-address system hunts us down:
"Will any editor please call Nina Totenberg on 2400? I need an editor. NOW!!"
"Sandy Ungar, your guest is in reception. Sandy, please, your guest is here."
"Studio Five engineer to Studio Five, please."
(Notice how polite everyone is over the public-address system?)
"Marc Rosenbaum, please pick up 2200. It's Ireland."
"Marc Rosenbaum, 2210 for Peking, please."

SCRE-E-E-E-E-E-E-E-CH. That's tape rewinding on production assistant Bob Wisdom's machine. He can't find the cut, and he's been trying for two hours. He pulls Jim Angle into the booth. Maybe a fresh pair of ears will help.
"There it is," says Angle. "Go from where she says, 'I never wanted to travel there in the first place,' right to, 'Two months later, there I was.' Cut all the junk about how she changed her mind and how hard it was to get the visa. Takes too long. And who cares, anyway?" Bob makes the cut. It works.
SCRE-E-E-E-E-E-E-E-CH. Same scene down the hall, in Neenah Ellis's edit booth. Maury Schlesinger has just listened to her edit of my Poland interview. "It's flat in the middle. Dump the stuff about the Soviets."
Marc Rosenbaum comes in to listen. "You can't dump that part. It's the news. Get rid of the stuff about Solidarity." Maury leaves. Marc leaves.
Neenah: "I listen to what Maury says. Then I listen to what Marc says. Then I cut the tape the way I think is right." Neenah makes the cut. It works.

Four o'clock. Most of tonight's tapes are in house and being edited. Only one is completely ready for broadcast. The program's lead story is missing: The news conference on the tax bill has now been postponed until four-thirty, and Linda Wertheimer will have to file her tax report live. Now she's not only frustrated, she's frazzled.
Director Jo Miglino is typing the run-down, a brief description of every item on tonight's program. Jo's rundowns are little miracles of precision and detail. This has not always been the case. A sample from a pre-Miglino rundown:

> SOVIET JEWELRY: SCOTT SIMON RPTS ON A CONF. WHICH ENDED YESTER-
> DAY OF THE NATL CONF. ON SOVIET JEWELRY.

Four-fifteen. Sandy and I use the rundowns to write our opening billboards, quick summaries of what listeners will hear.

Four-thirty. We go into the studio to record the billboards. They must fill a precise block of time. Recording (usually) assures that they do, and that they're flawless.

The opening theme rolls, with its four electronic dinks. We clear our throats. The ON AIR light flashes.

"Good evening. From National Public Radio in Washington, I'm Stuzan—"
"You ARE????"
"Could we take that again, please?"

Four forty-five. The billboards are taped. We make tea. Sandy likes Earl Grey. Today I have Constant Comment. As a matter of fact, *most* days I have constant comment. That's what they pay me for. I'm also pretty tense at four forty-five, and tea is soothing. The tension isn't mike fright—not after all these years. And it's not really worry about technical foul-ups, although that's always a possibility. It's concern that we get it right. Concern—after all the lobbying and joking and rushing around and concentrating—*that we get it right.*

Four forty-seven. At the producer's desk, Schlesinger and Angle read over copy, checking for errors, cutting.
    In the control room, engineer Lorraine Wilcox takes voice levels. Jo Miglino tallies time for each half hour, punching numbers up on digital clocks that will count down each tape by minutes and seconds. It's very quiet.

Four-fifty. Back in the studio, Sandy and I read and rewrite copy, call for clarifications and fact checks. It's very quiet here, too, and will be until six-thirty. The studio is an oasis of calm. Outside, the corridors are exploding, as everyone scrambles to deliver finished tapes to the control room.

Four fifty-five. The newscaster enters the studio, arranges his copy, clears his throat.

Four fifty-nine. In the control room, Jo cues Lorraine.
    "Ready with tape one. . . . Stand by. . . . Hit it!"

Five o'clock.
    DINK—DINK—DINK—DINK
    "Good evening. From National Public Radio in Washington, I'm Susan Stamberg."
    "And I'm Sanford Ungar, with *All Things Considered.*"

A.T.C. THEME

MARCH TEMPO

DON VOEGELI

© 1977 - UNIVERSITY OF WISCONSIN - EXTENSION

DON VOEGELI

Composer Don Voegeli has been working in public radio since 1938. He's based at the
Electrosonic Studio at the University of Wisconsin in Madison.

EVERY NIGHT AT FIVE

Listening for America

October 28, 1974, was Don Morris Day on *All Things Considered.* It was Veterans Day. Don Morris was a veteran of the war in Southeast Asia. In 1973, American troops had been withdrawn from Vietnam. I phoned Don Morris in San Francisco to ask whether anyone had given him a parade. A parade? Are you kidding?

> The only way I know it's Veterans Day is hearing about it on the news. Vietnam just doesn't seem to matter that much now. Maybe it was meaningless. Maybe it was worse than meaningless. Maybe everybody being involved in Vietnam made a big mess of our country.

During the 1976 presidential campaign, Cincinnati steelworker George Preston felt he had little choice.

> When push comes to shove, what it means is which rich man is going to be on my back for the next four years. I haven't seen a candidate come down the line that's my candidate. Not Ford. Not Carter. Jimmy Carter ain't no workin' man.

In September 1980, when his father learned the bluefish were running in the Connecticut River, nine-year-old Benjamin Alsop spent Sunday fishing. On Monday, I called New Haven to ask how many fish Ben had caught.

> "None."
> "None?"
> "The bluefish weren't running."
> "Well, that's too bad."
> "No, it was okay. There were crabs."
> "Terrific! Did you catch a crab?"
> "Nope. One caught me, though. Took my bait and pulled me right into the water."

People like Don Morris and George Preston and Benjamin Alsop help *All Things Considered* listen for America—to listen *in behalf* of the country, and to listen *to* the country. They talk about their readjustments, their politics, their fishing poles. They share grief over the war in Vietnam, betrayal during Watergate, joy at the hostages' return from Iran, shock at the shooting of a president. They describe where they live, what they do, and how they feel about it. Their voices are young, old, educated, plain, rich with the rhythms and accents of their regions.

We go out to listen: at political rallies, protest demonstrations, maple syrup tappings. Or people come to our studios to tell their stories. Listeners take part in the program: We read their letters on the air; we phone to ask about their favorite hamburgers. Contests help us listen. We run them regularly. No box tops, no prizes, but lots of listeners get their ideas and names on the air. We even pronounce them properly. The names, that is. Where they live (Sault Ste. Marie, Michigan!?) is entirely up for garble.

And commentators help us listen for America. We find them through the books and articles they write. Sometimes, they find us; they send a letter or a sample tape that will capture our imagination. Public figures or neighborhood folk, commentators are there to add spice to our air. They take stands, bristle with bias, entertain, raise hackles, delight, spur listeners to consider repacking their intellectual baggage. They are the opinion pages of our radio magazine.

Broadcasting this jumble of voices from many places, *All Things Considered* redefines the news. The program says news isn't just what happens in Washington or on Wall Street. News also happens in the small events of life: the cabbage popping up in Fletcher Cox's garden in Alexandria, Virginia; the kindergarten pupil in Baltimore, thrilled, the first day of school, to get her own cubbyhole.

All Things Considered has been listening for America for more than ten years. What we've heard is hustle, nostalgia, rage, serenity, optimism, confusion—a voice print of the country in the seventies.

What do you do while you listen to *All Things Considered*?

Thousands of men and women listen to *All Things Considered* in their cars. Bruce Marsden is one of them. Here, Bruce Marsden leaves work to drive home, in Oakland, California.

PRIMARY SEASON IN CLAREMONT, NEW HAMPSHIRE

(Traffic sounds/horns honking/cameras clicking)

Edward Kennedy   Hello, hello, good morning. I hear Boccia's Market is one of the oldest, finest stores in the community.

Woman   Well, we try.

Kennedy   Meet my nephew, Chris. This is Chris Kennedy.

Several women   Oh-h-h. Hello. How do you do? Pleased to meet you.

Woman   I'm going to ask you a question, Senator. You look pretty confident.

Kennedy   Ha, ha, ha.

Woman   What's the big priority once you get there?

Kennedy   I think it's basically the restoration of our economy. High interest rates, high rates of inflation. Maybe we'll get some information up to you that spells out how we can get to those goals, so that. . . .

It's 1980 and we're on the campaign trail. A great place to listen for America. Aim the mikes at voters as well as candidates, and you weave a tapestry of sounds: opinions, unguarded reactions, and the obligatory bad school band. (Nothing is quite as effective on the air as a high school band unable to reach a consensus on the precise notes of "America the Beautiful.")

All Things Considered has followed three presidential elections and four administrations—which means we've paid plenty of visits to New Hampshire during primary season. In February 1980, producers Betty Rogers, Art Silverman, and Larry Massett chose Claremont, New Hampshire, as their listening post. They spent almost two weeks there, taping the passing political parade: candidates arriving, mingling, making speeches; Claremont residents watching, listening, applauding the band; newspaper and network reporters, their pens and cameras poised, trailing the candidates and voters. The NPR crew recorded it all: hours and hours of tape, from which they created an eighteen-minute story for *All Things Considered.*

The piece is composed like a movie for the ear. One scene—a candidate politicking at a gas station—dissolves into the next scene—Rotarians singing their welcome to another candidate. After a brief stay (remember, sound only) at the Rotary meeting, another dissolve, this time to a gathering of senior citizens preparing to greet still a third candidate. The idea was to let listeners hear primary season as the producers had heard it, but to compress and arrange the hours of sounds into a coherent whole. Life, especially political life, is rarely coherent. Production and editing make it so.

The aural guide to primary season in Claremont, New Hampshire, is David Puksta, the mayor's son. Puksta is the secret weapon here. As local resident-*cum*-reporter, he lends a certain *Our Town* quality to the proceedings. In fact, that thought may help you read the piece. It's like reading a script, with sound effects pointing up changes of scene, and David Puksta, the narrator, coming in and out. Except it's radio. And David's not an actor; he's a student at Stevens High School, where he spent a good deal of time standing at the door watching the campaign limousines and buses pull up.

Few candidates missed the chance to visit Stevens High School. When they arrived, David ushered them in. He wore a Reagan button . . . a Carter button . . . a Bush, a Brown, a Kennedy, a Baker, a Lyndon LaRouche button. All the buttons were tucked underneath his lapels and cuffs. Each button came in handy, that 1980 primary season.

(Traffic/horns/band/cameras)

Campaign worker	Hi. Did you get your invitation to meet Governor Brown at the Pleasant Restaurant at lunch today?
Voices	Thank you. . . . Thanks. . . . What?
David Puksta	About this time during primary season, most people who want to become president feel some kind of urge to visit this little town of Claremont. About 14,000 people live here. It's called the city where the work gets done. It's pretty much a factory town— textiles, steel, paper, that sort of stuff. On Tremont Square is the city hall and chamber of commerce. We got a pet shop and a bookstore, a place to buy shoes. We renovated the old opera house. Years ago they had midget wrestling in there, but now they have jazz groups, ballet, operettas. We know a lot about hard work, low wages, and long winters, here. We know a lot about politics, too.

(Traffic sounds/cameras clicking)

Reporter	Is this your first visit to Claremont, Governor Brown?
Brown	Yeah, I'm here giving people a choice for president. Hello, Sir. How are you? I'm Governor Brown of California. What? You recognize me? Have you made up your mind who you're going to vote for yet?
Man	Well, I don't know yet.
Brown	You don't know? You think we need a change down there in Washington?
Man	I sure do.
Brown	I think I can make it. I'm not part of that mess.
Woman	Welcome back to Claremont, Governor.
Brown	When was I here last?
Woman	Oh, you were here at Stevens High School a few weeks ago, and before that—
Brown	Stevens High School?
Young person	What do you think of Claremont?
Brown	I love it. I've only been here a few minutes, but I love it. Is there an energy office in town? I'd like to visit it.

(Traffic/marching band/whistling/cameras clicking/applause/fade)

What Else was Said ↓

Puksta   Energy is probably the biggest issue all the candidates are latching onto this year. Last primary, about 10 percent of the people had wood-stoves; this time, about 65 percent. The cost of home-heating oil doubled in the last year, and it's still rising. One guy in town figured out how to heat a furniture factory by using the saw-dust from the machines. You see a lot of big vans outside the houses, pumping in insulating foam. The first gasohol pump just opened in Claremont, with a little help from Mayor Puksta and Howard Baker. Mayor Puksta, he's a supporter of Bush, but he comes out for all the candidates.

Mayor Puksta
(at gas station)   Over 25 percent of our work force works outside of Claremont, and they rely on transportation and travel. This gasohol could be a good thing for the entire area.

Howard Baker   Well, it's an important step. It really is, Mayor.

Photographer   Senator, would it be possible for you to just put that pump into the tank and put a couple of shots of gasohol into the car?

Baker   I don't know why not.

Photographer   I'm from United Press. Just hold up the pump.

Baker   But I'm gonna turn this thing on, and it's gonna squirt all over me, isn't it?

Photographer   Mr. Baker, how about a big smile?
(Camera clicking/gas pump)

Baker   There we go. That's another first in the campaign.

Mike O'Brien listens on his mail truck in North Springfield, Virginia.

(Laughter in background/conversation/cut to Rotary Club, singing)
R-O-T-A-R-Y,
That spells Rotary;
R-O-T-A-R-Y
is known on land and sea;
From North to South,
from East to West,
He profits most
who serves the best;
R-O-T-A-R-Y,
That spells Rotary.

Puksta   Rotary Club—we got one down on Broad Street there. John Anderson is speaking to them today. There are about sixty-six members, mostly businessmen. They do a lot of good stuff. Rotarians don't really mind candidates stopping by for lunch, but they are not so crazy about the old TV cameramen.

Rotarian   Okay! Ready for the ticket drawing here? We'll have Representative Anderson make the draw for us. Oughta have Mrs. Anderson. She's probably luckier. The number, the winning number, is 1353.

Kiki Anderson   Oh-h-h-h!!!

(Applause and laughter)

Puksta   Looks like Congressman Anderson's wife won the big jackpot down there. Ten big ones.

(Applause and laughter continue/cross-fade to elderly voices singing "God Bless America")

Puksta   The Congress of Claremont Senior Citizens is one of the best organized groups in Claremont. Last September, they opened up the Senior Congress Park, a new apartment building at the outskirts of town, better known as Earl's Paradise. Earl Bourdon runs the place. It's got a game room, wide-screen TV, greenhouse, arts and crafts, and five buses. It's a great place to live. Only requirements: Can't be too young, can't be too rich.

Elderly woman   Usually I go rap at the door. All of 'em know me. I'll say, "Gee, did you know Kennedy's coming down this afternoon?" So they'll say, "Well, gee, I have no way to go down there. I don't feel good." And we'll say, "Well we'll have somebody come up and we'll take you down, we'll help you up and we'll bring you back." And they still forget. You know, our minds aren't the same as they were when we were younger.

Earl Bourdon
(to crowd)   Please be in order. I want to be as brief as I can, but I want to welcome all of you and Senator Kennedy to Senior Congress

It's kinda strange, but it happens from the constable to the Congress and right on up to the president of the United States. As long as they're candidates, they want to be your servants. Soon as you elect them, then they begin to tell you what you can do. They immediately become superior to the people that elected them, and they get exalted and want to tell us what we can do and what we can't do.
—Ray Collins,
Baptist preacher,
Letcher County,
Kentucky,
February 1976

Park, a low-income senior housing project as a result of HUD's 202. And on behalf of the Congress of Claremont Senior Citizens, I welcome Senator Ted Kennedy.

(Applause/cheering/cameras clicking/Kennedy begins speech/fade to Bourdon voice-over)

Bourdon The purpose of the primary should be to afford the candidates the opportunity to say what they think, and the electorate to have a chance to hear it and to ask questions. But unfortunately the caucuses and the primary in New Hampshire have become media games. I think that's a bad thing. Obviously, a lot of people are too shy to ask questions of the candidate in front of sixteen different national TV cameras and forty-six different newspaper reporters. You got to find some way that you don't interfere with mass coverage of what people who are running for important offices are saying, but also you don't want to destroy that intimate relationship you can build between the people and the candidate.

(School bell)

School PA system Good morning. Congratulations to the boys' varsity basketball teams on their victories last Friday. Introducers for Governor Reagan, Senator Kennedy, and Senator Baker please report to the auditorium at eight this morning for practice.

(Fade to Puksta voice-over)

Puksta If you want my honest opinion about it, the best political shows in Claremont are right here at Stevens High, thanks to our civics teacher, John Scranton. He's got this primary business down to a science. We make phone calls, write letters, and then, when the candidates come, he's got everybody positioned where they should be: people who pass out pamphlets, put up posters, people who are standing out there parking cars. Ushers—that's my job. We have fun out there. We get to escort the candidate in, the Secret Service. We learn everything there is to know about him, down to the shoe size.

(High school band/applause)

John Scranton Jeff, can we get you over there behind the mike so that we can get you to practice up a few minutes? Start over here and look down at your dignitary section; look over there toward your press section; look up in there to the balcony. Okay?

Jeff Okay. . . . *(Trying out PA system.)* Today it is our privilege to have with us a man who has served and worked for our country for many years.

Scranton A little bit slower. The tone is good. Just slow it down, just a hair, Jeff.

(Jeff continues to practice, cross-fade to actual introduction/ cameras clicking)

Jeff And it's because of his past record, I believe, that this man could bring economic prosperity and peace to our country. It is with great pleasure that I present to you Ambassador George Bush. *(Loud applause)*

George Bush Thank you very much. Thank you. Thank you. Thank you, Jeff, for that very generous, warm introduction. You know what you got to do in life is get a good person with you, and that makes a big difference. That helps a lot. When Jeff sticks his neck out for me and helps in political organization. . . .

(Fade to band music/background noises/traffic/cameras clicking)

Puksta So that's what it's like in Claremont, during the primary season. Very busy here. Lots of things to see for a few weeks. Interesting things. Like, you notice the black limousines never get slush on them. The TV camera crew cars, they get slush on 'em; police cars get slush on 'em. Ordinary cars, they get slush on 'em. Politicians' cars, they never get slush on 'em.

(High school band/cheering to end)

STRIKE ONE FOR IZVESTIA

A Commentary by Melor Sturua

The politicking begins long before primary time, of course, which is how it happened that the Washington bureau chief for *Izvestia*, Melor Sturua, became a commentator on *All Things Considered*. We'd met one day in the summer of 1979, when a series of surprising resignations took place in the Carter Cabinet. Joseph Califano stepped down as head of the Department of Health, Education, and Welfare. W. Michael Blumenthal quit as secretary of the treasury. We couldn't understand all the musical Cabinet chairs. Neither could any of the political experts we consulted. Clearly, we needed a fresh perspective.

At our usual morning meeting, I remembered that U.S. Kremlinologists figure out changes in Soviet leadership by studying photographs of the line-up on the reviewing stand at the May Day parade in Moscow. Maybe we could reverse the procedure and get a Soviet "Potomacologist" to tell us what was going on in our government.

Enter Melor Sturua, who said President Carter ran those men out of the Cabinet so that Carter himself could run harder for re-election. Oh-h-h-h-h.

Naturally, we wanted to hear more from Melor Sturua, and so we invited him to share his views with us each week. We were intrigued by the idea of listening for America in a Soviet accent. When he joined us, Sturua had already spent three years as *Izvestia* bureau chief in Washington and had been a frequent visitor to the U.S. The topic he chose for his first commentary, in September 1979, was as American as apple pie.

Sturua
(*with heavy accent*)
Do you remember the old story about a man who saw for the first time in his life a giraffe in the zoo? "It's impossible," he said. Covering life in the United States for my Russian readership, I sometimes feel like a giraffe. The readers refuse to believe. "It's impossible," they write in their letters to me.

The last time I appeared in the role of an animal with a long neck was when I wrote a story [of] how Washington attorney Edward Bennett Williams bought the Baltimore Orioles for about $12 million. The first reaction was quite predictable. "It's impossible. We know," my readers told me, "that in the United States the players are bought and sold. But the whole teams? No, you exaggerate. You invent outrageous lies just to prove the point about the decadence of the contemporary American society."

I understand the sentiments of my readers, and I forgive them, because frankly I don't understand myself how one man can deprive the whole city of a baseball or basketball team. Yes, I know, the golden rule of sports: The guy with the gold makes the rules. But still, buying players, buying teams, what next? Buying the whole leagues? And why not! There is nothing in the golden rule of sports that prevents this. It's just a matter of money and impudence That's why I got so scared when I learned that seventy-six-year-old hamburger king Ray Kroc is also interested in

26

sports. Mr. Kroc is chairman of the board of McDonald's, and wealthier than Mr. Williams. He also can buy baseball or football teams. More than that, he can establish a completely new league like the McDonald's Hamburger League.

Now do you understand my troubles to explain to my readers how the American sports giraffe looks and functions? This is Melor Sturua for National Public Radio.

Stamberg Mr. Sturua, stay with us just a few minutes. We'd like to find out something about you. How do you approach your job—reporting home about what you're seeing here?

Sturua Well, my approach is to forget my bookish knowledge of this country, because this bookish knowledge sometimes is maybe more like a burden than help. It is easier to start discovering your country like Columbus did, from the first blank page.

Stamberg Did you have stereotypes about us?

Sturua I can give you a small example of it. Maybe it sounds very strange, but my perception of the United States was that it was a jungle of asphalt. No green. And now I live in Washington surrounded by the most green places.

Stamberg What about political stereotyping? How do you react to the kind of freedom of speech that you find here, the freedom of the press?

Sturua You have freedom of the press as you understand it, as it fits your philosophy, your way of life. It isn't freedom of the press as we understand it. The press in the United States belongs not to the people, but belongs to a few very powerful, very rich people; these newspapers are like hereditary kingdoms.

Stamberg We're going to get a lot of mail from listeners who will ask, "How is it that you are having, as a regular commentator on a government-sponsored, taxpayer-supported radio network, a man who is

Jules Feiffer exercises while he listens in New York City.

one and two and one and two and one and two and

27

the correspondent for *Izvestia,* which is essentially an arm of the Soviet government?" How would you answer those letters?

Sturua It's up to you to answer those letters, but I think your decision to have me on is quite understandable. You want the voice from another side of the fence. Maybe you regard me as a mirror, maybe a crooked mirror, but still a mirror, who reflects some parts of your body or face that you can't see yourself.

All commentators on <u>All Things Considered</u> are chosen as voices "from another side of the fence." Liberal, conservative, moderate, or satiric, commentators stay with us for months or even years. None of us agrees with all of them. Some of us agree with some of them. Agreement is never the issue. Their thinking makes us think.

The mail *did* arrive from listeners, who found Melor Sturua's commentaries either totally charming or thoroughly exasperating. The commentaries didn't last long, however. In the winter of 1979, Soviet troops and tanks moved into Afghanistan. The Washington bureau chief for *Izvestia* said it was a bad time for him to come to our studios. We called the next week, the week after, the week after that. We called for months. It was still a bad time.

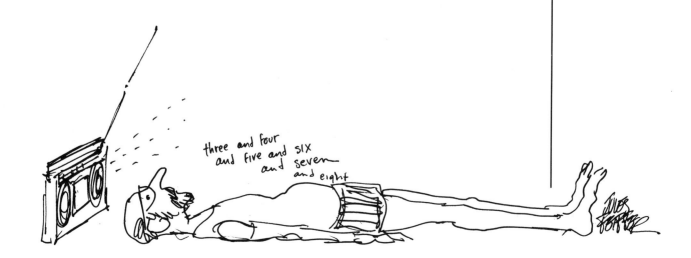

three and four
and five and six
and seven
and eight

SHOWING AMERICA
TO CHINA

A Contest

Contests came to *All Things Considered* via the Canadian Broadcasting Corporation's program "This Country in the Morning," hosted from 1971 to 1974 by the remarkably inventive Peter Gzowski. Our first producer, Jack Mitchell, used to listen to the CBC and swiped their contest idea early in our history. There were no prizes, but that didn't stop listeners from entering. They joined our romps delightedly. No one had ever asked them before. Here was their radio, wanting to hear from them!

Contest themes come from anywhere. A change in season led us to ask listeners for tips on keeping cool. (Listener suggestions: Wet down your leotard before you put it on; drink hot tea; revive flirtatious hand fans.) A chance encounter may spark a contest. One morning I was buying coffee in the snack shop next door. A man had a note pinned to his tie. He said it was his way of reminding himself of something. The next day *All Things Considered* asked listeners how *they* remember things. We ran a resignation contest. The winners resigned from anything they pleased—their job, their lawn, their diet, their moustache, their flat feet. We asked for good advice listeners had received over the years, and we got more advice than we could possibly follow. John Harris, of Meriden, Connecticut, warned: Never trust a man who has an initial for a first name. Four-and-a-half-year-old Joey Summerfield, in Jacksonville, Florida, firmly told us never to put lizards in our washing machines. Ruth Smestad, in San Francisco, made us reach for our shoes: "Never walk barefoot on the sidewalk in Fargo, North Dakota, or you'll get pregnant."

Sometimes a contest grows out of an item in the news. One of our most popular contests began with a news event and ended with a sense of America. Early in 1979, China's vice-premier paid a visit to America. Deng Xiaoping was scheduled to make official stops in Washington, Atlanta, Houston, and Seattle. We asked *All Things Considered* listeners to create an alternative itinerary—one they felt would give China's leader the true flavor of the country. We ruled out the obvious: Disney World, the Empire State Building, the Golden Gate Bridge, "Hollywood Squares," or sending out for Chinese food. Here's the itinerary listeners designed:

- a church service
- Billy Carter's service station, Plains, Georgia
- a major urban post office at midnight, April 15
- a hot tub in Marin County, California
- the Greyhound bus station, Indianapolis, Indiana
- the Greyhound bus station, Chicago, Illinois
- Union bus station, Champaign, Illinois
- Al's Breakfast, Minneapolis, Minnesota
- Blue Bell Drive Inn, Lavalette, West Virginia
- a prison
- an old-age home
- San Clemente, California
- Harlem
- Yosemite National Park
- Filene's basement, Boston

- the Grand Canyon
- a $200,000 mansion built on the San Andreas fault
- a Chicago slaughterhouse
- Los Angeles without a car
- a laundromat
- Studio 54
- a bluegrass concert
- Nashville and the Grand Ole Opry
- Arizona's London Bridge
- a ski resort
- a high school
- a family farm
- a Rotary Club meeting
- a Playboy Club
- an unemployment office in Philadelphia
- Barbara Efies's house in San Francisco, for carrot cake

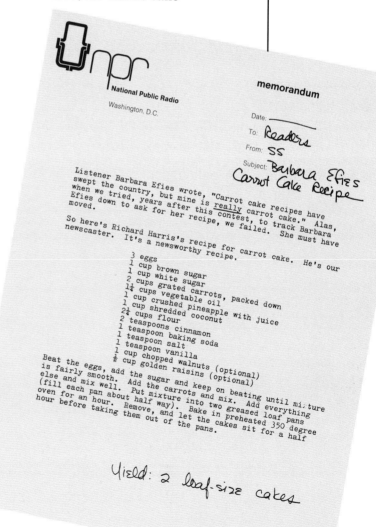

npr
National Public Radio
Washington, D.C.

memorandum

Date: _____

To: Readers

From: SS

Subject: Barbara Efies Carrot Cake Recipe

Listener Barbara Efies wrote, "Carrot cake recipes have swept the country, but mine is really carrot cake." Alas, when we tried, years after this contest, to track Barbara Efies down to ask for her recipe, we failed. She must have moved.

So here's Richard Harris's recipe for carrot cake. He's our newscaster. It's a newsworthy recipe.

```
      3 eggs
      1 cup brown sugar
      1 cup white sugar
      2 cups grated carrots, packed down
     1¼ cups vegetable oil
      1 cup crushed pineapple with juice
      1 cup shredded coconut
     2¼ cups flour
      2 teaspoons cinnamon
      1 teaspoon baking soda
      1 teaspoon salt
      1 teaspoon vanilla
      1 cup chopped walnuts (optional)
      ½ cup golden raisins (optional)
```

Beat the eggs, add the sugar and keep on beating until mixture is fairly smooth. Add the carrots and mix. Add everything else and mix well. Put mixture into two greased loaf pans (fill each pan about half way). Bake in preheated 350 degree oven for an hour. Remove, and let the cakes sit for a half hour before taking them out of the pans.

Yield: 2 loaf-size cakes

In Oak Ridge, Tennessee, Daniel Hulsey created an elaborate route for Deng Xiaoping:

> He should be chauffeured through downtown Knoxville on Interstate 40 during the evening rush hour, on his way to McDonald's on Cumberland Avenue, where he should personally order his dinner and be allowed to eat it in the car on his way to West Town Mall for an evening of American shopping. He should be given $10.00 to spend there.

In Florence, Massachusetts, listener Roger Sherman wanted the vice-premier to experience the Miss Florence Diner:

> It's beautiful, with lots of neon and waitresses who never write down your order. They just shout it. If you order a turkey sandwich, the waitress yells, "Chicken sandwich!" but you get turkey If you want chicken, she yells "Chicken sandwich!" and you get chicken. I can't figure it out.

And from St. George's Island, Maryland, Michael and Terry Evans extended a personal invitation:

> Let the Chinese visit us. We're a small and happy family, a husband and wife and three small children. We live in a little cottage on the water. We paid cash for the cottage. We run our own construction company. Our house is heated solely by a wood stove. We have no TV. We love America. We'll take a moonlight walk to the shore to hear the whistling swans. To understand us, you must walk with us, talk with us, work with us, and share with us. Let the people of America give our new Chinese friends something which our government cannot—a visit with the American people.

Bruce Marsden, still driving home, in Oakland, California.

THE NAZI RALLY

All Things Considered began broadcasting on Monday, May 3, 1971. That day, anti-war demonstrators tried to close down the city of Washington, D.C. More than 7,000 people were arrested. NPR reporters prowled the streets, taping the sounds of protestors, police and ambulance sirens, army helicopters; and questioning the police:

> **Reporter**   Excuse me, Sergeant. Jeff Kamen, National Public Radio. Is that a technique? Where the men actually try to drive the motorcycles right into the demonstrators?
>
> **Policeman**   Naw, it's no technique. We're trying to go down the road and the people get in front of you. What are you gonna do? You don't stop on a dime.

At the Pentagon, at the Lincoln Memorial, in hospital emergency wards, the demonstrators described their experiences:

> **Young man**   I was at Washington Square, and when the cop busted me and put me in the car I was peaceful. But then when they got me in the car they said, "You're stupid, kid." And the guy whacked me with a billy club.
>
> **Reporter**   Right there in the eye?
>
> **Young man**   I got eleven stitches.
>
> **Reporter**   Is this gonna stop you?
>
> **Young man**   No.

Voice after voice, sound after sound. It was guerrilla radio, taking the listener to the heart of the event. I can remember the production staff sitting around on desk tops outside the studio and control room, listening to that first broadcast, riveted. Demonstrations and rallies are standard, noisy, quick-action footage for television. On radio, *ATC* was *listening* to the demonstrators and hearing that rallies are more than a cacophony of sound.

Seven years later, in July 1978, NPR's Scott Simon spent an entire Sunday at an American Nazi Party rally in Chicago's Marquette Park. Scott roamed everywhere and recorded everything. He kept his tape machine running for seven and a half hours. At five in the evening, from a telephone booth near the park, he filed a short news report on the day's events. Then he went home and watched the news on television. The Nazi rally ran as the number-two national story of the day—a thirty-second spot that gave viewers the idea everything was all right because no injuries had been reported. Scott phoned his editor, Robert Siegel, in Washington, convinced that many injuries had occurred during the course of the day—not physical injuries, perhaps, but injuries to the spirit, to the idea of America. Siegel told Scott to put together the story of what went on beyond the speaker's platform, for Wednesday's *All Things Considered*. It didn't matter that the piece would run three days after the rally had taken place. The event had tapped themes that Siegel and Simon felt should be explored. Although the rally was over, the themes weren't dated.

On the air Wednesday night, co-host Bob Edwards introduced the piece, explaining that some twenty Nazis had been in the park, surrounded by 1,500 policemen and 3,000 to 5,000 men and women, many of whom denounced the Nazis, many of whom supported them. Scott's report began by underscoring the small number of Nazis present. He said there were more reporters than Nazis, more counter-demonstrators, even more police horses. "But what we want to examine now," Scott went on, "is the reaction of those people in the park last Sunday . . . thousands of people who were neither members of the Nazi Party nor members of counter-demonstrating groups; people who were there simply by choice or through circumstance."

Scott Simon The neighborhood itself is entirely white, encircled by areas now predominantly black. The residents work mostly in nearby assembly plants, factories, and small stores. Most own their own homes. In a city of apartment dwellers and racially mixed communities, Marquette Park is conspicuously different, and the park itself is considered to be a symbol of that difference.

First man Everybody wants to keep this park white. It's a peaceful park. It has zero crime rate—and we like it that way. I think most of the people around here support the rally.

Simon But these guys are Nazis.

First man I see 'em as representing white people, right now. It's true that they'd get more support without their swastika, but at least they're for white people.

Simon What do you think the Nazis are marching for today?

Second man I have no idea.

Simon What are you going to do when the march occurs?

Second man I'm gonna just do what I'm doin' right now.

Simon Work in the garden?

Second man Yeah, that's right. I don't give a damn if they kill one another.

(Airplane sounds/dogs barking)

Simon By mid-morning, police helicopters had come in low over the park, the wind from their blades spilling leaves from the trees and raising up picnic blankets. Lines of police stood along the sidewalks. Women, older men in knee-length shorts, and children in cut-off blue jeans filled the face of the small hill along the street leading into the park. Some had brought folding lawn chairs. On the opposite side of the park, store owners could be seen peering from under the shades of their windows. Heavy steel grates had been drawn across many shop doors. At Holy Cross Hospital, hospital directors spoke to the patients by closed-circuit television.

Hospital voice It's a beautiful day here in Marquette Park. But some of the activity outside is not so beautiful. We want to tell you a little about what's going on. You know that the Nazis are causing some problems in the area today and some other counter-marchers. Sister

Dorothy and the other sisters are present and would like to assure you that all is well and that you are safe here at Holy Cross Hospital.

(Crowd sounds/helicopters/traffic)

Simon Barricades had been set up to surround and protect the Nazis. The barricades were placed in the center of the park, near the public rest rooms. Beyond the barricades, thousands struck off over the small hills and spread-out spaces. Many brought signs reading SIX MILLION MORE or JEWS GO HOME. Youngsters wore T-shirts embossed with plain black swastikas and the words WHITE POWER. At the other end of the park, public buses brought in scores of authorized observers from Jewish-community and civil-liberties organizations. Police in riot gear escorted them from the buses.

Hospital voice In the meantime we ask that you join with the sisters in hoping and praying that we'll have no very serious injuries here this afternoon.

(Crowd shouts build)

Man's voice Give the Arabs back their land, you bunch of thieves.

Simon The Nazis arrived almost unnoticed in a white van pulled up to the entrance of the public rest room. The twenty Nazis, several of them only twelve to eighteen years old, entered the rest room in street clothes and came out in brown shirts and swastikas. Their speaker stood on the top of the van secured several hundred yards behind the sawhorse barriers and mounted police. The Nazis really were not heard nor seen by the several thousand people in the park. The people, their faces swelling with rage, were separated from each other and restrained by plainclothes policemen.

Man's voice Any one of you Jews wanta fight an Aryan—one on one? Better yet, two on one—I'll take two of you Hebes on. I'm an Aryan. I'm a white Irish American. I'm an Aryan.

(Applause and cheering from crowd)

Man's voice Six million wasn't enough. Jews go home.

Crowd *(chanting)* Jews go home. Jews go home. Jews go home. Jews go home. Jews go home. Jews go home. Jews go home.

Simon Also in the crowd were organizers from leftist political groups, wading into the lines of those who seemed in sympathy with the Nazis to argue that it was the commercial system that turned people against one another. They ignored the goading of racial and sexual epithets, stood up to those in white power T-shirts, and tried to disarm their anger. But the more they seemed to emphasize the effect of economics, the more their listeners seemed to return to race.

Crowd voices *(shouting)*   I worked for a Jew and all he wanted. . . . I worked at Ampleton Electric and. . . . I worked for. . . . You know what their religion is? Their religion is money, man, their religion is money. Everyone's religion is money. What religion is Rockefeller? A Jew will kill another Jew just to get his money. . . . And a Christian will kill a Christian to get his money, too. Am I right? . . . Wherever they can get working people fighting among each other, that's where the boss comes out on top. It's the oldest trick in the book, and they pull it out every time. . . . That's the damn joke about it. You are so concerned about it, and they don't care whether you're white or not. You come up against them, they'll beat you down just as hard as anybody else. And that's the joke. . . . Yah, yah, yah, yah, yah, yah. . . .

Crowd *(chanting)*   Six million more! Six million more! Six million more!

Simon   The Nazis seemed nearly ignored in all this, standing so far away, heard so feebly, moving almost like small string puppets as they gestured from the top of the van. But then one of the speakers raised himself to his toes and stuck out his arm, palm stiff, in the Nazi salute. And, on this bright Sunday in the middle of America, the audience of Americans wearing T-shirts, tennis shoes, denim shorts, and baseball caps responded with claps, cheers, whistles. shouts of "hooray," and strains of "The Battle Hymn of the Republic."

Crowd   *Sieg heil! Sieg heil! Sieg heil! Sieg heil!*

Simon   Half a mile away, police halted a march of about a thousand black counter-demonstrators en route to the park. The blacks sang and chanted as groups of white people came to confront them in the echoes of the underpass and were kept behind the three lines of police. The whites taunted the police and press photographers.

Man's voice   Get a lot of pictures, Jew boy? Will you tell them all stories about when you all killed Jesus, and all that?

Man's voice   I'm not Jewish.

First man   Oh, okay.

(Crowd shouting, yelling, screaming)

Simon   In Marquette Park there were more quarrels, snarling, and countless fights interrupted by plainclothes policemen. A black observer who somehow wandered into the park was set upon and beaten before he could be rescued. A black news photographer had to do his job encircled by police. As different groups threatened to push each other, the police would rush over and link

There are three kinds of survivors. One kind will forget it forever, like my friend in the south of France. She has two children, twenty and seventeen. They don't know their mother was in a concentration camp. The second kind still lives in concentration camps. They speak about it to one another day and night; they marry amongst themselves. They say, "You remember, on Monday the tenth, we did this and that and that." But I am the kind who wants to live in the present, *and* I want the world to know what happened. That's why all my life I have explained and told the stories of Auschwitz. So it would never, never happen again. That was the purpose of my life. I always knew that it would start again, that the fascism would come.
—Fania Fenelon, Auschwitz survivor, December 1980

hands in a human barricade. Each side pressed in on the other, the face of policemen straining red and steaming off sweat as they kept arguments apart by important inches.

Man	I ain't hit a kike in thirty seconds, man. I wanna hit somebody.
Man	Man, I'd rather shoot a nigger.
Woman	How come you wanta hit one so bad?
Man	'Cause they got no right here.
Woman	Why?
Man	And you don't have no right here.
Woman	Why?
Man	Do you live around here?
Woman	No.
Man	Then you don't have no right here.
Woman	Why?
Man	This is white—and we want to keep it white. We don't want no Jews or no niggers in here.
Woman	How come you can't share it?
Man	You got Skokie. You don't want us up in Skokie. We don't want you down here.
Other voices	Share it! How come you can't share it?
Man	I will squeeze the life out of you, you bitch.
Crowd	Whoo. Yah. Ray. *(Applause.)*
Man	You are no good. . . . You are white trash and we don't want you here. So why don't you turn around and walk out? I never hit a woman, but it's going to be a pleasure to cream you.
Woman	I care about you.
Man	Get outta my face.
Man	Here's somethin' you can write in your little papers and every-

John Spragens, Jr., listens in Berkeley, California.

	thing. We're all from different neighborhoods. Nobody knows everyone. But for the first time in a long time we've got a common bond. We're all white—we're all together.
Man	We're all together.
Man	And we're gonna stick it out until the finish.
Crowd	White power, white power, white power. (*Some applause.*) White power. (*More applause.*)
Simon	One young man slipped out from the arms of several policemen leading him to a paddywagon and leaped into the park's lagoon. swimming to the other side as Nazi supporters, Jewish counter-demonstrators, and bystanders applauded his escape. The swimmer bounded out to cheers and raised his arms in triumph before hurtling a fence to run off. No one knew who he was or why he was there, but it seemed for a time the only understandable moment of the day. The park began emptying, fights growing more wide-ranging and dangerous as groups kept separate earlier by the police now came upon one another in the streets. Four young men left, carrying a football, blankets, and a beer cooler.
First man	Today didn't prove nothing to me. Just an upset.
Second man	To me it showed one thing, that before the Nazis used to come into the park and everybody was for them. Now they had a little protest against them. Now they are thinking. If they didn't have the cops, there would have been an all-out riot. They would have gotten wiped over the floor.
Simon	The people who protested, were they all from outside, or were there people here who don't quite agree with what the Nazis were saying?
Second man	There were people around here who wouldn't agree with them.
Simon	There was a moment when, back of me and to the right, there was one black guy who somehow wandered in.
Man	Yeah, he's Jewish.
Simon	Some people swarmed over him and hit him. Why'd they do that?
Man	He was dancing with the Jews.
Simon	Because a black was dancing with a Jew, they've got to attack him?
Man	The ones who were with the Nazis attacked the black because he's black and because he's with the Jews. He had two things against him.
Simon	Does it make any sense to you?
Man	No. They don't know that particular guy's background or anything. They just know he's black and that's why they got him.
Simon	And, in a sense, that seemed the harshest thing, of all the

diatribes and epithets. That in the 1970s in the center of the country, it was still possible for someone to be beaten up simply because he or she was of a certain race. And to certain people, still, this seemed unexceptional and proper. *(Motorcycle and bus sounds/sirens receding.)*

The police removed their riot helmets and began to file into the row of city buses that had brought them into the park. The Nazis went directly back into their van and were taken, by escort, to their nearby headquarters four blocks west of the park. Large red iron doors shut tightly together, covering even the windows of the headquarters. No one acknowledged the ringing of the doorbell. The demonstration at Marquette Park was over. For National Public Radio, this is Scott Simon in Chicago.

A WIFE DIES

We listen for America in the stories people tell about their lives. Sometimes *All Things Considered* follows these stories for weeks and months. A young woman named Debbie kept us posted on her fight to lose 150 pounds. Farmers Floyd and Lucy Meeker described sales, one summer, at their produce stand in Bowling Green, Ohio.

The stories can be funny: Lee Garlington left a safe job (rare) and a cockroach-free apartment (rarer) in Washington to try to become a Hollywood star. Her second week there she got two film jobs on the same day. In one role she walked out of a bank as George Segal walked in. In the other, Lee and her van appeared in a traffic jam on the Santa Monica Freeway. ("What's George Segal really like, Lee?" "Short.")

And the stories can be deeply moving. Two very different men shared their grief with *All Things Considered*. They were men we had come to know. One of them, for several weeks in 1972, had described his retirement to us—how he passed his days. The other man had been a commentator on *All Things Considered* for years, a witty observer who expressed opinions on everything from Groucho Marx to the effect of Watergate on the hotel business. Now, speaking to us in sadness, each man helped us understand the experience of loss.

In winter, when the snow was six feet deep, Professor Jerzy Roman made the half-mile trek to his wife's grave in showshoes. He was eighty when *ATC* met him in 1972, a retired teacher of electrical engineering at Michigan Technological University in Houghton. Professor Roman visited the cemetery every day. One day, Joe Kirkish of member station WGGL went along and taped some of Professor Roman's thoughts, as he trudged through the snow:

> All the philosophers who want to solve the mysteries of life should come to the cemetery, far away from the noise of daily work. When my problems are building up, becoming more and more complicated, more subtle, only by kneeling down here do I find a little bit of peace.
>
> To my mind, every deep feeling demands some sort of liturgy. Bringing flowers to the grave of someone loved is that kind of liturgy. I am bringing flowers to emphasize to my wife that I'm still loving her, and loving her perhaps more than I did during her life. I'm bringing the very best flowers I can. And then I'm talking to her. I'm asking her to pardon me for all my mistakes I made during my life with her. I'm trying to excuse myself for not being the ideal husband I wanted to be.
>
> People are so deep in the daily work of life that they are forgetting that apart from this daily life there is some other kind of spiritual life. To learn to like the spiritual life is rather hard. You have to go through tragedy sometimes in order to find that out.
>
> When it's a windy day, the drifting snow whirls, and clouds

are coming toward me in the cemetery, telling me all sorts of things. They are telling me that this is the place where the sum of human sufferings has been buried.

It's not a place for young people, especially in winter. It's a place that can be really appreciated by old people. Let the young remain in life, enjoy dance, sport, song. Leave the aged people for the cemetery.

They were the Easy Aces—the popular comedy stars of early 1930s and 1940s radio. He the funny writer. She the mistress of malapropisms. Jane Ace was seventy-four when she died November 11, 1974. Her husband, Goodman, was a commentator on *All Things Considered*. Two months after Jane's death, Goodman Ace spoke about his wife.

She left without even saying good-bye. So unlike her. Even when she was off to a matinee with a friend, it was always, "See you later, dear." And always I said, "Not if I see you first." A family joke. And now a family of one.

November 11. Five days before our fiftieth anniversary. If she had known she was going to die, she would have stayed. But she hadn't known—hadn't even had an inkling.

Alone in the funeral home during all of the arrangements, there ran through my mind a constant rerun of a line that she had spoken on radio. She was talking about the brotherhood of man. In her casual malapropian style, she said, "We are all cremated equal."

Two limousines took us to the cemetery that cold autumn morning. A graveside service. The snow stopped the instant the last words were spoken. In His infinite compassion, He had the grace to celebrate her arrival with a handful of His confetti.

Finally back home. Home? House! Remembering to try to forget. But there was the mail, hundreds upon hundreds of letters expressing sympathy and comfort. Even now, two months later, the letters are spread around her photograph on the piano, treasured. Now and then, I pick up a few at random, to read and reread: "Haven't heard her in forty years, but I feel as if I knew and loved her." And one from a man who wrote: "I do not so much mourn the death of Jane Ace as I rejoice in the life of her."

Every letter a comfort and solace. Like time, they help to heal. So unlike the way Jane says it, or said it (excuse me please, I still can't get used to it): "Time wounds all heels."

And you want to hear the eeriest part of all? Whenever I open the letters again, for a split second I reach for the phone to read them all to her.

LISTENING UP

The telephone is journalism's most important tool. Phones connect reporters to sources, to facts, information, and verification. In radio, phones deliver stories directly to the listeners. In the early years of *All Things Considered,* when the reporting staff was small and travel budgets smaller, three-quarters of the program was done by telephone. The phone took us to places we couldn't afford to visit, and introduced us to people we otherwise couldn't have met That remains true. We still call faraway places, like Peking or Teheran or Kankakee, to ask what s going on there and report it the same day.

I've come to enjoy telephone interviews almost more than those done face to face. On the phone, I'm not distracted by the ugly tie, or the nervous tic, or the exquisite manicure. By phone, it's strictly voice to voice, and I can concentrate totally on what's being said. I also like the crackle of the phone line and the kind of electric punch it gives the conversations. Then, too, the telephone receiver is a microphone everyone knows how to use. People are relaxed and comfortable speaking on the phone, and that quality comes across. A recording studio, with all its equipment and electronic gear, is a pretty intimidating place. All kinds of people (children, especially) just freeze up in a studio. Call 'em on the telephone, though, and they'll curl right up for a chat.

Sometimes you find folks with nothing better to do than talk on the phone. That certainly was true in 1974, when I called Vernon Woodrich in Los Angeles. But the conversation was over my head.

Stamberg	Where are you, now, Mr. Woodrich?
Woodrich	On top of a thirty-foot flagpole.
Stamberg	Why?
Woodrich	I'm trying to break a record. The current record is 115 days. I'm going for 120. I've been here 25 days so far.
Stamberg	How do you do it?
Woodrich	I have a six-foot platform up here. I'm not sitting on top of the ball of a pole or anything.
Stamberg	Oh, that's good, because that would be uncomfortable.
Woodrich	Yeah.
Stamberg	Yes. How do you eat? How do you sleep? How do you go to the bathroom?
Woodrich	Well, I have a chemical toilet. I have a sleeping bag and a four-inch-thick foam-rubber mattress. Food is sent up to me in a bucket on a pulley. I have a telephone, so I can call down in case of an emergency. I can talk to my wife, and I have a radio and I have a TV.
Stamberg	So it's really sort of life as normal except you're thirty feet higher than any of the rest of us.
Woodrich	And on a six-foot square.
Stamberg	What's the hardest thing about being up there?

Woodrich	Not being able to go for any walks.
Stamberg	What is the thing you find yourself thinking about the most?
Woodrich	Each day getting shorter.
Stamberg	When you're not sitting on a flagpole, how do you spend your time?
Woodrich	I usually work in a restaurant.
Stamberg	How did you get off from your job to do this for 120 days?
Woodrich	I was unemployed at the time.
Stamberg	I see. So it was the perfect opportunity.
Woodrich	Yeah. I have a slight case of high blood pressure, and I have to relax and take it easy. This is a good way to do it.
Stamberg	Your doctor is not worried that sitting on a flagpole for 120 days might be dangerous for your blood pressure?
Woodrich	Nope. I'm not under any tension or hypertension up here. I'm not getting aggravated.
Stamberg	Is it a nice place to be for a while?
Woodrich	Well, if you can learn to live with yourself and not become bored, it's not bad.
Stamberg	Was that hard for you to do?
Woodrich	I'm learning. Each day it gets a little easier. The first few days were so long that I didn't know what to do with myself. And I went through one or two days of depression where I was almost on the verge of coming down. When I finally began to relax and stop trying to hurry everything, everything became fine.
Stamberg	Mr. Woodrich, when I called you, I thought what you're doing was crazy. Now I'm starting to envy you.
Woodrich	Lots of people end up feeling that way.

All Things Considered never checked back to see whether Vernon Woodrich made it through the full 120 days. Putting the book together so many years later (he went up the flagpole in 1974, remember), we got curious again. No listing in the *Guinness Book of Records*. No information from the *Los Angeles Times*. No Vernon Woodrich in the Los Angeles telephone directory. The mail carrier says there's no flagpole at the address we had. Nothing.

Vernon Woodrich, if you're reading this, please get in touch and let us know what happened. We're starting to wonder whether you really were on that flagpole in the first place. Telephone interviews do have their limitations.

A LIFE IN CRIME

Bob Kingsley let us in on an underside of American life. Kingsley was chief cook at a private school in Fargo, North Dakota, when Bill Siemering spoke with him in December 1977. But in an earlier incarnation, Kingsley had been a safecracker. He'd gone to jail four times, for a total of eight years. Crime, as Kingsley described it, is a kind of art form:

In the beginning, it was the money I was after. But the first time I opened a safe by myself was like discovering sex. I said, "My god. This is something I did all by myself." I don't think I've ever spoken to a safecracker who said that he didn't enjoy it. Most of us feel that we're in a hierarchy, too. You're not just a rip-and-tear burglar. You're going in there specifically to do a specific thing. We take pride in the fact that it's not an armed robbery. Anybody can take a gun and walk in and take some money away from a person. But not anybody can walk into a place at night and open a safe and achieve what he set out to do.

After a while, the money became kind of secondary. I mean, once you've accumulated a certain amount of money and you've met what you feel are your needs, just to open that thing up is the primary function.

The life I lived was a lot faster paced than the average person's. It wasn't necessary for me to make thirty-six payments in a thirty-six-month period to buy a car. I'd go out and get the money and I bought it right then. My partner and I had a goal of $1,500 a week. Every week we made $1,500. If it took us seven days to do it, we were out every night for seven nights. If it took us one day, okay. We retired for the rest of the week. And I never really thought about the penitentiary. I was thinking about buying a new car. It's like anything else in life, you have little drawbacks, and going to the penitentiary was one of them.

Most professional criminals feel the same way. As a matter of fact, some of them go to the extreme of building up little bankrolls for their families because they anticipate that within the next five years or so they're going to be busted and they're going to have to serve four or five more years. So they make allowances for these things. But the goal inside the penitentiary is to get back out again.

Rehabilitation as it exists today is just a fraud. We play these little games in the penitentiary. If you don't make waves, you're back out in the street again. So you play the games. But that hasn't changed your attitude any or given you a new set of values. I mean, if you go to church, it's not for God to hear your prayer. You hope that some guard is going to report to the board that you're really a devout individual. Then you get out faster.

One New Yorker's Guilt
I feel guilty about not getting to work on time. I feel guilty about getting to work too early. I feel guilty about getting to work on time and making other people feel that they should have gotten to work at the same time. I feel guilty about getting up too early in the morning, because I might wake somebody up. I feel guilty about sleeping too late, because they might have to creep around and not disturb me, and I don't want them to feel bad. You see what I mean. Once you're into it, the whole world opens up for you.

One of the philosophies is that you go in there and you become a hell-raiser, cause quite a bit of trouble for the first six months. Then, slowly but surely, you change. You start accepting the programs, you start attending church, seeing your social worker; and then this beautiful conversion record is shown to the board and they release you. And I know in my heart that those board members sitting up there say, "Well, at least we got him to play the game." They're not dummies. They know what's happening. But they've got to make room in the penitentiary for the new batch. It's just a flow of people through the doors, in and out and back again.

If a person is truly going to be rehabilitated I would think that the first thing that the person would have to know is that he did something wrong. The first thing the alcoholic has to do is admit that he is an alcoholic. I think the first thing the criminal has to do is admit that he did commit a crime. The majority of us have a lot of other words for it. It's not "stealing," it's "hustling," it's "making a buck," it's "doing your thing." The only time you use "stealing" is when somebody takes something from *you*. So the criminal has to become aware that he did something to an individual that he wouldn't want done to himself.

My wife's the one who keeps me from going back to safecracking. She's a social worker. Funny combination, the social worker and the burglar. But it works. We have deep feelings for each other.

It used to be difficult for me to handle waiting for anything. As a matter of fact, it's still a little difficult sometimes. If my wife and I are talking about taking a trip to New York or buying some stereo equipment, I don't really want to wait for it. She has to slow me down and say, "Hey, wait a minute." It's still a pattern. It's there. I think I'm breaking it slowly but surely, but it's there.

I'm not earning nearly as much money now as I did cracking safes. But I'm a lot happier. I know one thing: When I was out there stealing I used to go through a bottle of Rolaids a day. That's a hundred tablets. I'd walk out to my car and just touch the handle of my car, and my stomach would go into a knot. I haven't had those problems lately.

THE BEST HAMBURGERS IN AMERICA

A Contest

Keep your Two-All-Beef-Patties-Special-Sauce-Lettuce-Cheese-Pickles-Onions-on-a-Sesame-Seed-Bun, or

> *"Nobody sent us a hamburger. Only scores of wonderful descriptions of hamburgers. I know. I read them all. I am the hamburger editor."*
>
> — Paula Schiller

In February 1978, *All Things Considered* told its listeners where to find eighty-two of the best hamburgers in America. Why we didn't come up with a plump, juicy, perfectly rounded one hundred candidates, I'm not quite sure. Maybe the mail was slow.

ATC weekend hosts Noah Adams and Jackie Judd had invited listeners to name and defend their favorite burgers. Production assistant Paula Schiller collated the entries. Two books Noah was reading that winter prompted the contest: Calvin Trillin's *American Fried,* and *Where to Eat in America* by William Rice and Burton Wolf. Trillin's theory is that the best hamburgers in the world are served in the hamburger stands of childhood. Trillin told Noah that the all-time best hamburger was, and still is, served at Winstead's in Kansas City.

Trillin   I made a firm decision about where the best hamburger in the world was when I was fourteen, and I naturally haven't changed my mind. I think anybody who changes his mind after the age of fourteen on a matter like that is a deviate, a backslider, a security risk, probably.

Adams   If I came to New York and asked for a good place to get a hamburger, what would you tell me?

Trillin   I would tell you to fly to Kansas City.

Noah gave equal hamburger time to food writer William Rice.

Rice   Having gotten on an airplane and having gone to Kansas City, I have to differ with Trillin about Winstead's. Winstead's hamburger is not worth the voyage. In fact, in Kansas City we recommended a place called Fred P. Ott's for hamburger. Winstead's hamburger is all right, but it's not an extraordinary hamburger.

Adams   We have a letter from James Mark Palmer, a listener in Athens, Ohio, who says, "At the top of my list of excellent hamburger emporiums is Winstead's of Kansas City."

Rice   Ah ha! This is Calvin Trillin writing under an assumed name. I think we can take that for granted.

Adams   If someone told you to go anywhere you please to get the best hamburger in the country—expense is no object—where would you go?

Rice   For the operation, the ritual, and dedication attached to it—in a town where plastic food is the norm—I'd go to Cassell's in Los Angeles.

Does Your Butcher Love You?
You can tell stores care about the consumer if they clean their hamburger machines every day.
—David Frampton, butcher, Richmond, New Hampshire

45

So much for the professionals. Then the real experts spoke. Our listeners. According to them, the *most* best hamburgers are found in the Midwest—maybe because most of our listeners live there. John Nolan, in Iowa City, gave high marks to Hamburger Inn #1 and #2 when he was interviewed by Jackie Judd:

> **Nolan** It's just a plain hamburger. It's not adulterated with the frills and garbage that ruin otherwise perfectly good hamburgers.
>
> **Judd** What do you mean?
>
> **Nolan** Mayonnaise.
>
> **Judd** How about onion rings?
>
> **Nolan** Filler. Now, I don't mind something like lettuce or onion.
>
> **Judd** But you draw the line at mayonnaise?
>
> **Nolan** Mayonnaise is too much. That's the Californication of hamburgers.

Lerk's Bar in Afton, Minnesota, got the most votes from listeners around the country. Doug Johnson of River Falls, Wisconsin, described it:

> Lerk's Bar is a sleazy riverman's bar on the St. Croix River. Other than a sweep and mop, it is in its original state. Lerkburgers are fried—not baked, broiled, or electrocuted. They arrive on paper plates with onions and potato chips, nothing else.

Charles Zelle, of the District of Columbia, told how you get to Lerk's Bar:

> Well, you go on a highway through Afton. Afton's a pretty nice town. It has a lot of curvy roads near a stream. When you hit the edge of town, there's a small bar there. I'm not even sure if there's a sign outside. As a matter of fact, if you didn't know it was

there, I don't think you'd be able to find it. It's not hyped up. Everybody just knows that's where the Lerkburger is.

Small and unpretentious, most of the hamburger places are located near parking lots, busy shopping centers, or down by the tracks. No china plates, no cloth napkins. The point is food, not atmosphere. Some places offer dozens of extras; others, like Louis' Lunch, sell only two kinds of burger—with and without cheese.

Louis' Lunch is a historical monument in New Haven, Connecticut. The hamburger may have been invented there. The place has been in business long enough —since 1899—and the original cooker is still in use. Jack Eiferman of West Trenton, New Jersey, described how hamburgers are made at Louis' Lunch:

> Two (or one, three, four, whatever) balls of meat are pressed, seasoned, imbedded with a thin slice of onion, and then placed in a vertical broiler, to be cooked on both sides at the same time. Then the burger is placed on freshly toasted Pepperidge Farm white bread (no tasteless muffins with obnoxious sesame seeds). Finally, if you so desire, a nice tangy cheddar cheese spread is available. Or some nice fresh tomato. No special sauce, pickle, chips—and *most* important, no catsup!! This is a hamburger for those who like hamburger, not junk that covers up the flavor of freshly prepared and properly broiled ground beef.

Finally, here are the favorite places, the quintessential hamburger joints, heavens, etc. Those that have closed will live on in our collective memory:

Alabama	*Birmingham:* The Dairy Snack, Milo's
Arizona	*Tucson:* The Chuck Wagon
Arkansas	*Pine Bluff:* John Noah's
California	*Los Angeles:* Cassell's, Tommy's, Hampton's Kitchen *East Los Angeles:* Chronis Hamburger Stand *Northeast Los Angeles:* Pete's Blue Chip *West Los Angeles:* The Apple Pan *Studio City:* Fat Jack's *National City (south of San Diego):* Jimmy's Family Restaurant
Connecticut	*New Haven:* Louis' Lunch
Florida	*Fort Lauderdale:* Jack's Hamburger House *Palm Beach:* Hamburger Heaven
Indiana	*Bloomington:* Hinkle's *Marengo:* Marengo Tavern *Valpariso:* The Olde Style
Iowa	*Iowa City:* Hamburger Inn #1 and #2
Kentucky	*Ashland:* The Bluegrass
Louisiana	*New Orleans:* Camellia Grill

Massachusetts	*Cambridge:* Mr. Bartley's Burger Cottage
Michigan	*Ann Arbor:* Fleetwood Diner, Del-Rio Bar
	Beaver Island: Circle M Supper Club
	Dearborn: Miller's Bar
	Detroit: Checker Bar
	Lansing: Kewpee's
Minnesota	*Afton:* Lerk's Bar
	Coates: House of Coates
	Mankato: Hilltop Tavern
	St. Paul: Haberdashery, The Frontier
Missouri	*Columbia:* Ernie's Steak House
	Rolla: Maid-Rite
Nebraska	*Belleview:* Stella's
New Hampshire	*Claremont:* Pleasant Restaurant
	Hanover: Hopkins Center Snack Bar
New Jersey	*Point Pleasant:* Skokos Drive-In
New Mexico	*Albuquerque:* Blake's Lotaburger
	Farmington: George and John's
	San Antonio: The Owl Cafe
New York	*NYC:* The Cedar Tavern, P. J. Clarke's, Jackson Hole
North Carolina	*Pantego:* Mrs. Lee's
	Plymouth: Eva's Diner
Ohio	*Cincinnati:* Mecklenburgs
	Glendale: Century Inn
	Greenville: Maid-Rite
	Rocky River: Herb's Tavern
Oklahoma	*Oklahoma City:* Split-T
Oregon	*Portland:* Yaw's
	Rice HIll: D & B
Pennsylvania	*Selinsgrove:* Biff Burger
	Springfield: Charlies
	Tunkhannock: Shadow Brook Dairy Bar
South Dakota	*Brookings:* Nick's
Texas	*Austin:* Grove Drug
	Waco: The Health Camp
Washington, D.C.	Gallagher's Pub
Wisconsin	*Cedar Grove:* De Smidt's
	Green Bay: Kroll's
	Madison: Plaza Tavern
	Sturgeon Bay: Babe and Ray's
	Waupaca: Simpson's Restaurant
	West Sweden: West Sweden Bar

What's There to Do in Murray, Kentucky, on Saturday Night?
It's a little path. Go down to Burger Chef. Come back. Go out to the court square and just see what's happenin'. Look at crazy people. I've seen lots of 'em doin' lots of things on the court square. There's a guy stood right there on that corner and danced for a long time. He's good, too. Just do what you want to do. If you don't want to do it, don't worry about it.

GONE FISHING

A Commentary by Gamble Rogers

I would like to sing a hymn of praise to one of the most seldom celebrated groups of American heroes—men for whom the noble concepts of free determination, personal integrity, and Yankee ingenuity are as natural as breathing. I am speaking, of course, of the commercial fishermen of Big Lake George.

Big Lake George, Florida, is right down the Oklawaha River from Eureka, near Palatka. Well, it's a big mother. Sixteen miles long.

Early of an A.M., when the lake is gun-metal gray spangled with burgundy, and gossamer streamers of sunlight shaft skyward through the palmetto and cypress fringe, and the noble blue heron and the sassy anhinga leave the sanctity of the rookery in search of sustenance, you can hear these water-borne good ol' boys whipping over the surface of the lake. Each one sits tall in his forty-year-old, flat-bottomed, paint-flaked, plywood fishing skiff, the bow piled high with crab traps, trot lines, and fish weirs. He's got a Winchester rifle. If he catches some pilgrim rustlin' his crab traps, he'll perforate his sorry carcass and sink him in the sanctified waters of the mystic lake. For he flat do not give a damn! I can see him now, his horny, callow right hand wrapped reposefully about the throttle of a 175-horsepower Mercury outboard motor with a quicksilver lower unit, stirring a paper plate full of pot-liquor and grits nailed down to the seat at his left side, whipping through the Florida atmosphere at eighty-three miles per hour, his mouth a thin, white line, nostrils flared.

He say, "She-e-e-e-e!"

Well, now, one day I'm hanging around the Gulf Oil pumps in Georgetown, and one of these commercial fishermen whips in off the Tarmac, pulling his rig behind his Dodge Club Cab pick-up truck. You know the Dodge Club Cab— that's the stretch version of your common pick-up, so you can carry *two* gun racks. He opens the door and eases out, a symphony in pastoral grace. I was up for the encounter. I had on my Johnny Cash belt, my boots, and my Blue-Bell Wrangler shirt with the pearl snap buttons. As he came toward me, I sized him up.

I said, "Howdy."

He looked me over. He said, "She-e-e-e-e!"

I said, "Buddy-buddy, you must catch right smart of crabs and fish to buy a big kicker like that."

He said, "Pilgrim, I didn't get that outboard motor catchin' no crabs!!"

That's where the second part of the tale commences.

Winding out of the Georgia Piedmont like a malignant magic carpet of concrete is Interstate 75. It bores relentlessly southward, splits the sovereign beauty of Florida asunder, heads off toward Tampa past the greatest commercial concession ever articulated in the entrepreneurial visionings of modern mankind, a monument to the legacy of Mickey Mouse. Disney World, Disney World, a $500 million jukebox in the honky-tonk of life!! Disney World!!

And, here comes the average American tourist in his Winnebago Camper. He's got two Yamaha trail bikes on the front bumper. He's got an Old-Town canoe lashed to the left side, four snowmobiles on the roof, a pair of L.L. Bean polypropylene snowshoes crossed on the back door. He's got Savage Anschutz .22 rifles, Shakespeare fishing rods, Zebco spinning reels, Uncle Josh pork rind, Coleman double-mantle lanterns, Barlow knives, air mattresses, sleeping bags, pup tents, and pack frames. He's got Naugahyde upholstery, shag carpet, Panasonic television sets, and two point six (2.6) children. And if that's not enough, he's towing a Cobia Fiberglas family runabout with an Evinrude V-4 Starflight outboard motor. He is sitting tall at the helm of his motorized Conestoga, wearing a Pendelton Mackinaw, smoking a Marsh-Wheeling cheroot. He looks down at his lovely bride.

He say, "Mama, we are the great, the chosen, cosmic consumers. We're packing everything we'll ever need right here on our backs!"

They get down to the Lake Monroe Bridge on the St. John's River and run into a forty-five–mile traffic jam winding all the way up from the front gate of Disney World. And a solid phalanx of fools swelter in the Florida sunlight. And a malodorous mantle of exhaust fumes diffuses itself abroad over the land of flowers. But this man is up to any contingency.

He say, "Mama, let us take advantage of this hiatus and go fishing."

So, they back the Cobia runabout into the water and set out trolling with 1,500 other pilgrims. You could walk across the water on outboard motors. Ain't nobody caught a fish in that part of the river for twenty years. Too many pilgrims!

He trolls down to Big Lake George. Here's one of those commercial fishermen in his hook-nose skipjack. He's got his foot up on the gunwale. He's got his transistor radio hooked on a rusty nail, tuned into WCKY, listening to Merle Haggard sing, "It's Not Love, But It's Not Bad," and he is whittling a minute, functional, wooden chain out of an Ohio Blue Tip match, with a

Barlow knife. He looks up and sees all the pilgrims coming.

He say, "She-e-e-e-e!"

One of the tourists insults the appearance of the commercial fisherman's boat. The next thing he knows, he's racing that good ol' boy, pink slip for pink slip, title for title, boat for boat.

The sun goes down on beautiful Big Lake George. The noble blue heron and the sassy anhinga return, satiated, to the sanctity of the rookery. And the commercial fishing fleet returns to the docks at Georgetown—each one of those good ol' boys packing one and a half pounds of catfish filets, four frog legs, a six-inch stringer of perch, and . . . towing *twenty-six* Cobia family runabouts. Bright and early Monday morning, he trades all that trash in at the Evinrude dealer in Palatka, takes the cash down to the bank, renders it into travelers' checks, sends 40 percent of the proceeds back to Pascagoula to cover alimony arrearage, and buys Mercury outboard motors with the rest.

Commentator Gamble Rogers says, "The Lord gives me grace, and the Devil gives me style." Rogers was born in Florida, where he still lives. A troubador, he takes his personal observations, stories, and music on the road about 225 days a year. This one came our way in December 1976.

What's There to Do in Murray, Kentucky, on Saturday Night?
We usually come up here, just find out how everybody's doin', make sure everything's okay, you know. Everybody just likes to keep in touch. Don't talk about nothin' special. Just gettin' together. Most of us work and we don't get to see each other during the week. On the weekends we just all get together and reminisce. Whatever happens, just let it happen.

WHO WANTS TO LIVE
IN NEW JERSEY?

It was a gloomy February morning in 1979. The bulk of the news had to do with the Iranian revolution, oil shortages, and human rights violations. On such days, when the news is mostly grim, we make a special effort to lighten things up on *All Things Considered*. Those are the days on which I take it upon myself to say, firmly and frequently, "Where is the JOY in this radio program?"

Luckily, someone noticed that Gannett News Service had asked New Jersey residents whether they would rather live in another part of the United States if they could. Fifty-two percent of the New Jerseyites surveyed said yes. Joy??! Well, maybe not for the 52 percent. But definitely for *All Things Considered*. In the first place, the poll was irresistible to our staff of Easterners. Second, our producer that month was from New Jersey. But more than that, the survey gave us a chance to do something typical: deliver information and have some fun at the same time.

We raced to the phone to call Thomas F.X. Smith, the mayor of Jersey City and a self-proclaimed New Jersey chauvinist. How did he react to the suggestion that the Garden State just might not be Eden?

Smith	First of all, I have some very serious questions about the validity of that percentage. But if there is some validity to it, the only account I could give for it would be that quite honestly, Sue, in the last twenty or thirty years there has been a suburbanization of the community and a lot of our open spaces have begun to disappear.
Stamberg	Not only have they disappeared, Mr. Mayor, they've taken on a certain aroma. When you take the Jersey turnpike into New York, you hit a stretch where you can barely breathe. You have to hold your nose, it smells so foul from all the factories and smokestacks. Maybe that's why 52 percent of those people would rather live somewhere else.
Smith	Well, quite honestly, Sue, you're just isolating certain sections of New Jersey. I think in any state you'd probably run into the same kinds of problems. But, by and large, you've got one of the finest beaches in the world in New Jersey. You have some of the finest lakes and some of the finest mountains in the world in New Jersey. And, quite frankly, we have something no other state has.
Stamberg	What's that?
Smith	The Manhattan skyline.
Stamberg	But how come I never met anybody from New Jersey who left and who had a nice thing to say about it?
Smith	Ah, no. I disagree with that very, very strongly. They don't come from all over the world to see Boise, Idaho (I know they're going to be mad at me in Boise), or Bangor, Maine (I know they're going to be mad at me there, too). But they do come from all over the world to see just what we have right here in New Jersey, on that beautiful Hudson River.

What's There to Do in Murray, Kentucky, on Saturday Night?
Where we come from, it's a little town. There's nothin' there. I mean, like, they roll the sidewalks up at three o'clock in the afternoon. Everybody does this. Just rides around. They don't have nothin' to do, you know. Movies is all you can do on a date around here.

Stamberg	I came to New Jersey once, to Hackensack, and I caught chicken pox.
Smith	Ha, ha, ha. Maybe you brought it with you, Sue. Where're you from?
Stamberg	Well, Mr. Mayor. I have a confession to make to you. I was born in Newark.
	(Pause)
Smith	You were born in Newark?
Stamberg	Yes.
Smith	Oh-h-h-h-h. Well. Then you know how wonderful New Jersey is!
Stamberg	Thomas F.X. Smith, the mayor of Jersey City.

What's There to Do in Murray, Kentucky, on Saturday Night?
You go down south 'til eleven-thirty. To Tennessee for beer. Then you come back here and usually you eat. You git a pizza. You drive around town two or three times. Nothin'. You go home. That's it.

"It's Susan Stamberg, at National Public Radio. She wants to know if you want to defend yourself on the airwaves tomorrow."

The New Yorker Magazine 1978

What's There to Do in Murray, Kentucky, on Saturday Night?
There's nothin' else to do in Murray. They don't let you stop on the parking lot. If there was something else to do, we wouldn't be up there on Saturday night driving up and down the street.

MAPLE SUGARING

Noah Adams At just about the right time, at the time it really needs to, spring begins to come to New England. The snow still falls, but it's softer and wetter. The sun is up earlier and stays later. The frozen ground gets muddy. The nights are still cold and crisp, below freezing, but daytime temperatures climb into the forties and the low fifties. On the snow-covered hillsides, deep inside the sugar maple trees, the sap begins to flow. The sap of a sugar maple contains about 1 or 2 percent sugar. If you drill a hole into the tree, the sap drips out. If you collect the sap and boil it down, you've got maple syrup. Boil it some more, you've got sugar. It takes about thirty-five gallons of sap to make one gallon of syrup. It works out just about like this: Each spring one sugar maple tree will produce enough sap to make one gallon of maple syrup.

In late February, in the Connecticut River valley of Vermont and New Hampshire, the farmers get ready for their first crop of the year. Donald Crane of Washington, New Hampshire, likes to tap a couple of trees early, as a test. Then each day he checks the buckets. A couple of weeks back, in March, Art Silverman stopped by the Crane farm to see how the 1978 season was going to be, to see if the sap was flowing yet.

(Creaking/groaning/sap dripping beats)

Silverman Where're the buckets that you have up now?

Crane They're right here beside the road. You didn't notice them?

Silverman No.

Crane You're not very observant.

(Walking/snow crunching)

Silverman Let's concentrate on not falling down and not stepping in anything.

Crane Well, it's a good idea to look down because you have two things in sugarin' that bother your footin'. One's ice. The other's mud.

Silverman And if you have a few oxen there might be a few other things?

Crane Well, that's why a farmer never looks up. *(Bucket sounds/walking)* I tapped this tree three days ago. See that little icicle right there? That means the tree's willing, but it can't do it. And this one over here is just as dry as can be. You see, this tap is a little more to the west; that one is a little more to the southeast, and it apparently just hasn't got warm enough right here yet. Those trees are froze clear through, you know. So it takes a little time to get 'em loosened up.

(Tapping sounds/clanking bucket handles)

Adams For those who are involved in the sugaring, the beginning of spring means about six weeks of hard work for everyone in the

	family. Someone has to cut the firewood. Someone has to haul the sap buckets. And there's another problem: Almost everyday is laundry day.
First woman	Because maple sap is very sticky, and when it's boiling away it seems like it's a rather nice pretty cloud of white steam coming off the evaporator, and it's very tempting to lean over and kind of smell that steam coming off the evaporator.
Second woman	But, unless you want to look like a candy-coated apple, you don't do it.
First woman	You don't do it. Nope.
Second woman	No.
First woman	No. Because that steam is very sticky. It's pretty and it smells really nice, but it gets on everything—*everything!* Everything you own smells like maple syrup after a while.
Second woman	Right.
First woman	And it takes so long. The amount of time that they spend preparing the maple syrup doesn't include the hours that those of us who don't tap and collect and boil spend supporting the people that actually do those things. By "supporting" I don't mean just feeding them, but I mean washing their clothes, getting their meals, picking them up, driving them home to sleep for four hours before getting up and driving them back up to the sugar house so that they can boil some more. Dealing with meals for lots and lots of people.
Second woman	Hearty meals that are going to be served to all of the people who come help. Instead of pay.
First woman	Regular meals.
Second woman	Regular.
Reporter	That's a lot of work. Is it worth it? Do they make much money?
First woman	Not at all.
Second woman	No.
First woman	They wouldn't do it if they really had to make a living at it, because they wouldn't be able to. Takes too much time. It's a passion, and that's the only reason they're doing it. Something happens when you start tapping a tree and you see little stuff drip-

Vermont Baklava

Take one slice of good-quality white bread.
Toast it.
Pour pure maple syrup on top.
Eat it.
Repeat the process until you're full.

	ping out of it, drip-drip-drip, and then a few days later you pour it out of a can. There's just some magical thing that happens, and they all get addicted.
Second woman	In the springtime, when the trees start to operate, you want to be in on it. You want to watch spring start up right from the beginning. You want to watch the sap starting to run. And during sugaring season, you're just so intimately involved with the coming of spring, it's like you breathe the coming of spring.
Reporter	You forget everything else?
First woman	Yeah. You don't even worry about mud season anymore.
	(Music/tapping/whistling)
Teacher	Can you get maple syrup out of any other tree except a maple tree?
Children	No! No! No!
First child	You can get it out of an oak tree.
Second child	You can only get oak out of oak trees. Eric's being ridiculous.

JOHN LENNON, A MEMORIAL

A Commentary by Vertamae Grosvenor

Moments after they heard the news that John Lennon had been shot and killed, fans began gathering spontaneously in front of the Dakota, his apartment building in New York. They stood there in shock, in tears, throughout that night of December 8, 1980, and for days afterward. Citizens around the country mourned Lennon profoundly and personally: "He was everything there was to be when I was a kid." "He was a poet. They shouldn't kill poets." John Lennon was their ideal, their artist, their adventuring hero, a part of their emotional experience.

Lennon's widow, Yoko Ono, asked fans throughout the world to observe ten minutes of silence in his memory at two o'clock on the Sunday afternoon following the murder. Her request was honored in many ways by millions of Beatles fans. Some spent the time alone. Others met with close friends. Several radio stations signed off the air for ten minutes. And at least 100,000 men, women, and children came together in New York's Central Park to stand in silent vigil.

The day after the silent observance, _All Things Considered_ commentator Vertamae Grosvenor said she had not planned to get caught up in the Lennon memorial.

Vertamae Grosvenor

I believe in magic and, yesterday in an Upper West Side bistro, I saw it happen. Because my 1960s were sit-ins not love-ins, because for me it was not Beatles and Monkees but Panthers and Young Lords, because my song was "We Shall Overcome" not "I Want to Hold Your Hand," I felt it would be a bit hypocritical for me to go to Central Park and light a candle for John Lennon. But because I believe that John Lennon was a righteous brother, I wanted to do something. So I met with several of my friends for brunch around one-thirty. Nobody announced when two o'clock came. But when it came, we knew. A remarkable thing happened. The café became absolutely silent. For ten minutes. The magic transcended generations and color and culture and politics. Former flower children, black ex-militants, old long-haired Marxists, young short-haired advertising executives, shallow bar flies, and deep intellectuals all came together in grief and fell silent. I swear I heard Aretha singing "Peace Be Still." Some folks actually prayed out loud. Most had their heads bowed. A few shed tears. None was embarrassed. I had the feeling that people prayed for John Lennon's soul, and their own. I know I did. In these troubled times, when a pair of shoes costs as much as a month's rent, the cost of a Christmas tree equals that of a week's groceries, the Klan is on the rise, children are disappearing, men's hearts are being cut out, I prayed for John, and me, and you. I prayed for change.

The 1960s are over. Let's not lament the loss of innocence and youth. If we can come together in peace and love for ten minutes, let's try to hold on to the feeling a little longer.

My Grandmamma Soula used to say, "Prayer changes things." And for ten minutes yesterday, it did.

Commentator Vertamae Grosvenor was born in the Carolina lowlands and now lives in New York. She is a poet, writer, culinary anthropologist, and the mother of two teenage girls.

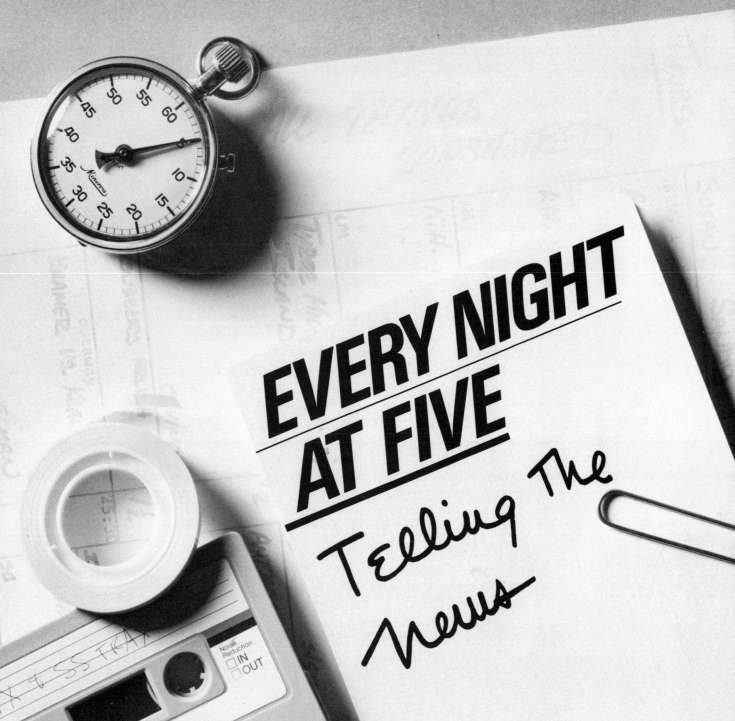

EVERY NIGHT
AT FIVE

Telling The
News

"What happened today?"

That's the first question *All Things Considered* tackles. Our answers always start with the day's major events—the official statements, the vote in Congress, the election returns. Then we move on to how those events affect the public.

News touches our lives. Today's White House economics decision shows up on the grocery store tab four months from now. The Congressional debate on abortion will determine the size of an inner-city family. We ask people what they make of the tax cut, the threat of radioactivity, Watergate. And we keep going back with more questions. The news event itself may be over, but its impact doesn't evaporate. People still have to make adjustments after the flood, the war, the accident at the power plant. We want to hear how they're doing.

Their reactions are barometers of the political climate. Lyndon Johnson is supposed to have said that when Walter Cronkite criticized his Vietnam War policy, he knew he'd lost "Middle America." During Watergate, when a Nixon voter in Manhattan, Kansas, told us he'd lost faith in the president, we knew Richard Nixon was suffering heavy losses.

All Things Considered also tells what happened today by telling about some things that happen every day—events that take place without ceremonies or press releases or news conferences. In the 1970s, the economy squeezed family budgets; kids spent more time watching television; the divorce rate spiked; and so did the suicide rate. There was an increase in teenage pregnancies. There's news in what worries us and how we think and feel. We make time to talk about the events of living.

We hear reactions from our own reporters. Personal journalism is a rarity on *All Things Considered,* but it can happen when a reporter and editor feel it would be dishonest, given the context of the story, *not* to speak personally. Linda Wertheimer, covering the Congressional abortion debate, was distressed by the insensitive language of the proceedings, and said so on the air. When Cokie Roberts came back from Three Mile Island and wondered aloud whether to burn the blue suit she'd worn there the week of the accident, listeners shared her anxiety.

We also invite informed observers to analyze the news. A report on a change of government in France is followed by conversations with experts about the French political system, about the effect of the new government on U.S.-French relations. Spending more time, going deeper into a story, makes its importance clearer. When the Equal Rights Amendment was proposed, we asked psychologists about the impact of women's liberation on men; we discussed sex-role divisions in childhood games. These conversations on tangential topics helped us explore the brouhaha over ERA. On the day the United States formalized relations with the People's Republic of China, *All Things Considered* asked a single question: What difference has it made that we haven't had relations with China in thirty years? Some answers from China experts here and abroad: The wars in Korea and Vietnam might not have occurred; the isolation was essential for the success of China's revolution. The answers went beyond the facts of the event to its meaning.

Facts alone are rarely interesting. They're vital, but they don't nourish. Ideas, on the other hand, give you something to talk about.

On *All Things Considered,* telling the news means mulling over issues in the course of interviews, hearing the opinions of commentators, and presenting the views of just plain folk down the block. Plus a contest or spoof thrown in for good measure.

Most of today's news either wraps fish tomorrow or vanishes into the very air through which it's broadcast. If the news told here stays, it's because of something in the telling.

THE WAR WAGED ON

The war in Vietnam had begun to wind down by the time *All Things Considered* went on the air. Five months after our first broadcast, in October 1971, the Pentagon reported that "only" eight Americans had died in Vietnam that week, the lowest weekly casualty toll in six years. NPR's Doug Terry responded to the news with a bitter commentary, unusually personal for a reporter but reflecting the rage and grief many young journalists felt about the war:

I think the characters in daytime television are trapped there, forever condemned to guess the price of a refrigerator, forever condemned to walk in at the moment Mary tells Barbara about Betty's impending divorce. There they are, inside that little box, day after day, week after week, year after year. They can't come out. Puppets on an electronic string, condemned for a time to wander in between soap and soup commercials, in a land as playlike as everything else. Maybe, if they scream just the right way when they win that dishwasher, if they lose with just the right mixture of humility and hatred, if they cry on cue for the ninth time about Billy's accident, they're released from their torture right in front of the scanning tubes of the color camera.

Into this realm of ghosts for the last eight years has come something called the Vietnam War. The tube cannot distinguish among the electronic signals it sends, each just an electronic impulse away from the other; the impulses of war footage are no different from the impulses of a deodorant commercial. It has been one of the new agonies of this age that we've had to watch our sons, our friends, our brothers, our lovers die on the screen only a few minutes after the soap operas end.

And now they tell us only eight have died this week—eight, only! Only sixteen parents to grieve, only eight wives, girlfriends —and how many never-to-be friends?—to cry. And those, over the years, who died on the screen may be trapped, too, in our minds, in our consciousness, in the heart of the nation. They are certainly trapped in that death, that TV death. They are as trapped as we are, sitting there waiting for Walter or Chet to come back and to go on to the next story. Having to watch.

Like the characters in daytime television, like the soldiers in their televised, useless deaths, we are trapped in the Vietnam War. What will it take for some bureaucrat or would-be leader to find a means to get us out? We wait. We wait for the end of our nightmare. Somewhere in the endless corridors of official Washington there must be a computer that keeps track of statistics on the Vietnam War. Someday, somehow, when the numerical truth adds up to the simple reality of human suffering, the computer will print out: ENOUGH. But when?—This is Doug Terry.

WATERGATE

Wade Horton	The fact that you called me about the thing is what makes me so mad, see!!!
Stamberg	Why?
Horton	For the simple reason that you media people are trying to create this whole thing. You people are doing this, and *you know* you're doing it. You have complete control of what you say and what goes on. What *I* say is not going to come out the same way it goes in.

Wade Horton never minced his words. I liked that. We were having the first in a series of discussions about Watergate—the most relentless, longest-running story *All Things Considered* has told.

From the bungled break-in at Democratic National Committee headquarters in Washington, D.C., in June 1972, to Richard M. Nixon's resignation in August 1974, Watergate twisted slowly to its historic conclusion. Like other news programs, *All Things Considered* told the news from the White House, Congress, and the courtrooms. But added to these reports were reactions from a family of citizen-commentators assembled by the program: men and women who lived in various parts of the country. Wade Horton, Jan Saecker, Charlie White, and others represented public opinion for us, as a president moved inexorably out of office. We phoned them throughout Watergate, asking for their opinions, determined that what they said would "come out the same way it goes in."

Wade Horton called himself a "devout Republican," a staunch Nixon supporter. He said nothing could shake his faith. He was sure the president was not personally involved in the Watergate break-in, or cover-up.

On April 30, 1973 (a week after our first call to Horton), John Ehrlichman, H.R. Haldeman, Richard Kleindienst, and John Dean resigned from top White House positions, and, in a speech to the nation, Richard Nixon said he wasn't personally involved and hadn't known how serious Watergate was until a full nine months after the break-in. We called Augusta, Georgia, to talk with Wade Horton again.

Horton	He must think we're a little naive if he thinks we'll believe he didn't know anything about this until March 21st.
Stamberg	You mean you have doubts about that?
Horton	I think so. I think he knew about it probably before then.
Stamberg	Then what was the purpose of a speech like the one he made?
Horton	Well, I think he thought he did enough.
Stamberg	You are a Nixon supporter. Did he go far enough to satisfy you?
Horton	I think it's just been blown out of proportion. If the media would go after both sides . . . I think this is the only way. All of this is going to do more harm to the country, and it's going to hurt us a lot. As he said, we've got a lot more important things to do. We've got inflation. We've got foreign policy.

Stamberg   I don't think you answered my question, Mr. Horton. Are you, as a "devout Republican," satisfied with the president's speech last night?

Horton   Well . . . I was hoping I wouldn't have to answer that. I may not be satisfied. I really don't know. But it's the . . . the reason if I . . . if there is any indecision on my part, it's questioning whether or not I know enough about it, you see?

What did the president know, and when did he know it? The questions became a national refrain. The Senate Watergate hearings began on May 17, 1973. On May 22, President Nixon admitted he had ordered some aides to limit the investigation of Watergate, to protect national security. The president again denied he had had any prior knowledge of the break-in. This time I called another Nixon supporter, Charlie White, a rancher in Manhattan, Kansas. His reaction:

White   You know, Susan, I just have a hell of a time believing all of that. I really think that the guy knew. He maybe didn't know exactly what was happening, but he had to know that there was something being done. If he came right out and said, "Yes, I did know that it was going on and I was not in favor of it," or *was* in favor . . . whatever . . . I would stomach it a whole lot better than his beating around the bush forever. I never have liked that and never will.

In the following weeks, former White House counsel John Dean and thirty-four other witnesses testified at the Senate Watergate hearings. The White House accused Dean of orchestrating the cover-up. The president himself refused to appear before the Senate Watergate Committee, or to give them his taped recordings. An impeachment resolution was introduced in the House. On August 15, 1973, as President Nixon again prepared to speak to the nation, I called Nixon supporter Charlie White once more:

White   Listen, you probably already misqualified me when you said I am a Nixon supporter. I *was* a Nixon supporter. As for what he has to say tonight, it's probably going to be basically the same thing that we've read about, that we've heard about for the past . . . I don't know, it seems like years. He's going to talk about Watergate. He's probably going to talk about why he didn't turn the tapes over, what he feels his powers are as far as his being the president, why some things that maybe he knows or has access to can't be made public knowledge. Do you want to know if that's going to satisfy me?

Stamberg   Yes.

White   No.

Marshall McLuhan on the Senate Hearings Ehrlichman is a very poor TV image. He's too hot. It's like Nixon himself. You see, Nixon's problem all along has been that he's a private image in a public role. Nixon doesn't have a corporate image to offer. He is merely, like Ehrlichman, a private image suddenly put into a very public role for which he has no image at all. To be a public role player, you have to be a bit of a ham. You have to be able to play. The ability to play is the ability to put on a role and hide yourself completely in the role. Ervin is a superb role player, with a wonderful capacity for ham. Ehrlichman is dead earnest, no capacity for hamming at all. Just a very poor TV image.
—July 30, 1973

That night, President Nixon publicly denied any guilt in the Watergate affair . . . again.

But the president had loyalists, too, among our citizen-commentators. On the same day Charlie White said he was a *former* Nixon supporter, Richard Larson, a photographer in Las Cruces, New Mexico, told us he was keeping the faith:

> **Larson** Nixon doesn't have to say anything to satisfy me. I wasn't dissatisfied to begin with. I never thought he really knew what was going on. I have always believed what my common sense dictates: that he did not know the particulars of the Watergate scandal, and, just like everyone else, he is sorry about the disgusting turn of events. It just couldn't be that anyone that has performed as Richard Nixon has could be such a dog as to sanction something as criminal as what went on. I think he's after the culprits as much as anyone else is, because they stabbed him in the back.

Seven months passed. Spiro Agnew resigned as vice-president, and Gerald Ford took his place. The House Judiciary Committee began to consider possible impeachment proceedings. Richard Nixon's resignation was called for by the *New York Times,* the *Detroit News,* and *Time* magazine. The White House agreed to make tapes available to Judge John Sirica in U.S. District Court in Washington. An eighteen-and-a-half-minute gap was found in one tape. Richard Nixon told newspaper editors, "I am not a crook."

On March 7, 1974, when I phoned Richard Larson in Las Cruces, New Mexico, he still kept the faith.

It's not so serious. Nobody was shot or killed, after all. And who knows why they were trying to break in at the Watergate? Maybe the Democrats were planning to blow up the Senate chambers or something.
—William Menton,
Los Angeles, California,
April 24, 1973

Janitor J, of the J & S Janitorial Service, listens in Veradale, Washington.

Larson It's going to come around full turn, the events, and we'll find that President Nixon wasn't the culprit everyone is so ready to condemn him for being.

Stamberg What evidence do you have for that?

Larson Well, I think one thing that is in his favor is his steadfast position. He never wavered. He *never* wavered! He kept telling the same story. Every time you've got someone that's got a crooked story going, the story changes; it gets mulled around. It never does with him. It's continuous. I'm happy for the man. He's done a good job.

Stamberg Specifically, what do you mean?

Larson Well, when you take a look at the hellacious problems he's dealing with right now. . . . It would be very easy for the fuel crisis to get out of hand. We could be on rationing stamps right now. Look at Europe. Look all over the world. There isn't another nation that has it still as good as we do. I think it's because of the level head at the helm. He's not flying off the handle. He's doing a damn good job with the fuel crisis and, I think, with inflation. And in overseas affairs he's doing a darn good job.

It would be another five months before Richard M. Nixon resigned from office. During those months, as the House Judiciary Committee gathered material for its impeachment inquiry, I called Jan Saecker, a housewife and mother of three in Markesan, Wisconsin, to ask if she thought impeachment would threaten the democratic system.

Jan Saecker listens in Markesan, Wisconsin.

Saecker No. No, I don't. In fact, I think it would be more of a safeguard. If we don't approach questions of legality openly and honestly, we're in more danger.

Stamberg Are you worried about world reaction to an America that might impeach its president?

Saecker No. I worry about world reaction to the kind of America we've had in recent years, where there seems to be so much hanky-panky, where we say one thing and support another.

Watergate was not without its lighter moments. In June 1973, after John Dean told about the White House enemies list—men and women in politics, media, labor, and show business thought to have worked against the Nixon administration—*All Things Considered* spoke with a prominent figure whose name was not on the list, to ask whether he felt slighted.

Art Buchwald I not only feel slighted, I am starting a class-action suit for all the people who were not mentioned on this list. It's very damaging to be eliminated from a list of this importance. It's hurt me journalistically. I feel that there was a conspiracy in the White House to keep my name off that list just to embarrass me.

Stamberg Do you consider that you are a legitimate enemy of the administration, Mr. Buchwald?

Buchwald Of course. And when they don't take you seriously, it hurts you personally. I feel that I won't be invited out anymore. There are a lot of my friends on the list who are making life very miserable for me now.

Stamberg Oh, is that so? Why?

Buchwald Because I didn't make it. They're laughing at me, they're holding me up to ridicule. That list is very shocking. Sidney Harris is on it. He hasn't written a political column in twenty-five years. And Herb Block is *not* on that list. Oliphant is *not* on that list. Russell Baker is *not* on that list. It's an outrage! I heard the list was coming out. I told everybody I would probably be on it. I can't tell you how disappointed and hurt I am. I've never been so insulted in my life.

As Watergate dragged on, it got harder to laugh. Finally, on August 8, 1974, the story came to an end. Richard M. Nixon announced his resignation.

Nixon To continue to fight through the months ahead for my personal vindication would almost totally absorb the time and attention of both the president and the Congress in a period when our entire focus should be on the great issues of peace abroad and prosperity without inflation at home. Therefore, I shall resign the presidency effective at noon tomorrow.

Early on August 8, in anticipation of that announcement, crowds had begun gathering outside the White House. National Public Radio kept vigil on the air all day. A coast-to-coast telephone party line was created, and, hour after hour, citizens called in to express themselves. Many wrote out what they wanted to say, as they waited their turn and listened to others. They spoke quietly and thoughtfully, and said they were grateful for the chance to share these final hours. There was the feeling of a wake about the day.

Most callers were pleased the president was leaving office, and the overwhelming majority felt he should also be punished:

> I don't think they should let Nixon worm his way out of this. He's going to get a life pension. This guy who has desecrated an office is going to be paid for the rest of his life.
> — Peter Curland
> Nashville, Tennessee

> I feel as if I've awakened from a bad dream. The last two years have been the most traumatic experience I've ever had. I'm sixty-four years old. I've lived through two wars and the Depression. And the feeling that I have had toward this president (and I am a Quaker) has been one of complete horror and disbelief and fury. He should have resigned a year ago. He should never have been elected.
> — Woman
> Leavenworth, Kansas

The callers also included men and women who supported the president and felt he was being badly treated:

> I've been appalled at the vindictiveness on the part of the people of this country toward him. He has suffered more than any criminal prosecution could bring on him. In this long Watergate process, we've lost a great deal of perspective about its true importance.
> — Robert Wessel
> Fairfield, Ohio

> My wife and I are very depressed. We thought much of Mr. Nixon. We both cried today. We are in our eighties. We think he was the best president we ever had. We can't understand why a thing like this Watergate can be blown up to the point where they can retire him from office and humiliate him. I think it's purely political, and I can't think any other way.
> — Howard Lill
> Corvallis, Oregon

And one caller looked ahead to the impact of Watergate on Richard Nixon's private life:

> The most interesting and far-reaching consequences will be for Nixon, who will become, in every sense of the word, a man without a country and without the refuge of anonymity. To use Orwellian terminology, he will really be an "un-citizen."
> —Woman
> Washington State

In September 1974, a little more than a month after Richard Nixon resigned, he was pardoned by the thirty-eighth president of the United States, Gerald R. Ford.

Jan Saecker I think we've been gypped. Somebody stole our sense of proper legal procedure. And, whenever we're robbed of something really precious or basic, we're left with the feeling of frustration.

Stamberg On the other hand, let's assume the pardon had not been granted. What good do you think it would do to put Mr. Nixon in jail, or to fine him, or make him go through an extensive series of trials?

Saecker It might have cleared the air. Here we have one of the greatest dramas of American history, and we're missing Act Three.

Stamberg You feel the story is incomplete?

Saecker Yes. Only the king can do no wrong, and that was no Camelot we went through.

HUBERT H. HUMPHREY IS DYING

It's no secret that news organizations have obituaries on hand for prominent citizens who are perfectly alive and well while the obituary is being prepared. Newspapers keep some obituaries set in type, ready to go to press on an instant's notice. Radio programs have the obituaries pre-taped, sitting on a shelf, quickly airable should the need arise. Similarly, when a prominent man or woman becomes ill, assignments are made to get the obituary prepared. It's a ghoulish but pragmatic part of the business. And so when word came that Hubert Horatio Humphrey had inoperable cancer, reporters got to work on the obituary All Things Considered would air when Humphrey died.

Humphrey knew he was dying. He went home to Minnesota for treatment, then came back to Washington. His return to public life in the city where he'd collected friends, enemies, and allies for thirty years created a unique national experience.

In December 1977, shortly before Humphrey's death, NPR's Robert Krulwich considered how the senator was spending the remainder of his time and how those around him were reacting to the news of his numbered days. Krulwich assembled a series of tapes from some of Senator Humphrey's public appearances during the last phase of his life. The premise was intriguing. Not yet an obituary, not really a memorial, Krulwich's piece paid tribute to Humphrey's political life, even as it measured the loss to the nation.

Krulwich	Hubert Humphrey's decision to come back to Washington brought this city, and the country, face to face with his imminent death. He looks frail. His head, that round dome that used to be so popular with cartoonists, is now bony and drawn. Yet only a year and a half ago he was the most popular Democrat, the best hope to stop Jimmy Carter, the one man who could be wicked to Jerry Ford but do it nicely.
Humphrey	My dear friend the president played on the University of Michigan football team against the great Golden Gophers, back in the days of Bernie Bierman, when we were good. What position did he play? He played center. Now, when you're playing center you're leanin' over, you know, and you're looking through your legs and everything is upside down. *(Cheering and applause from crowds)* So, dear friends, what ought to be up is down. What ought to be down is up. And he thinks it's right. *(More cheering)* Prices ought to be down and they're up. Employment ought to be up and it's down. He doesn't know he's wrong. *(Laughter)* After you've been in that position long enough, it looks normal. *(Loud laughter)* So you and I've got to straighten him out! *(Applause)*

Krulwich	A few weeks after he gave that speech, Hubert Humphrey withdrew as a candidate for president. A few months later, at a private dinner with President Ford, Ford said his two and a half years were too short a time in the White House. Humphrey answered, "I would have given five years of my life to have had two weeks or two months in this office." Last January Humphrey ran for majority leader of the Senate and lost. And two months ago came the announcement that he had terminal cancer. James Gibbons is chaplain at the University of Chicago. He is a confessed Humphrey fan and has studied the process of death and dying. Reverend Gibbons says that when Hubert Humphrey returned to Washington, the terms had changed.
Gibbons	Political differences don't matter much anymore, or affect how people treat him. They figure he's probably not going to be around long enough to be an important adversary. Now he's in a period of transition from being simply a politician, simply a public figure, into being a man. And people are beginning to conclude some of their business with him as a man.
Krulwich	Jimmy Carter, who'd beaten Humphrey to the nomination, brought him home on *Air Force One*. The Senate that refused to elect him majority leader gave him a formal welcome and, before that, an honorary title and a limousine. Senator Robert Dole, a conservative Republican who had opposed him on countless issues over the years, sponsored a bill to name a major federal building after him. The act of dying produces guilt in the living, says Reverend Gibbons—the guilt of surviving, of being relieved and at the same time ashamed that someone else is dying and not you, the need to make amends for old mistakes. It is this guilt his friends may be trying to exorcise now. But, at the same time, Senator Humphrey is aware that these tributes are also good politics. It doesn't hurt their careers to be photographed being kind to Hubert Humphrey. Humphrey even joked about this at a public appearance with his friend, Vice-President Walter Mondale.
Humphrey	By the way, Fritz always expresses his gratitude for these occasions because he says he gets so much television coverage. *(Laughter)*
Krulwich	But these events serve a function for Hubert Humphrey, too.
Gibbons	He's living out a fantasy that each of us has: "What will happen when I die? I'd like the assurance that my life has meant something. The way I will know this is by knowing how my death will affect other people, how my not being here any longer will affect

other people. That will tell me that my life has been of some value." With the cooperation of friends, and media, and government, Hubert Humphrey is certainly managing to live out these fantasies. He's attending some functions that he imagines would be appropriate, and even indicating the words that would be appropriate for his obituary.

Humphrey I have to digress for just a minute. Fritz said, "How long are you going to talk?" I said, "Why ask a foolish question like that?" I'm going to tell you something. When Fritz introduced me, he left out a couple of good quotes. I was peeking at his notes. He had a wonderful one from Emerson that I thought would have really sort of enriched the whole occasion.

(Laughter)

But he said he's saving it for another time. He figures they might want to dedicate a tennis court or something.

(Laughter)

Krulwich And then, of course, Hubert Humphrey has his own accounts to settle. He was speaking recently at the dedication of a building. In the audience were a thousand government workers, about a third of the Senate, and most of the Cabinet. But in the middle of the speech he paused and looked around: first at his wife, who was sitting near him on the podium; and then at his sister, who was down in the audience, watching from the first row.

Humphrey I do also want to say very quickly that the struggle that we've been going through these months has been a special challenge, but it's really one that we're beginning to win. I never could have done it—I couldn't have kept up my spirit—without my Muriel, and I'm everlastingly grateful to her. She's put up with me for forty-one years of married life.

(Loud applause)

My sister Frances, here, who fills in for me so many times and is so often forgotten by her brother in his busy life . . . I want Frances to know how much I love her and how grateful I am.

Krulwich And if Humphrey is trying to exorcise his guilt, so, as it happens, are thousands of people around the country who've never even met the man. The Chicago *Daily News* reported this week that thousands of people are writing to Senator Humphrey and many are apologizing, saying they're sorry for having been angry at him, for having been rude to him during the anti-war years. They're asking that he forgive them so that they can make their peace with him.

Senator Humphrey has been told that there's a 10 to 20 percent chance that he'll live another five years. He says there are some moments in the morning when he looks in the mirror and sees his gaunt face and gets depressed. Then he says he has to use an act of will to regain his confidence and good spirit. But, however much longer he has, Senator Humphrey seems unafraid. He's up and down sometimes, but he seems to have made his peace.

The frequent public appearances make some people uneasy. They wonder why he doesn't "do the decent thing" and go away and die out of our sight. Again, Reverend James Gibbons.

Gibbons Throughout history, death was always a rather public event. People died in the sight of other people, not in institutions. Privacy at the time of death is relatively new, a matter of a hundred years. Now there's a kind of leper image that hangs around the dying. Death has become taboo—an unseen, untalked-about phenomenon.

Krulwich But Hubert Humphrey has always been even more public than most politicians and says his approach to death is perfectly consistent with his life. He's always liked a good fight.

Humphrey I want to make it clear that while some people have said of me, "You're a good loser, Hubert," I'm really not. I don't like to lose at all.

(Chuckles in audience)

I know that I personally have been what you call a good loser only because I've always been determined to return for another fight. Apparently people do not identify only with winners. They also identify with warmth, with enthusiasm, with folks who lose a round or two but who fight on against the odds.

Krulwich Tonight Hubert Humphrey will be honored at a $1,000-a-plate dinner hosted by the president and the vice-president of the United States. The proceeds will help establish the Hubert H. Humphrey Institute of Public Affairs at the University of Minnesota. Fundraisers are calling it a living memorial to the senator.

On January 13, 1978, a little more than a month after that report was broadcast, Hubert H. Humphrey died.

IT'S TEN O'CLOCK. ARE YOUR CHILDREN WATCHING TELEVISION?

In the early 1970s, Jerzy Kosinski did experiments on the impact of television on children. Kosinski's novel *Being There* is the story of a naive gardener who knows life only from watching the small screen. The gardener becomes a presidential candidate. Kosinski says it may be the most horrifying of all his tales, since it focuses on what he considers *the* evil demon in our society: television. On *All Things Considered*, in February 1979, Kosinski described his experiments with public-school children, ages nine to fourteen. He compared what they did in private with what they did when he told them they would appear on television.

Kosinksi   If I asked, "Do you masturbate?" or "Do you steal?" they would not talk about it privately. Then, the child was put on television. We brought in cameras, lights, an entire set-up. They were told, "You are going to be on a talk show. The show may be run nationally, but, if not, it will at least be seen by your friends and your parents. I will ask you certain questions. You don't have to answer them." Then, on camera, I asked them the same question I'd asked in private: "Do you masturbate? Do you steal?" And, with the cameras rolling, they absolutely opened up and answered everything in great detail with nice Johnny Carson—like smiles.

        The most horrifying experiment was when I was being televised telling a group of children an interesting story. I had arranged that, in the middle of the story, I was to be assaulted by a man breaking into the classroom. Now, as I was telling the story to the children, they had a choice of either watching me "in person," as I sat in front of them, or watching me on two giant television screens we'd placed on either side of the room. As long as I was alone and nothing bad was happening, they looked directly at me. The minute the assailant came and started to punch me and I started to bleed, most children in the classroom turned toward the TV screens. Suddenly I was without any help from anyone. They refused to look at me. They chose instead to watch the assault as a television show.

Stamberg   The only way they could deal with the violence was to remove themselves from it?

Kosinski   Yes. And become passive observers.

Stamberg   But how do you explain the first business: their being able to admit on television what they wouldn't discuss in private?

Kosinski   They were responding to the unreality of it. They were removed from the normal.

Stamberg   But research shows that very young children will turn from passively watching television to being extremely aggressive toward brothers and sisters or parents. They don't, in fact, remain passive in real life.

Kosinski   Because they can't just "watch" real life the way they watched me getting beaten on TV. They have to deal with it, and they're not equipped. They're very immature and they're not building bridges to maturity when they sit all day watching television. So they have these fits of aggression even into their early twenties. In the late 1960s, the first true television generation grew into adulthood. They had about 18,000 hours of television watching behind them. That would correspond with about nine years on a job. These kids were only eighteen or nineteen, and you could see they were absolutely different.

Stamberg   But this was a generation that took to the streets, that went out to protest.

Kosinski   There was no sustained effort there; no sustained political party developed; George McGovern was not helped. They screamed for him, but they didn't register later to vote for him. I was there. They just didn't show up. They were already bored. They'd gone from one program to the next.

Stamberg   It did have some impact.

Kosinski   Yes, of course it had impact—on other generations. But, in terms of their own doings, they remained basically very sporadic, drifting from one activity to the next, quickly bored, moving to another program. They lack sustained attention to their own lives. They are not tense enough about themselves. They waste a lot of spiritual time and physical time. They are inner drifters.

Stamberg   And no residue is left? There is no layer of experience that stays?

Kosinski   Very little. They discard things very quickly.

IT'S TEN O'CLOCK. IF THEY'RE NOT WATCHING TELEVISION, WHAT ARE THEY DOING?

Announcer You are about to hear a very explicit discussion of sex among teenagers. The conversation includes advice parents might consider giving teenagers about having sexual intercourse. We want to advise listeners that some might find the discussion provocative.

That's a listener advisory, an on-air warning that we're about to broadcast sensitive material. Sometimes, tapes will be fed down the line to stations twenty-four hours before air time. If the local station decides the piece is too controversial to be carried in its community, it substitutes something else—music or local announcements—to fill in the time slot. Before this interview with Eleanor Hamilton ran in 1979, a group of stations in one state decided not to broadcast it. Afterward, a listener in the area called to ask, "What could _ATC_ broadcast that was so terrible that we weren't allowed to hear it?"

Hamilton Last year we had something like a million teenage pregnancies and 400,000 of the girls were under the age of fifteen. They are certainly acting sexually in ways that have not been very constructive to them. There has to be a better way. I don't know any fifteen-year-olds who are equipped to be parents.

Stamberg Psychologist and sex therapist Eleanor Hamilton has a controversial solution to the problem of teenage pregnancy. Her solution is both permissive and conservative.

Hamilton Only about half the people of the world are married at any one time, and _all_ the people of the world are sexual from the time they are born until the time they die. I say there has to be some ethical form of sexual expression at every age and stage in life, and I don't think that intercourse is the ethical or even the desirable form of sexual expression for young teenagers. In fact, I think that probably not till they're seventeen or eighteen are they anywhere near ready for intercourse.

Stamberg What does "not ready" mean? Not ready emotionally? Surely they are ready physically.

Hamilton I think they are not emotionally ready, and as far as their physical readiness is concerned, I've never known a girl fifteen or under who came to orgasm by the intercourse route. Most women don't come to orgasm by intercourse. This is very much a male form of sexual completion.

Stamberg Ordinarily, orgasm for women comes through clitoral stimulation?
Hamilton Primarily, yes.
Stamberg Eleanor Hamilton formerly shared a marriage counseling practice in New York with Wendell Pomeroy of the Kinsey Institute. Now sixty-nine and a grandmother, Dr. Hamilton operates a counseling center in Sheffield, Massachusetts; a summer camp in

Nova Scotia; and a clinic in the British West Indies. *Sex, with Love,* her most recent publication, was a Book-of-the-Month Club alternate selection. It's written for readers between the ages of ten and fifteen, and their parents. Dr. Hamilton says that adolescents should be discouraged from seeking intercourse, but they should be encouraged to seek emotional and sexual satisfaction. And Dr. Hamilton says that one path to such satisfaction is masturbation.

Hamilton That's a nasty word for a nice act. Some nasty-minded adult at some time in history gave that perfectly good act a bad name. We should remove the stigma.

Stamberg So you would encourage teenagers to stimulate themselves to orgasm?

Hamilton Right. I would also very much increase the amount of body contact in what I call "intimacy experiences"—hugging, massage. . . . I think children, like adults, have skin hunger that needs satisfying. The only way they think of satisfying it, the only way they've heard of, is sexual intercourse. And I don't believe that is the only way. They really are more hungry for intimacy than they are for sex.

Stamberg Isn't that more true for girls than boys? Girls in their teens really want closeness, they want to be cuddled. But the boys want something quite different. They really do want the experience of intercourse.

Hamilton They want the experience of sexual fulfillment. But they've been brainwashed that the macho thing to do is to "put it in." I think they need to be taught that they can have full sexual satisfaction without endangering the girl. And intercourse does put the girl at risk.

Stamberg You were listing various alternatives: auto-eroticism to orgasm, massage. . . . What's the next step?

Hamilton All right. I think around the age of fourteen or fifteen very often girls and boys think they are in love, and they want something more than hugging. At that point I think petting to orgasm is one of the answers. I'm sixty-nine years old, and when I was a teen we used to pet, all right, but when we became stimulated, we would stop. Anything more was a no-no. But I think, if they can pet right straight through to orgasm, the boy will have complete sexual fulfillment and there's a good chance the girl will have sexual fulfillment, too.

Stamberg You mean you would urge parents to tell their children that auto-eroticism and petting to orgasm are all right?

Hamilton I would not only do that, I would give them some information on *how* to pet to orgasm, so that they don't run the risk, say, of

What They Don't Know Can Hurt Them
They just don't have good, correct information. They just have a lot of myths they've heard from their friends. One kid asked me if it was okay to wash out a condom and use it over again; he said he had ecological concerns. I said, "Well, save your concerns for something else. Condoms are only supposed to be used once."
—Carolyn Alkire, counselor, Planned Parenthood Teenage Hotline

ejaculating near the entrance to the vagina, which is always a possibility. I would give them some good books to read on lovemaking. And when a child is somewhere around sixteen, seventeen, or eighteen, and seriously developed enough to be insisting on intercourse, then I would certainly see that they understood birth control.

Stamberg   Dr. Hamilton, you can't really think that parents will suddenly see the light and start encouraging all this sexual activity in their children!

Hamilton   I think that parents have to take a look at the options. The present situation is leading to a million teen pregnancies a year. And there's more harm than that. If they buy the ethic of waiting until marriage for sexual activity, what are they going to end up with? The average age of marriage today is twenty-two, and the average age of physical maturation is twelve. If you take any function as vital as sexuality and put it on the shelf for ten years, what you're going to get is a very large number of people with sexual dysfunction.

Stamberg   Dr. Hamilton, we've been talking so much about—

Hamilton   *(Interrupting.)* We've been talking about sex instead of about loving!

Stamberg   Yes, but more than that, we've been talking about physical satisfaction, and really not looking closely enough at emotional development.

Hamilton   I would like to turn our attention to that. I define love as that condition in which the well-being of the beloved is essential to your own well-being.

Stamberg   But I know *adults* who can hardly live out that definition: thirty-year-old women who are just now having children and having a hard time "giving" to them. If adults can't find that emotional maturity, how can fifteen-year-old kids find it?

Hamilton   They've got to have some education. I believe we could spend a lot more time, all of us, as a nation, learning how to love a little bit better. I'm not talking about physical satisfaction now, but responsible loving.

A lot of the tension between parents and children during the teenage years comes from sexual disagreements. The children are experiencing all kinds of sexual feelings, and the parents keep telling them no. The children feel that the adults are taking away their happiness and that they have to fight the adults. And they fight them on all sorts of levels.

How different it is, in the families we've worked with. The adults and children are together in ways that you just couldn't

They have to get used to the changes in their own bodies—they reach for a glass of milk, and they're so awkward they knock it over. Their voices go up and down. And while all that is happening to them, adults demand that young people study very hard and that they make life choices, religious choices. We dump everything on them all at once.
—Margaret Mead

imagine—the warmth, the love and appreciation. If you give kids the right to experience their own sexuality safely—both physically and emotionally—they feel wonderful toward you.

This conversation with Eleanor Hamilton had quite an impact. People wrote of their shock and disgust that such subjects were aired during the dinner hour. We answered the letters politely, arguing that the topic had been handled thoughtfully and with taste. I felt it was important to talk about it.

Betty Pollock listens in Daly City, California.

THE CONGRESS DEBATES ABORTION

NPR Congressional correspondent Linda Wertheimer followed and reported on the abortion debate for years. She became increasingly appalled by the tone of the discussion, the crudeness and insensitivity of some of the participants. She faced a personal dilemma: As a reporter her job was to present objectively the news of any day's deliberations, but those deliberations had become so disturbing that finally, in November 1977, she had to tell listeners about the callousness she was witnessing day after day. It was a departure for her to offer this essay in a tone of quiet outrage.

For five months now, twenty-seven members of the House and Senate—all men, average age sixty-one—have been talking about abortion in a House-Senate conference. The bill they are discussing bans federal funding for abortion, with certain exceptions. The exceptions have been the basis for prolonged discussion over the summer and fall. The conferees agreed to permit abortions in cases where the pregnancy endangers the life of the mother. But, beyond that, they and the houses they represent have not been able to agree.

They disagree on the question of whether or not to permit federal funding of abortion in cases where the mother's health might be damaged. They are at odds over cases where the baby, if it were born, would have a genetic disease or defect, like Tay Sachs disease or mongolism.

They disagree on whether federal funding could be used for abortions in cases of rape or incest.

For five months, these men have met and argued about what to do. For five months, they've exchanged painful stories of defective children slowly dying of incurable genetic diseases, examples of bungled abortions, and arguments over the right to life. The debate has been a difficult and brutalizing one for all the participants, those who oppose abortion and those who do not. Every day's debate has demonstrated the difficulty of settling, through legislation, a socially sensitive and medically technical question.

Watching and participating in the abortion discussions requires a strong stomach. Phrases like "backroom butcher" are among the mildest. It's become apparent that the men who make the decisions have, in some cases, an imperfect understanding of female sexuality and physiology. During one session a male Senate staff member whispered to a female colleague, "Is ovulation the same as orgasm?"

A member of the House complained that the measure currently on the table went too far in permitting federally funded abortions. Gesturing toward a table of male colleagues, he observed:"Under this bill anyone in this room could get an abortion."

The conferees have made harsh jokes. Should the rape exception include teenagers who are not forcibly raped but who are victims of statutory rape because of their age? One member cracked: "It's not a question of consent. The question is whether she enjoyed it."

Does medical treatment for victims of rape or incest include abortion procedures like dilation and curettage? "It would," another member replied, "allow a quick scrape." Talking of abortions in cases where the mother's health might be damaged, one member told his colleagues that the language before them was too liberal. "We don't want a woman who wakes up with a hangnail to be able to get an abortion," he said.

One congressman proposed that federally funded abortions should be available to pregnant teenagers. To guarantee that, he proposed permitting abortions for girls aged sixteen and younger. When that was rejected, he tried fifteen, then fourteen, then thirteen. At that point, his colleagues rebelled. "You are trying to make us look bad," one shouted. "Are you going to take it down to age one?"

The arguments in conference and the six floor debates on abortion have been more than some of the civilians who watch the Congress can bear. I'm thinking of a staff member who logs debates in the House. When abortion is discussed she arranges for someone else to take her place.

Senator Edward Brooke of Massachusetts has led the fight to permit certain federally funded abortions. He told reporters that the irony of middle-aged men sitting in a room and determining what poor women may do with their bodies has not escaped the twenty-seven conferees. This may be. But the debate goes on. I'm Linda Wertheimer.

In 1977, the Congress finally banned federal funding of abortion, except in cases of rape, incest, or danger to the mother's life. But decisions on funding bills are renewed each year, as is the painful discussion of exceptions.

SILVER SCREEN DIVORCE

A Commentary by Richard Elman

The other night I saw *Kramer vs. Kramer*. Meryl Streep leaves Dustin Hoffman and their adorable son, to go "find herself" in California for eighteen months. While she's gone, Dustin learns how to be an adorable father. Then she comes back and wants the kid, but by then he thinks he's a better mother than she is.

I found the movie disagreeably cloying. Both parents seemed so well-intentioned toward each other and their offspring, when in fact it has been my experience that the only time I ever seriously contemplated committing murder was during the time of my divorce. There simply isn't enough rage in the picture to give an accurate sense of what a custody fight can be like. And one wonders, coming away from the theater, how that kid could have survived his depressed mother and psychopathic father to be so cute and kissy, even before the divorce.

I think people who work in advertising do not make suitable parents. I feel the same way about successful sportswear designers, nuclear engineers, and dieticians. But that issue was never raised in the film.

The problem with such ordinary, everyday people as Dustin Hoffman and Meryl Streep is they behave too well during their divorces. If they behaved as badly as most people, their agents would be worrying about finding them future work.

At various times, during various divorces, I have known friends who did things that would be perfectly consistent with the action of the average Elizabethan revenge play—*Hamlet* or *Timon of Athens*. Cruel, vengeful, spiteful during the litigation, they did not hug and talk nice to each other when it was all over. Divorce is an experience that hurts quite a lot; it destroys time and feeling. Its only justification is that it's really better for kids to grow up with parents who manage to be hateful to each other from a distance than to remain in a home where things are tight and cozy and nasty . . . as they are in most American homes.

Movies like *Kramer vs. Kramer*, which sentimentalize the parental role (whereas what we really need to know is where to get a good baby-sitter), are finally doing a terrific disservice to all of us, as sentient, mature human beings. Maybe Hollywood ought to consider making a movie about people who don't have $60,000 a year to cushion their divorce, and who are angry at each other, brutal, and oppressive to their children. That's a little more like what the average U.S. divorce is about.

Commentator Richard Elman, who contributed this piece to *ATC* in February 1980, is the author of numerous novels, books of poetry, stories, articles, and essays. He writes, reads, and goes to the movies on Long Island.

TAXES AND LIFE'S LITTLE LOOPHOLES

The news in January 1977 was that President Carter proposed a $50 tax rebate. The news in April 1977 was that President Carter *withdrew* his proposal for a $50 tax rebate. Oh, well. Easy come, easy go. But the rebate stuck to our wallets just long enough for us to tell listeners what they could have bought with $50 if the president hadn't changed his mind:

- a seventy-one-mile metered taxi ride from the middle of Manhattan to Ellisdale, New Jersey
- six marriage licenses in Murfreesboro, Tennessee
- 150 McDonald's hamburgers—the plain ones
- 385 13¢ stamps
- a fifty-minute hour with a psychiatrist
- two and a half bags of groceries
- ten six-pound bags of chicken feed
- eight copies of the King James Bible
- twenty-eight six-packs of Pabst Blue Ribbon beer
- seventy-seven gallons of gasoline
- a twelve-and-a-half minute phone call to New Delhi
- four nights at the YWCA in Omaha
- ten pounds of coffee
- one share of General Electric stock
- the services, for one week, of the NPR research department, consisting of Rob Robinson (he helped compile this list)

Edwards
And $50 will buy the entire city council of . . .
Stamberg
Bob, we warned you about that.

Tax time is news on *All Things Considered,* rebate or no rebate. In April 1980, we tried at least to get listeners laughing all the way to the IRS. NPR's Robert Siegel, whose life's dream it is to be referred to in print as a "wag," wrote a series of totally false tax tips. To introduce the series, director Maury Schlesinger created a pastiche of sounds: screeching violins, agonizing screams, and the rat-tat-tats of adding machines. Over the sounds, a deep-voiced announcer intoned, in 1940s documentary style, "Life's little loopholes . . . erroneous answers to the most common questions about preparing your taxes." The announcer also warned, "If you use this information, you'll have no one to blame but yourself."

When Should You Itemize Your Taxes?

Early in January, if you can; mid-February at the latest. Itemizing takes time. Time to straighten your records and get your receipts in order. If you served pretzels to business contacts and people who worked for you, save the cellophane bags for claiming the business entertainment deduction. And make sure to shake the salt out before you send the bags to the IRS.

Always remember to file the name of the medical school your doctor attended, and the branch of the service he was in. Get to know the mother's maiden name of all the people with whom you have tax-deductible transactions. If you move, in order to take a new job, and claim the moving-expense credit, include the route that the van took going from your old house to the new one. If your belongings were shipped, attach the appropriate nautical map to your returns, with information on currents, tides, and weather. If you're claiming a loss due to theft, be sure to include the boxes or bags the stolen goods were wrapped in when you bought them. The Styrofoam molds might help, too. Send along a photograph of you or your spouse in the act of buying the stolen good, or a photograph of the two of you taken in your house with the article, before it was stolen.

Can You Claim an Energy Tax Credit for Your Honda Because It Saves Gas, or For Your Wood-Burning Stove?

No. The energy tax credit is not nearly so widely applicable as many people think. There are four basic cases that are covered by the energy tax credit.

Case One: If you build a solar-heated home on a golf course in Utah for the purpose of holding religious services.

Case Two: If you outfit an old house with a new hydro-electric plant that you built with your own money.

Case Three: If you build a new house, or move your old house to the top of a volcanic hot spring.

Case Four: If you build a windmill on a family farm or condominium *and* you are a widow, filing under Schedule Z.

Can You Claim a Boyfriend or Girlfriend as a Dependent?

Under nearly all circumstances, no. The rare exceptions involve incestuous relationships with members of your immediate family or sprees with promiscuous in-laws or distant cousins who come to live with you in your household without the specific intention of having illicit affairs.

You might consider, though, the numbers of men and women who can't be your dependents but who can provide both loving companionship and favorable tax treatment. Your psychiatrist, for one. His bills are deductible, and they can often be for good times spent in a pleasant, candid, one-to-one relationship. Other kinds of medical doctors, dentists, optometrists, and physical therapists can improve your physical well-being, your love life, and your tax picture all at once.

When you take a health professional to dinner or a play, he or

A Legitimate Tax Tip: How to Deduct Your Child
If you are accumulating money for your kid's college education, get him or her a social security number and transfer some of your income into a savings account or a trust fund for the kid. Then let the kid pay income tax on the interest that money earns. That way, the tax shouldn't amount to anything.
—Barry Steiner, tax consultant, 1977

she might oblige with a bogus receipt, making your entertainment deductible as a phony medical bill. If you decide on a fraud like this one, remember: Stick to the tried-and-true professional, so you don't draw attention. Keep all your receipts. File on time. And don't use an accountant whose socks match his shirt.

What Is the Marital Status of Two People Who Are Married but Separated, and Hate Each Other's Guts?

According to recent statistics, that status would have to be called increasingly typical. But it's not a way out of the so-called marriage tax: the standard deduction that is smaller for two married people than for two single people. There are, however, some other means of relief. If you've been carrying your spouse as a no-show employee of a company you own, you can always have him or her fired. You might try filing individually as a married person and deducting as stolen property the value of articles taken by your estranged spouse to the new abode. If a home owned in your name is occupied by your estranged spouse, you can try charging rent and depreciating the house. It probably won't work, but it might make you feel better.

Another Legitimate Way to Deduct Your Child
If you work at home, running your own business, put your kid on the payroll and take a tax deduction on what you would normally pay for an allowance. Get the kid to vacuum your office or something.
—Barry Steiner, tax consultant, 1977

Noah Adams, All Things Considered's weekend co-host, is our most avid reader. We fear he will eventually leave radio to open a bookstore or write a novel. He comes from Lexington, Kentucky, and has worked at various radio stations as an announcer, disc jockey, sales manager, production manager, program director, and general manager.

Bill Buzenberg reports on foreign affairs for NPR. A former Peace Corps volunteer in Bolivia, he studied international relations at the University of Michigan and the Johns Hopkins School of Advanced International Studies in Italy. He was also city editor of the Colorado Springs Sun. Bill's gentle manner is deceptive. Sources remark on his uncanny ability to spot a scam.

Neal Conan was born in Beirut, Lebanon, and has worked in radio since 1967, in New Jersey and in New York. He produced All Things Considered from 1978 through 1979, left it a better program than he found it, then became NPR's New York bureau chief. He loves Manhattan, although it's not the easiest place in which to pursue three of his major interests: baseball, horseracing, and missiles.

Robert Krulwich, NPR's business and economics correspondent, uses mice (our taped voices played back at double speed) to demonstrate the heating-up of the economy. Robert went to Oberlin College and Columbia University Law School, and was formerly Washington bureau chief for Rolling Stone magazine and national bureau chief for Pacifica Radio.

David Molpus, a minister's son from Belzoni, Mississippi, reports on religion, the South, labor issues, and defense policies. He attended the University of Mississippi and holds a graduate degree in journalism from American University. David's the only one calmly editing, typing, and thinking at three in the afternoon.

Cokie Roberts grew up in the U.S. Congress. Her father was Representative Hale Boggs, Democrat from New Orleans; her mother, Representative Lindy Boggs, continues the family political connection. Cokie specializes in reporting public events through people's reactions; they respond to her compassionate attention. She studied political science at Wellesley, lived in Greece for three years, reports for television and magazines.

Ira Flatow, *NPR's science correspondent, was born in Queens, New York, studied engineering at the State University of New York at Buffalo, and believes that baking soda and science do mix. He has produced radio series on the workings of the brain, science in China, and Antarctica.*

Richard Harris, *All Things Considered's newscaster, works the late shift. He arrives at one, presents the news at five and six o'clock, stays on to update his two newscasts at eight and nine o'clock, and stands by until nine-thirty, watching the AP, UPI, and Reuter wires for breaking news. He had more regular hours when he was public-affairs producer at member station WOI, Ames, Iowa.*

Jackie Judd *was weekend co-host of All Things Considered (with Noah Adams) from 1977 to 1979. Jackie was raised in Baltimore, studied journalism at American University in Washington, D.C., and has reported the news for several radio stations in New England. A model of serenity in the midst of our chaos, she left All Things Considered to become a daily newscaster on NPR's Morning Edition.*

Robert Siegel *is NPR's London correspondent. Before he began referring to subways as "tubes," he was ATC's senior editor and ran our morning meetings in part like Socratic dialogues, in part like the lectures in Contemporary Civilization he attended at Columbia College.*

Scott Simon, *NPR's Chicago bureau chief, includes elements of an event that you're really not supposed to hear. A report on a speech begins with the ambient sounds of the public-address-system man: "Test, one-two-three—is this mike on?" Suddenly you're in the auditorium, waiting for the speaker. Scott went to the University of Chicago and has reported for television and Newsweek.*

Nina Totenberg, *NPR's legal-affairs correspondent, continually surprises judges and lawyers with the fact that she has no law degree. Nina has aggressively revealed secret court votes and deliberations, and relishes a good story. She was raised in New York's Westchester County and Boston, writes for newspapers and magazines, and once sang with a band.*

Linda Wertheimer, *NPR's senior correspondent, is the first broadcaster to have reported live from the Senate (during the 300-hour Panama Canal debates). She understands the workings of Congress as thoroughly as any one of its members, and thrives on the Byzantine intricacies of its rules and power shifts. Linda grew up in New Mexico, graduated from Wellesley, and worked at the BBC and WCBS in New York.*

EDWARD R. MURROW, REPORTER

When Edward R. Murrow told the news, he set new standards for broadcast journalism. Murrow was the first great radio reporter, a model for all of us. His vivid eyewitness accounts of World War II popularized radio as a source of up-to-the-minute information.

As CBS bureau chief in Europe during the late 1930s, Murrow did not usually speak on the air himself; rather, he hired reporters to tell listeners the events of the day. But Murrow happened to be in Austria in 1938, and so it was he, live on the air, who told the news of Hitler's take-over. He continued his broadcasts from London, reporting the war for his American audience.

Murrow pioneered the use of the microphone as an instrument for conveying the sounds of a story. To illustrate what it was like to be in a blitz, he set his microphone down on a London sidewalk. The mike picked up sirens, anti-aircraft guns, and something else: the footsteps and conversations of the British people going about their daily business as the guns thundered. Listeners could hear that, in the midst of war, the people were not panicked. Current events leaped out of the radio with new immediacy.

Murrow's reports let listeners visualize events. In April 1975, on the tenth anniversary of Murrow's death, Bob Edwards's tribute to the distinguished broadcaster included vintage recordings. Here's Murrow, from a London rooftop:

> At the moment everything is quiet. Off to my left, far away in the distance, I can see just that faint, red, angry snap of anti-aircraft bursts against the steel-blue sky.

I can look across just at the building not far away and see something that looks like a slash of white paint down the side, and I know from daylight observation that about a quarter of that building has disappeared, hit by a bomb the other night. Streets fan out in all directions from here and, down on one street, I can see a single red light and, just faintly, the outline of a sign standing in the middle of the street. I know what that sign says because I saw it this afternoon. It says DANGER UNEXPLODED BOMB. Off to my left, still, I can see just that red snap of the anti-aircraft fire.

I was up here earlier this afternoon, looking out over these housetops, looking all the way to the dome of St. Paul's. I saw many flags flying from staffs. No one ordered these people to put out the flags. They simply felt like flying a Union Jack above their roofs. No one told them to do it, and no flag up there was white. I can see one or two of them stirring very gently in the breeze now.

You may be able to hear the sound of guns off in the distance, very faintly, like someone kicking a tub. Now they're silent. Four searchlights reach up, disappear in the light of a three-quarter moon. Everything is quiet. More searchlights spring up over to my right. I think probably in a minute we shall have the sound of guns in the immediate vicinity. The lights are swinging over in this general direction now.

(Boom boom)

There they are, still a considerable distance away, moving just a little closer.

(Louder explosions)

The searchlights are stretching out now in this general direction. I can hear just a faint whisper of an aircraft high over head. Again, those guns are a considerable distance away. You hear them just vaguely in the background.

(Explosions)

That was an explosion overhead, not the guns themselves. I should think in a few minutes there may be a little shrapnel around here. Coming in, moving a little closer all the while, the plane is still very high, and it's quite clear that he's not coming in for his bombing run. Earlier this evening *(louder shots)* we could hear, occasionally—again, those were explosions overhead— earlier this evening we heard a number of bombs go sliding and slithering across to fall several blocks away. Just overhead now, the bursts of the anti-aircraft fire.

(Shots)

The searchlights now are feeling almost directly overhead. Still the nearby guns are not working.

(Shots booming)
There they are. That hard stony sound.

Simply, yet dramatically, in that resonant, steady voice, Edward R. Murrow talked about the war for his listeners. He radiated a sense of integrity. Listeners could hear that he cared, that he was disheartened by much of what he saw, but that he could be cheered, too, by something like the quiet heroism of the British people flying their Union Jacks.

Fred Friendly, who worked with Murrow on television, spoke of his effect on an audience: "People identified with Murrow and were able to stitch their reactions to his. They saw in him their own conscience."

Technological advances let today's broadcasters travel farther from the studio than rooftops and sidewalks to tell the news. Lightweight, portable, battery-operated recorders can tape sounds on water, even in the air. But Edward R. Murrow's integrity—his responsibility and sturdy conscience—can only be emulated, never surpassed.

THREE MILE ISLAND

> *In this accident, the amount of releases of radioactivity have been very small. The total dose to the public has been so small that if you take all the lifetimes of the people around the area, you may get one extra cancer out of several thousand cancers. This is an extremely small consequence of what was a major industrial accident.*
>
> — Richard Wilson, Professor of Physics
> Harvard University
> April 1979

> *My neighbor's supposed to deliver a baby in May. She said to me, "I just thought of a good reason for having a baby, finally. It means my son will have a sibling. If he develops leukemia there'll be a chance for a bone-marrow transplant." I felt like I'd been punched in the stomach.*
>
> — Patricia Street
> Middletown, Pennsylvania
> October 1979

In the spring of 1979, there was an accident in the cooling system of the Three Mile Island nuclear-power plant near Harrisburg, Pennsylvania. The plant is owned and operated by the Metropolitan Edison Company. Radioactive water had leaked out as a result of the accident, and detectable amounts of radiation were measured in the area near the plant. Conflicting information about the accident came from Metropolitan Edison, local and state officials, the Nuclear Regulatory Commission, proponents and opponents of nuclear energy. No one knew precisely what was happening inside the reactor. The lack of precise information created a terrifying chain reaction of confusion and misinformation.

One year after the accident, *All Things Considered* broadcast a fifteen-minute summary of the events of that week in March at Three Mile Island. Producer Gary Covino sorted through tapes recorded at TMI the week of the accident. There were the voices of the officials involved—their public statements and their recorded conversations with the Nuclear Regulatory Commission. There were reports from the scene. Covino arranged them all in chronological order, and wrote a brief script, which was narrated by NPR's Steve Curwood.

Curwood Four A.M., Wednesday, March 28, 1979.

Man I saw a plume of steam rise several hundred feet in the air. You could see it—white steam—from the lights around the plant. And it roared. It woke me up. I looked out the window and I saw this huge column going up in the air and roaring.

Curwood The worst commercial nuclear-power accident in history has begun.

Official Everything is under control. There is and was no danger to public health and safety.

Pennsylvania Lt. Gov. Scranton There was a small release of radiation to the environment. Metropolitan Edison has been monitoring the air in the vicinity of the plant constantly since the incident. No increase in normal radiation levels has been detected.

Curwood But when a Nuclear Regulatory Commission team reaches the scene, they report to their superiors that things inside the reactor are anything but normal.

Men's voices on phone *(garbled)* Sam?
Yeah.
Couple of radiation levels.
Okay.
200 R per hour . . .
Yeah . . .
. . . inside containment building.
Holy Jesus!
That all the numbers you got?
Yeah. Those are the only numbers.
Okay. Keep us posted. That's a serious, serious damn event.

Curwood Thursday, March 29. Pennsylvania Governor Richard Thornburgh reassures local residents.

Thornburgh There is no cause for alarm, no threat to the health or food supplies in the area. We regard the situation as being stable and under control.

Curwood Most people take the governor at his word. But Met Ed representatives find themselves surrounded by skeptical reporters. The news conferences become more crowded.

Met Ed We do not refer to it as a nuclear accident because it was not that.

Reporter How can you say it's not a nuclear accident when radiation is being detected as far away as sixteen miles—excess levels of radiation?

Met Ed Well, that does not constitute an accident. It wasn't an accident. It was a failure of a piece of machinery.

Curwood Friday, March 30. A day some will refer to as Black Friday. Three Mile Island has sent out another burst of radiation.

Thornburgh *(broadcast announcement)* I am advising those who may be particularly susceptible to the effects of any radiation—that is, pregnant women and pre–school-age children—to leave the area within a five-mile radius of the Three Mile Island facility until further notice.

Curwood Saturday, March 31. More frightening news. The director of systems safety for the NRC urges a general evacuation. He says the

core could be hours away from a melt-down, the most serious kind of nuclear accident. There's been a hydrogen explosion at the plant, and there could be another. Met Ed disagrees. An exodus is underway.

Resident My family is on its way to New York City to stay with relatives. The gas stations are flooded, the banks are busy, people are withdrawing some of their money so they can get out of here. The group that operates the plant is saying, hey . . . no problem. Another regulatory agency is saying, hey . . . there might be a problem. And the state government doesn't know which way to go right now. There's a group of people around a fifteen- to twenty-mile radius that are starting to get in their cars, get gas, and just leave. They're heading to Pittsburgh, they're heading to New York, they're heading north, whatever.

Curwood Sunday, April 1. Fifty thousand people have already fled the Harrisburg area. President Carter comes to town.

Carter The primary and overriding concern for all of us is the health and the safety of the people of this entire area. If we make an error, all of us want to err on the side of extra precautions and extra safety.

Curwood Monday, April 2. Officials report that the gas bubble is shrinking and the nuclear fuel is beginning to cool.
Tuesday, April 3, a week since the accident. The NRC says there are no further significant safety problems. Families begin to trickle back. Debate begins about what to do with Three Mile Island. Schools are about to re-open.

Child They told us to lock our doors and keep the windows and doors shut.

Reporter Were you scared?

Child Nope.

Reporter Why not?

Child The teachers didn't tell us to be frightened.

Reporter Was anybody here scared?

Children I was! I was! I was!
I wasn't! I wasn't!
My dad works there. He wasn't scared.

Reporter Think your mom was scared for him?

Child Yes.

Reporter What did she say?

Child Well . . . nothing. But she was crying.

Another child Sometimes in the nighttime I just go in bed and I start dreaming they'll come in and get us. See, our door has a crack in it, in the screen. I dream that stuff's coming in and trying to get us.

Cokie Roberts was one of the NPR reporters who originally went to Three Mile Island to cover the accident. She returned to TMI six weeks later to file a series of follow-up reports. Excerpts from her reports show the psychological effects of the accident. Counselor Holly Davenport at the Hillcrest Clinic in Harrisburg said pregnant women in the area were especially worried.

Davenport Women who knew they were pregnant had the option of leaving. Women who didn't know couldn't make that decision. We're seeing a lot of concern on that basis now. Our pregnancy tests are up. A lot of people are coming to us because they've missed a period and are afraid they were pregnant during that time. What those women will eventually decide, it's too soon to tell.

Twenty-five percent more pre-school children than usual had come to the county mental health agency. And, as agency official Lenora Stern told us, there were other emotional problems.

Stern Families who had disturbed relationships prior to the incident, who were just kind of on the brink, TMI just kind of pushed them over the edge. Thousands did split, and one of the contributing factors was the process of decision making—to stay or not to stay, who should handle the kids. Those tough decisions were the final blow to the marriage relationship.

But other residents reacted differently. Some opened tourist concessions, selling posters of steaming cooling towers, T-shirts reading HELL NO, I DON'T GLOW and I CAME, I SAW, I SURVIVED, and tins labeled ORIGINAL CANNED RADIATION. Resident Vickie DeSanto had some second thoughts.

DeSanto In a way I'd like to capitalize on it. Then again, I feel like these people are making money off of something that I went through

Steven and Barbara Schenck listen in Claremont, California.

and that I have very personal feelings about and very strong objections to. It's like they're endorsing what happened, selling T-shirts. If I get a T-shirt, it's not going to say I SURVIVED THREE MILE ISLAND or anything catchy. It's going to say something I want it to say, like I WANT TO LIVE, NOT MERELY SURVIVE.

Bruce Phillips, manager of a drugstore in Middletown, thought all the upset about the accident was silly.

Phillips All right, so what if we get cancer from it? What's the difference? See this ceiling tile here? That's made of asbestos. That school that you went to probably had asbestos chips in the walls, and asbestos tile. Practically everything that you eat today has something in it that can cause cancer. Everything that you breathe has something that can cause cancer. Water today has cancer-causing agents in it, chemicals. The clothes that you wear. What's the difference?

But for everyone it was a struggle to get back to normal.

DeSanto I try to convince myself that I'm getting over it, that I am starting to forget about it. And yet the towers are still always there. Even if you have your back to them, you're aware of them over your shoulder. And you have to keep looking back there.

In 1980, one year after the accident, Cokie Roberts again traveled to Three Mile Island. The reactor containment building remained sealed up, the debate over past and future dangers continued, and officials considered venting radioactive gas into the air to begin the clean-up process.

In the Harrisburg area, property values rose again, elementary-school enrollment grew daily, and businesses flourished. The observation center across the river from the plant welcomed summer tourists. Families could picnic at redwood tables as they looked at the towers. Then they could see a Metropolitan Edison film, explaining that no one was hurt in the accident.

Middletown residents saw their monthly utility bills rising. Some, like Micky Minneck, organized protests against nuclear power and Metropolitan Edison.

Minneck They just got a $55 million rate increase. They're applying for another $50 million rate increase to pay for the clean-up and replacement power. Look, we didn't cause it. We don't want to pay for it. It's like, if I were Jewish, asking me to pay for a retirement village for the SS troops. Well, they're potential murderers. That's how I feel about Met Ed.

And mistrust ran high. Mistrust of the experts, particularly on the issue of health.

DeSanto What's the incidence of leukemia going to be? And who's it going

to hit? My boy is a likely candidate. He lives this close. He's been through all this. Who knows what could happen to him because of something that happened when he was eighteen months old?

Cokie Roberts   You come away from Middletown with a sense of people feeling out of control, angry, ill-served by government and the utility company. And, worst of all, they feel worthless.

De Santo   We don't hear sirens out here, so the only way I know there's something going on at the Island is if any of the dogs in the neighborhood bark. I listen for them. They can't expect to evacuate everyone under those circumstances, so we're the expendable ones. It really lowers your opinion of yourself to go through this, because everything they're doing makes you feel so insignificant. I feel like I don't matter at all.

I hate being a guinea pig . . . and that's what we are. Nothing like this has happened before. They don't know what the effects are. The statistics they use, if there are any future accidents, are going to be based on us. We didn't volunteer for this experiment.

     — Young wife
     Middletown, Pennsylvania
     March 1979, the week of the accident

RUMANIA DOESN'T ANSWER

The chill of the Cold War entered our studio one June afternoon in 1977, when Constantin Rauta came in and tried to make a phone call. NPR's Nina Totenberg and Robert Krulwich sat in the studio with Rauta. Their report was introduced by co-host Bob Edwards.

Edwards Every week, Constantin Rauta tries to call his mother in Rumania.

Operator Okay, go ahead now.

Rauta *Mămica?* (Mom?)

Mother *Da, mamă, da.* (Yes, dear, yes.)

Rauta *Ce s-a întîmplat cu telefonul? Alo?* (What went wrong with the telephone? Hello?)
(Click/phone line goes dead)

Rauta What happened?

Operator I couldn't tell you what it is, sir. She says something. You hear her, right?

Rauta I understood her. She said to speak fast.

Edwards Constantin Rauta has to speak fast. Every week he calls his family, but within seconds someone in Rumania pulls the plug and he's disconnected. NPR's Nina Totenberg has learned that Rauta is something of a human pawn in the power games of the United States, Rumania, and the Soviet Union.

Totenberg In 1973, the Nixon administration was trying to thaw its relations with a number of Iron Curtain countries. In part, the policy was an expression of détente. In part, it was an attempt to drive a wedge between the Soviet Union and its satellite countries. One of those countries is Rumania. Rumanian President Nicolae Ceausescu was due here for talks with President Nixon. The Rumanians badly wanted to be granted "most favored nation" status, which would entitle the country to trade advantages. Several weeks before Ceausescu was due to arrive, a Rumanian advance party came to the United States. One member of that party was Constantin Rauta. Rauta wanted to defect from Rumania. The problem was that his wife and son were still there. They had been refused permission to travel with him. Rauta devised a plan. He got off the plane in New York and went immediately to a police station. Rauta took with him his country's diplomatic pouch, which contained valuable top-secret documents. He hoped to use the pouch in a trade for his family.

Two Rumanian-speaking FBI agents came to see him immediately. They were soon joined by Jay Katzen, a Rumanian-speaking State Department official attached to the United Nations mission. According to Rauta, Katzen wanted the briefcase returned to Rumanian officials. Katzen feared that, otherwise, the Rumanian

	president would cancel his trip to the United States. Katzen took the briefcase, but he made Rauta a promise.
Rauta	Yes. He promised the United States government to do everything possible to bring my family out of Rumania.
Krulwich	He even said that President Nixon would ask the Rumanian president to bring your family to America?
Rauta	Yes. That was his example of what can be done instead of using that suitcase.
Krulwich	So you thought you'd won?

Rauta   Well, the people in Rumania with the sense for human rights are living with the feeling that this is a society with people, and especially the government, which you can trust. So when I go to police station and am introduced to the State Department official, and he states in front of the FBI (there were three or four people in the room) that he speaks in the name of the United States government, maybe I'm wrong, but logically there was no reason to suspect anything.

Totenberg   The next day, Rauta says, he had an appointment to meet Katzen at the immigration office, but Katzen didn't show.

Rauta   I tried to contact Mr. Katzen. I insist to those people to put me on the phone. I reach him over the phone and he said he is busy, he cannot come.

Krulwich   You had a sense that the whole thing was lost?

Rauta   I sensed that . . . let's say it this way . . . that I wasn't told the truth.

Totenberg   State Department sources confirmed Rauta's version of what happened. I asked State Department spokesman John Trattner if Henry Kissinger had made the key decision in the Rauta case.

Trattner   The decision to return the pouch was made at a senior and authoritative level of the State Department.

Totenberg   You cannot tell me whether or not it was Dr. Kissinger?

Trattner   I cannot specifically take you that far, no. I have said a senior and an authoritative level.

Totenberg   For those of us who don't normally cover the State Department and for the several million listeners out there who don't understand State Department code, why can't you tell me any more than that?

Trattner   Well, because sometimes we choose not to. But in this case I think that the point is that the decision was made responsibly, authoritatively, and at a very high level. It was not a decision taken lightly at a middle level or a working level.

Totenberg   Why was the decision made to return the diplomatic pouch? For some time this man had planned a strategy that he thought, rightly

	or wrongly, would give him leverage to get his family out. The State Department really took his leverage away by simply giving the diplomatic pouch back to the Rumanians.
Trattner	Well, I would like to point out that protection of the inviolability of diplomatic pouches is a firm obligation under international law —the Vienna Convention on Diplomatic Relations to be exact— and it is an essential condition for the effective conduct of foreign relations. The diplomatic pouch held by Mr. Rauta was returned, unopened, to the Rumanian government in accordance with that obligation and practice.
Totenberg	Are you telling us that everything we have ever seen on television or read in spy novels is wrong? That when we get a pouch full of valuable information from a country that is not an ally, we would not look inside that pouch?
Trattner	I'm telling you what the international law obligation is and how we act under that obligation.
Totenberg	The Nixon administration granted "most favored nation" status to Rumania. Overall emigration from Rumania increased. And the Carter administration asked Congress to extend Rumania's "most favored nation" status by another twelve months. But what about Constantin Rauta? We asked Mr. Trattner.
Trattner	The case that we're talking about here is highly regrettable, and we hope that something can be done very soon to resolve it favorably for the Rauta family.
Totenberg	Mr. Rauta's wife and four-year-old son remain in Bucharest under constant pressure. Rauta described for us his wife's attempt to visit the American Embassy in Bucharest in 1975.
Rauta	She was stopped, physically prevented from going in the embassy, threatened with being beaten. She was brought to a police station and kept for a couple of days in jail. She was asked to sign a divorce paper. Of course, my wife refused to do that. After two days they allowed her to go home. There was a lot of other day-by-day harassment that forced my wife to give up her job. Now she's waiting for an exit visa.
Totenberg	You told me that the American Embassy had been very kind to her. She'd made visits to them and they'd made visits to her. But that has now stopped?
Rauta	In the last two months my wife was threatened by the Rumanian authorities that if she will speak with somebody from the embassy she will be beaten.
Totenberg	Are you afraid that your wife may just give up?
Rauta	I know my wife. I hope that everything will be solved well, will be a happy ending.

Totenberg NPR has repeatedly called the Rumanian Embassy in Washington trying to get some explanation of the treatment of the Rauta family, given the improved relations between the two countries. After the first call, a Mr. Horodincă promised to get back to me with a response. He has never called back. Nor has he answered repeated messages left for him. As for Mr. Rauta, he has a job as an engineer. He sends money to his wife through an intermediary. And every week he tries to call his wife and his mother.

Rauta Some of the time I can hear my wife answering, but at the same time the Rumanian operator is saying the phone is out of order.
(Phone ringing)

N.Y. operator May I help you?

D.C. operator Party on the line for Rumania.

Rauta Hello, operator. I wish to place a call to Bucharest, Rumania, please.

N.Y. operator One moment.

Totenberg I sat with Rauta as he tried to place a call to his wife. After a minute or so a connection was made.

Wife *Alo.* (Hello.)

Rauta *Alo, Catişor.* (Hello, Kathy.)

Wife *Alo.* (Hello.)

Rauta *Nu te-aud bine.* (I can't hear you well.)

Wife *Alo. Să nu ne-ntrerupă.* (Hello. I hope we don't get cut off.)

Rauta *Alo!* (Hello!)
(Clicks/phone disconnected)

N.Y. operator Hello, sir? Is that your party?

Rauta Is my party, but I cannot speak with her.

N.Y. operator She hung up. Did you tell her something, sir?

Rauta I didn't have a chance.

D.C. operator Can you please get the number for me again, Bucharest 56893.

Rumanian operator But that was a Mrs. Rauta on the line, wasn't it?

D.C. operator Well, she hung up. He's on the line, but I don't know what happened. She hung up.

Rumanian operator Ah-h-h-h. One moment, ma'am.

Totenberg The second phone call to Bucharest was no more successful than the first.
(Operator speaking in Rumanian/phone ringing)

Rauta *Alo, Cati, Catişor.* (Hello, Kathy, my little Kathy.)

Wife *Alo?* (Hello?)

Rauta *Ce s-a întîmplat?* (What happened?)

Wife *Ce să se-ntîmple, Doamne, Dumnezeule.* (What do you think happened? Oh god, dear god.)
(Clicks/phone disconnects)

Totenberg	Again, the connection was made and again it was cut off. Rauta tried his wife one more time, but this time the phone rang and there was no answer at all. A Rumanian operator came on the line and Rauta asked what was happening.
Rumanian operator	I don't know, dear, but I think this number is out of order.
Rauta	Operator, can you give me another phone number? I wish to talk with my parents. I have another number. The number is 239 in Alba Iulia. It's in Transylvania.
Rumanian operator	One moment. For anyone?
Rauta	Mrs. Rauta, R-a-u-t-a.
Rumanian operator	The same name? Yes. One moment. *(Phone ringing)* Go ahead, please.
N.Y. operator	Thank you very much. Speak up now, sir.
Rauta	*Alo.* (Hello.)
Mother	*Da.* (Yes.)
Rauta	*Mămica?* (Mom?)
Mother	*Da. Mamă.* (Yes. Mother.)
Rauta	*Alo.* (Hello.) *(Clicks/phone disconnects)* Hallo! Hallo!
N.Y. operator	No.
Rauta	What's happened, Operator?

Margaret Rodgers and Sunny, of Coraopolis, Pennsylvania: "*ATC*** was high on my list of NPR programs, but four years ago, when I became blind, it became the only newspaper I ever read. Sunny is my seeing-eye buddy."**

N.Y. operator	I don't know, sir.
	(Phone ringing)
Totenberg	Rauta tried to make another connection with his mother. The phone rang at the same number she had just answered, but this time no one picked up. The American operator came back on the line.
	(Phone ringing)
N.Y. operator	Hello, sir.
Rauta	Yes, Operator.
N.Y. operator	Are you sure that they want to speak to the United States? Because they'd be talking on the line and she hears you and you hear her, but all of a sudden she hangs up. I really don't think that they want to speak to you.
Rauta	Operator! You are New York operator?
N.Y. operator	Yeah.
Rauta	Operator, yes, they want to speak with me.
N.Y. operator	But, sir, you know this seems mighty strange.
Rauta	It's my mother!
N.Y. operator	Hello? Hello, Bucharest!
Totenberg	This is Nina Totenberg in Washington.
N.Y. operator	Hello, Bucharest? Bucharest?

As of this writing, Constantin Rauta is living in a suburb of Washington, D.C. His wife and child finally joined him in the United States in the summer of 1979.

WHAT IF THE BOMBS FELL?

Stamberg	What is the most staggering piece of information in your report, *The Effects of Nuclear War?** If all Americans read it, what would be the one thing that would keep them up nights?
Dr. Peter Sharfman	Well, the most staggering piece of information is only implicit in the report, and that is that nuclear weapons are real. They exist. I myself think that nuclear war is very unlikely. But it's possible. It could happen. And the consequences are simply beyond anything that Americans have ever experienced.

As a prelude to Senate debate on the Strategic Arms Limitation Treaty, the Senate Foreign Relations Committee asked the Congressional Office of Technology Assessment (OTA) to prepare a comprehensive study on the effects of nuclear war. The premise was that before making crucial decisions, policymakers had to understand what is known, and what is not known, about nuclear war.

Dr. Peter Sharfman was program manager for national security at OTA. Sharfman and his staff were asked to think the unthinkable. What, precisely, would happen if the bombs fell? In June 1979, *All Things Considered* asked him to share his findings with our listeners.

Sharfman	It's possible to calculate what the effects would be. But we found that the effects you can't put numbers on, the ones you can't calculate, are in all probability just as important as the effects that you can calculate.
Stamberg	What are you thinking of?
Sharfman	Let me give you a couple of down-to-earth examples. One is that radioactive fallout depends tremendously on the weather—which way the wind is blowing and how strong it is. We imagined that a single nuclear weapon exploded in the city of Detroit. If the wind were coming from the southwest, most of the fallout would go into Ontario, Canada, over essentially uninhabited areas. There would still be a lot of damage, but it wouldn't be devastating. But if the wind were from the northwest, the fallout would go directly over Cleveland; over Youngstown, Ohio; and over Pittsburgh. If you want to know how many people that single nuclear weapon would kill, you have to know which way the wind is going to be blowing at the exact hour the weapon is detonated.
Stamberg	But there's no way ever to know that or to be able to control it.
Sharfman	That's right. We can't even predict a snowstorm a day in advance.
Stamberg	Let's say that the wind is blowing toward Cleveland and Pittsburgh. What does it mean for the family in Columbia, Missouri, or Miami, Florida?
Sharfman	Imagine a big attack. Thousands of weapons detonated. Tens of millions of people would die virtually instantaneously. Additional

---

* *The Effects of Nuclear War* was published by the Government Printing Office in 1979.

tens of millions of people would die as a result of radioactive fallout, which is not instantaneous. Even if you get a fatal dose of radiation it takes several days for it to actually kill you. Beyond that, there would be people, millions certainly, possibly tens of millions, who would get a dose of radiation that would not immediately kill them but that would lower their bodies' resistance to other kinds of diseases. At the same time the medical facilities of the country would be largely destroyed. Most hospitals, most doctors, most medical researchers are in big cities and would have died immediately. With no factories producing antibiotics, a lot of people might die from flu or from typhoid, because they were weakened by the radiation and the medical system of the country was unable to care for them. Then you would have additional people who would be fine until the stocks of food in their immediate area ran out. The trucks that normally carry food in from the farming areas of the country wouldn't be running anymore.

Stamberg But the food that they would be eating would be contaminated at that point, wouldn't it?

Sharfman No, not necessarily. Canned food is hard to contaminate. To get a sense of what might happen in a specific community, we asked a very good journalist named Nan Randall to come and read the materials we had been gathering—in effect, to study up on nuclear war—and then to go to Charlottesville, Virginia, and create a fictional study of what would happen if there were a nuclear war in which Charlottesville was not a target.

In the scenario she created, the nuclear attack did not come as a complete surprise to the nation. Relations between the superpowers had deteriorated to the point that citizens were deserting the cities weeks before the bombs fell.

When the sirens sounded, most of Charlottesville hurried to shelter. The sky to the east and north glowed brilliantly, following the attack on Washington and Richmond. At first no one knew how extensive the damage was—that more than 4,000 megatons had destroyed military and industrial targets, and close to 100 million U.S. citizens had been killed.

Imagine 100,000 people in shelters. That's 30,000 who are there to begin with and 70,000 refugees. They are extremely uncomfortable, to put it mildly, and probably contracting diseases of various sorts from poor sanitation. It's too hot or it's too cold. They are undergoing terrible psychological trauma, packed together and giving each other diseases. But most of them are alive.

After a couple of weeks the fallout diminishes to the point where they might as well come out. Not that it's safe. There is some statistical risk of getting cancer. But since every place in the country is going to be unsafe, you just have to come out and put up with it.

In our Charlottesville scenario, three weeks after the nuclear attack almost all the residents had returned home. The refugees could move out of shelters, but still had to camp out, waiting in endless lines for food or use of the bathrooms. Emergency authorities ordered local residents to take in refugee families. Resistance to the order was strong. In the meantime, the need for food was becoming acute. There was no refrigeration, and much food had spoiled. Food prices skyrocketed.

The number of radiation deaths increased, and mass funerals took place several times a day. The city set aside several locations for mass graves.

Stamberg So Charlottesville has now become a crippled population, not only decimated but crippled physically, mentally, psychologically, in all ways.

Sharfman That's right. Exactly. There's another thing to consider. Apart from direct damage, a lot of people's jobs have disappeared. What's the use of owning a shoestore if you can't buy shoes to resell to people? There would probably be a mismatch between the tremendous amount that would need to be done and what the survivors would know how to do.

Stamberg What kind of a timetable do you put on our ability to reorganize in some way?

Sharfman Well, that's the real question, of course. Social organization is really the crux of the matter. There would be surviving people.

Lynne Harrison and his kitten, Laslo, listen in Mercer Island, Washington.

There would be surviving things. The problem would be getting them together to start the work of rebuilding. Remember that, after a few generations without machines and training, people forget how machines work. So we will have survived biologically, but our way of life is going to be unrecognizable. In several generations the U.S. could resemble a late medieval society.

Stamberg   Is it a possibility that the actual situation might be better than the fictional Charlottesville scenario?

Sharfman   Sure. Or worse. I tend to think we picked a somewhat optimistic scenario. We assumed that civic spirit survives; that people for the most part treat their neighbors well; that you don't have riots or anarchy or mass looting or martial law. But you can't be sure. Remember, in a nuclear-war environment you're talking about tens of millions of people dying. In such an environment, one of the things that goes by the board is the attitude that a single human life is precious. I suppose that one of the ways you would know that the war was over, that the recovery period was over, that the survivors had gotten over the war, would be when human life could again become precious. That could take a very long time.

(Long pause)

Stamberg   As I listen to you and become increasingly chilled by what you're saying, I feel I must ask you a personal question. What has it meant to you, working on this report? What are your dreams like these days?

Sharfman   Well . . . that's a hard question to answer. I guess there is a trick to doing any kind of disciplined work on an unpleasant subject. You insulate yourself. As we wrote the study, we tried to avoid drifting off into easy abstractions. You get a phrase like "a bomb would inflict a million fatalities." And I sat there with my little pencil and changed it to "a bomb would kill a million people." You have to keep reminding yourself of that. But, at the same time, killing a million people is no more comprehensible to me than it is to anybody else. And I suppose that, in a funny way, I would lose more sleep if one particular individual I knew and was attached to was simply in pain than I would at the thought of a million people whom I don't know dying. It's a strange sort of thing, but I think that's the way human psychology works, and what that means is that your gut reactions are not a sound guide to policy. That is, you can get fascinated by these weapons. You can get fascinated by the fun of trying to imagine things different. You can also get horrified, turn away in repulsion. Neither the fascination nor the repulsion is a very good guide to figuring out what would make a good foreign policy.

One way or another, ever since I was in college, I have been professionally concerned with foreign-policy matters, with issues relating to war and peace. I decided a long time ago that if war was possible, it was better to think about war and try to understand what it is that hangs over all of us than to just try to pretend it isn't there. So I don't think that doing the study has directly affected what I dream about. You can't lie awake at night worrying about nuclear war without going nuts. What I really would hope is that, as people go about their normal business, they bear in mind that avoiding a nuclear war is important. That nuclear weapons are real. That they are serious business.

The Senate debate for which the Sharfman study was prepared didn't take place in 1980, as scheduled. In December 1979, Soviet troops moved into Afghanistan. President Carter asked the Senate to delay debate on SALT in retaliation for the Soviet action.

TELLING THE NEWS IN 2076

A Contest

<u>All Things Considered</u> listeners told the news of their times when they helped us create a Tricentennial time capsule. It was a few months before July 4, 1976, and Bicentennial piety was running high. I asked listeners to stop for a moment and think about the symbols of America in its 200th year. What could be put into a time capsule now that would represent America when the capsule was opened in 2076?

- the White House Watergate transcripts
- a 1976 Sears catalogue
- seed packets
- the *New York Times* for July 4, 1976
- birth-control pills
- frisbees
- faded, patched blue jeans
- *TV Guide*
- a pocket calculator
- a piece of the moon
- a handgun
- marijuana
- a $2 bill
- credit cards
- 13¢ stamps
- pantyhose
- Henry Kissinger
- the Pentagon Papers
- Valium
- Beatles records
- an aerosol can
- a rural mailbox
- Martin Luther King, Jr.'s, "I Have a Dream" speech
- waste from a nuclear reactor
- a list of predictions of what life will be like in 2076.

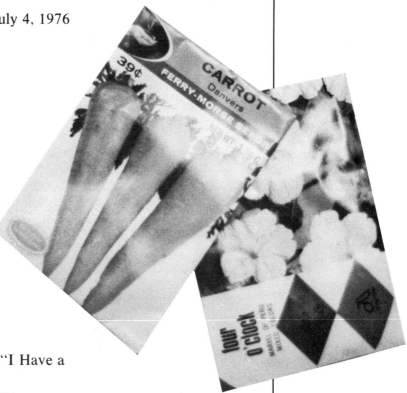

Listener Tony Chaves of Hyattsville, Maryland, offered an inscription for the Tricentennial time capsule:

> This capsule contains some symbols of our problems. If you've solved them, you can look back to our pessimistic times and laugh. If you haven't, we understand. If you've created new problems, you can call these the "good ole days." If all three are partly true, the pattern of our civilization remains constant and unchanged.

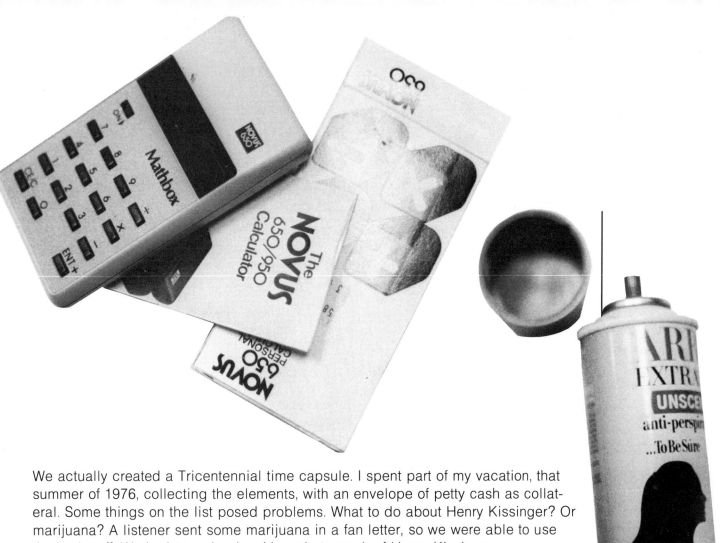

We actually created a Tricentennial time capsule. I spent part of my vacation, that summer of 1976, collecting the elements, with an envelope of petty cash as collateral. Some things on the list posed problems. What to do about Henry Kissinger? Or marijuana? A listener sent some marijuana in a fan letter, so we were able to use the real stuff. We had to make do with a photograph of Henry Kissinger.

The capsule itself was a closet in our producer's office. The key to the closet was offered to a child born on July 4, 1976. Four years later, the closet and the office were demolished in reconstruction. We barely managed to salvage the results of my shopping spree.

Today the items are all crammed inside a rural mailbox (see list), and the _All Things Considered_ Tricentennial time capsule sits on the radiator in my office.

Last Christmas she sent a small disco purse—red, with metallic threads. The Christmas before, a scarf and hat in soft heathers. Shirley Ricketts and her crochet hook haven't missed a Christmas since 1971. In 1974, she even crocheted a present for my son—a bright, multicolored muffler and a cap with a peak. Sending warmth from Minneapolis, Shirley Ricketts has been a loyal and giving listener. She's also been an inspiration. Sometimes the inspiration is more important than the gifts. Especially when our ideas run thin.

For at least the last three weeks of December, Christmas is the major news in many listeners' lives. *All Things Considered* recognizes that preoccupation each Christmas season, and we look for news around the holiday table as well as on Capitol Hill. But how many new things can you find to say? Christmas is, after all, a 2,000-year-old current event.

We've tried. And tried. We've discussed traditions and customs. Priests and ministers have retold the Christmas story on *All Things Considered*. We've wondered why people act differently at Christmas time. (The behavior is not always loving. A policeman in Detroit told us the homicide rate soars. Families get together and rekindle old hostilities.) We've talked about Blue Christmas: depression at holiday time. Once we tried a slightly sadistic short story about the murder of Santa Claus, to mix some vinegar into the seasonal treacle.

New gift ideas are no easier to come by. We've suggested alternative, non-commercial Christmas gifts: a book of coupon promises—five free nights of baby-sitting, lessons in driving a stick shift—presents that take time and attention, not cash. We've even figured out what it would cost, on the twelfth day, to give your true love all seventy-eight items in the song "The Twelve Days of Christmas": $391,200.04. Dave Zornow of member station WAMU-FM in Washington arrived at that total in 1977.* He had some trouble with swans, as in "seven swans a-swimming."

> Swans are out of season, but one source says that when you can find them, they cost $175 apiece. That does not include the pool in which they a-swim.

Three French hens also gave Zornow difficulties. He called several French butchers, who muttered things to him in their native tongue. He was unable to understand the mutterings but suspected they had little to do with French hens. Zornow finally had to settle for Cornish hens, at $1.69 each, $5.07 for three.

After ten or more radio Christmases, though, it gets tougher and tougher to come up with something to say. There's a great temptation to finesse the whole thing and settle for a few quick choruses of "Silent Night." What's true at Christmas is also true for Thanksgiving, April Fool's Day, Easter, and the times when the seasons change. All are challenges to our powers of invention.

Many of our listeners live closer to the weather than we do in Washington. They're in the country—especially in the middle of the country—on farms, in small towns,

The Perfect Gift for a Child Fourteen Months Old and Over
A Ping-Pong ball's the thing. It makes interesting sounds when it rolls around on a wooden floor. It rolls a lot, with very little input. It feeds into the child's interest in his motor mastery—he must practice throwing, and walking to get it and carry it back. It's also nice for getting a game going with another person—playing ball with Mom or Dad. And most of all, it's a whole lot of fun for just a few cents.
—Dr. Burton White, child psychologist, Cambridge, Massachusetts

---

* Just to remind you of what happened to the cost of living in the 1970s, in 1972—just five years earlier—the gifts totaled only $25,000. Maybe we added wrong.

places where tall buildings don't get between them and the sunshine. We've celebrated with them the variations in temperature and the landscape. One autumn, we phoned a foliage hotline in Vermont to ask where to drive for the best fall colors. One winter, the president of the Burpee Seed Company reassured us that the seeds in the seed packets wouldn't freeze in our mailboxes. (They don't freeze when they stay on the ground all winter, so why would they freeze in the mails?) In summer, we've talked about summer romances, whether anyone still sews labels on kids' camp clothes, and how, on a hot day, it's not so much the lemonade that cools you off; it's looking at the patterns you can trace on the glass pitcher as it sweats on a summer porch. Still, what can we say next year?

But just when it seems the seasons hold no more surprises, and the holiday tinsel is tarnished, up pops the thought of Shirley Ricketts . . . and the ideas begin flowing once again. If Shirley Ricketts doesn't run out of things to crochet for us at Christmastime—and she never does—*All Things Considered* can't run out of things to say to Shirley Ricketts.

WHAT WILL YOU DO WITH YOUR LEAP SECOND?

A Contest

Atomic clocks have gained on earth time. Or the earth has slowed down. Whichever way you want to look at it, each year the earth gets out of step with an atomic clock by almost a second. So we have to add a second to precision timepieces to even things out. It's sort of like a leap year, when you put an extra day in. Well, this is called a leap second. You put an extra second into the clock. They make the change at the end of December.

> — Dr. James Barnes
> National Bureau of Standards
> December 1979

The extra second is added at midnight on New Year's Eve. Rather like a special present from nature, it costs nothing but shouldn't be spent lightly. *All Things Considered* asked listeners how they would spend the leap second. Eager to look a gift second in the mouth, most listeners decided to spend the time kissing sweethearts a little longer. Other answers:

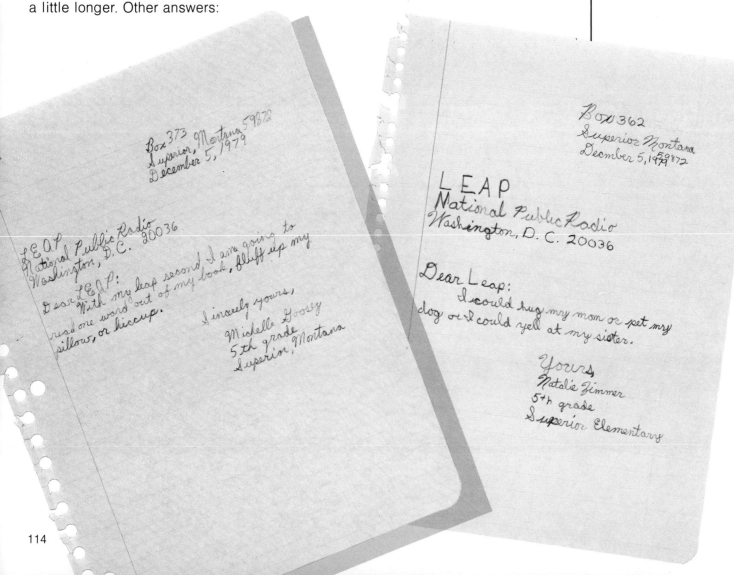

Box 373, Montana 59872
Superior, Montana
December 5, 1979

LEAP
National Public Radio
Washington, D.C. 20036

Dear LEAP:
With my leap second I am going to read one word out of my book, fluff up my pillow, or hiccup.

Sincerely yours,
Michelle Goosy
5th grade
Superior, Montana

Box 362
Superior Montana
December 5, 1979 59872

LEAP
National Public Radio
Washington, D.C. 20036

Dear Leap:
I could hug my mom or pet my dog or I could yell at my sister.

Yours
Natalie Zimmer
5th grade
Superior Elementary

I will spend my leap second contemplating all the virtues of the Nixon presidency. But I'm non-partisan. I could also spend it listing the major achievements of the Carter presidency.

—Chris Morris
Hilton, New York

I'll count my blessings. I haven't figured out what to do with the time I'll have left over after that.

—Paul Netherwood
Joppa, Maryland

I was crocheting when I heard about the contest. I'll use the extra second to make an extra stitch in my afghan. That way I'll have a stitch in time.

—Therese Young
Silver Springs, Maryland

I'll have second thoughts.

—Judith Stone
Chicago, Illinois

LEAP
National Public Radio
Washington, D.C. 20036

Superior Elementary
Superior, MT 59872

Dear Leap:

During leap second I am going to NOT THINK about all these kids!

Sincerely,
Jackie Boslka
Teacher

NEW YEAR'S RESOLUTIONS OF A SPORTS FAN

A Commentary by Robert Lipsyte

1 I will not watch the Super Bowl this year with an intellectual. Intellectuals spoil football. Either they say that the Super Bowl reaffirms the truth and beauty of America's technological progress, or they say that the Super Bowl exemplifies America's oppressive jockocracy. If I watch the Super Bowl at all this year, it will be with a Neanderthal mush-brain who knows that the Super Bowl is merely a passion play designed to resolve our lack of spirituality.

2 I will not get into any discussions regarding premeditated violence in hockey. I don't think there is anything premeditated about hockey, violent or otherwise. I don't even understand how those people keep their balance.

3 I will not even speculate on rumors that the East Germans have built a breeding farm for their Olympic athletes. I think it's all a ploy by American athletes to get their own breeding farm.

4 I will not answer questions regarding Muhammad Ali's plans to retire, although I find it hard to believe that a man who owes his soon-to-be-ex-wife more than a million dollars can retire from anything. I will also not answer questions regarding his future opponents, other than to say that I have no plans to challenge the heavyweight titleholder myself. At this time.

5 I will take no sides in the growing debate among players, owners, agents, television programmers, journalists, and fans over the future of big-time pro sports. All I'll say is that everyone should make as much money as they can before their legs give out. Incidentally, I know of no owners, agents, or journalists forced to quit because of bad knees.

6 I will not be drawn into any conjecture regarding the possibility that two all-pro quarterbacks, a starting guard in the National Basketball Association, and four Most Valuable Players in baseball are among the thirty-four women currently playing major-league sports as men. I don't even want to know the names of players who refuse to take showers after a game.

Commentator Robert Lipsyte, a former sports columnist for the *New York Times,* was born and raised in New York City. He made these New Year's resolutions from his home in suburban New Jersey in 1977.

How to Cure a Hangover, Really!
**This cure was discovered in England during World War II. Take a gram of vitamin C before you go out drinking. Take another gram of vitamin C when you return home. The vitamin C will make you feel refreshed and ready to go the next day.
—Carl Johnson, professor of chemistry, Wayne State University, Detroit, Michigan**

ALASKA WINTER

My special affinity for celebrating the seasons on *All Things Considered* goes back to my radio debut, in 1963. It was long before *All Things Considered,* long before there was an NPR. I was working at WAMU-FM in Washington (the station became part of NPR in 1971, when the network was founded). My job—my first in broadcasting—was as a producer, working behind the scenes, organizing programs, lining up guests, writing copy for others. Then one day the weather girl got sick. No one else was around. It was up to me.

I was so nervous I forgot to dial WE6-1212 ahead of time, to find out what the weather was. This was a low-budget station. No meteorologists, no fancy radar screens. To announce the weather on the air, what you did was dial the weather lady, write down what she said, and then take your notes into the studio and read them on the air. Not only were there no meteorologists, there were no windows in the studio, and so I couldn't even look out to see whether the sun was shining. All there was was the telephone, and I had forgotten to call. When the ON AIR light went on, I did the only thing I could think to do. I made up the weather. It was February. I said the temperature was sixty-two degrees, the humidity 60 percent. Then I had to repeat it. But I'd forgotten what I'd said the first time. So I made it up again: twenty-four degrees, 40 percent humidity. No one called, which probably meant that my seven listeners weren't tuned in that day. Thank goodness. But I learned some important lessons from that auspicious radio debut: Never lie to your listeners; never go on the air unprepared.

We don't do weather reports on *All Things Considered.* But we do talk about the weather a lot (even though talking doesn't change anything). One chilly winter, Paula Schiller did the talking for us. Paula had been a production assistant in Washington. In October 1978, she went to work at KUAC, the NPR station in Fairbanks, Alaska. Four months later, she sent us her first tape. Her voice, so familiar in our halls, suddenly had a faraway quality to it. The tape made us realize she was indeed speaking from thousands of miles away. Perhaps if you put on a pair of dark glasses while you read her essay, you'll get a visual equivalent of how she sounded. Earmuffs might help, too, for other reasons.

It's so cold that all the moisture in the air freezes instantaneously. Even as I speak, the moisture from my breath forms a small cloud around my head. If I were a team of panting sled dogs, I'd be completely hidden by my own white breath. The phenomenon is called ice fog. It reduces the visibility to less than five feet. It's like trying to see through Vaseline.

Last fall, ice fog was just another mystery of the far north to me, like the Aurora Borealis, or forty below. Since I've moved here, I've discovered that forty below is an interesting temperature. It's about when the worst ice fog begins. My Arctic Survival Guide says that at forty below exposed flesh will freeze in thirty minutes. Forty below also appears to be the cut-off temperature, separating the residents from the tourists or, in the local idiom, the sourdoughs from the cheechakos. For example, when I would answer, "Yes, I like it here. So far so good," the sourdoughs would look wise and say, "Just wait until forty below." Well, it's been forty below or colder for fourteen consecutive days this month, tying the all-time record for cold days in February.

At forty below, cars don't start at all. Most won't do much at twenty below, and mine begins to refuse at minus fifteen. So what you do is have your car winterized. It costs $150 to $200 and involves changing all the car's lubricants, wheel-bearing grease, steering-column fluid, and engine oil to lighter weights. That often means replacing rubber parts with silicone axle boots, gaskets, and seals. It means installing a thermostat and a whole heat register and putting in some kind of battery warmer. It means hooking up a security heater to keep your engine's precious bodily fluids flowing. The whole system gets plugged into outlets that most employers and some public places provide. They turn on the juice at zero and the car's vital signs are monitored by little lightbulbs.

I'd find the whole business of plugging in sockets, winding up cords, screwing in fuses (all the while encumbered by heavy mittens — skin sticks to metal at forty below, too) pretty unbearable if I didn't think it was a little bit funny. It amuses me to look at litters of cars attached to feeder boxes by heavy-duty Underwriters' Laboratory Approved umbilical cords. They suck the current, their little lights glowing and head-bolt heaters purring contentedly.

One twenty-below night, I had to crawl around under the car in the snow to put the chains on. The well froze on Christmas Day. During a power failure, my oil heater went out and I didn't know how to relight it. So far, though, that's been about the worst of it.

I'm hoping that the first sound of spring will be the dripping of my shower, frozen since February 3. I would appreciate an early thaw, so the water that runs into my kitchen sink can once again exit through the drain, instead of through the door by way of buckets. Maybe someday I'll be able to unstick the coffee cup frozen in a brown puddle on the floor mat of the car, and I can go out and paint my name on the mailbox, and tear the plastic off the windows. I may even get a few of those chores done before next winter.

Alaska Thanksgiving
**This Thanksgiving is an extra-special day for giving thanks. Some friends have skied or dog-sledded out these cold thirty miles to continue our tradition of celebrating our friendship together. The temperature is still above zero, but this time of year it could drop to twenty below tonight. A home-grown turkey, some winter squash from Gail's garden, some honey from Eric's bees, sourdough muffins, and pumpkin-pie crust made with pure black bear grease. It's going to be a fine meal. Relatives are far away and here in Alaska we adopt friends to round out our families. I give thanks for friends that are near, and families that are near in heart.
—Mary Shields, Goldstream Valley, Alaska**

WARM AND DRY

A Contest

Stamberg	A pepperoni pizza with extra-hot peppers and extra anchovies.
Edwards	That's warm.
Stamberg	And the place has run out of beer.
Edwards	That's dry.

Winter after winter, _All Things Considered_ has tackled the topic of cold-weather management. We've given tips on how to dress for it (nose muffs), how to sleep in it (flannel sheets), and how to treat your cat in it (keep her indoors). But the winter of 1978 was so merciless, we were driven to meditation. Perhaps, if we all _thought_ of enough things that were warm and dry, the thoughts themselves would make us cozy.

Edwards	A listener named Peggy Stevens Becksvoort says warm and dry is a clean diaper.
Stamberg	Yeah, but not for long.
Edwards	Bruce Easton, in Inglewood, California, says warm and dry is you're snowed in at an old relative's house in Buffalo, New York, watching _Lassie Come Home_ on television. The heater is stuck on high, and all there is to eat is popcorn and salted nuts.
Stamberg	Nancy Veglahn says it's standing over a floor furnace and hugging someone you love.
Edwards	Warm and dry is snuggling with your sweetie under a down comforter.
Stamberg	Who says that?
Edwards	Gary and Marilyn Johnson, in Bloomington, Illinois. They also say it's listening to _All Things Considered_ at the kitchen table.

Paul Johanson listens on his commercial fishing boat off Provincetown, Massachusetts.

What to Feed a Cold
Try the famous eighteenth-century Two Hat Cure. Take a bottle of gin (or bourbon or rum or brandy), go to your bedroom, and throw your hat on the bedpost. Then sit down and drink your gin . . . bourbon . . . rum . . . brandy until you see two hats. Get in bed and stay there until the cold is gone.
—Jim Swan,
Buffalo, New York

Stamberg	They're equating *snuggling* with this radio program?
Edwards	You got it.
Stamberg	In Springfield, South Dakota, Jan Krizan says warm and dry is the cat in the clothes dryer . . .
Edwards	. . . a guppy flopped out of the water under a Gro-Lite . . .
Stamberg	Or putting on long johns, sweat pants, two sweat shirts, wool socks, heavy-duty overalls, boots, down mittens, a hood, and a jacket, and getting a hot flash.
Edwards	Gene Stoughton, in Oak Ridge, Tennessee, says warm and dry is being left under the dryer an extra twenty minutes in a back-porch home beauty parlor in Tucumcari, New Mexico. In July.
Stamberg	And this, from Bruce Easton, in Inglewood, California.
Edwards	He already had a turn.
Stamberg	After being kidnapped by a weird political splinter group, you are confined in the giant rug dryer of a laundromat and fed chili and croutons five times a day.
Edwards	That's warm and dry!

Warming Your Ears

I've been sewing earmuffs for, let's see, twenty-five years. It's not an easy job. You have to be an experienced stitcher to make an earmuff. You want me to show you how I work? How I go around one of these? What I'm doing is, I'm putting elastic around an earmuff to give it a tension, to cup it up. So we insert a centerpiece to make the complete earmuff. You understand? Let me just show you what happens.

(Sewing machine sound)

That's an earmuff, right there.

—Freddy, L & G Manufacturing Co., Boston, Massachusetts

National Public Radio

Warming Your Heart

When you get right down to it, chicken soup is at the heart of any real relationship. Say you're walking down the aisle some day, and you get to the "I do" part. At that moment, ask yourself whether the person you're about to marry would fix you a bowl of chicken soup when you catch a cold. If the answer comes up NO, I think you should turn right around and walk out.

Susan

VALENTINE'S DAY

This piece was broadcast on Valentine's Day 1979. Freelance producer Madeleine Lundberg had gone out, days earlier, to ask some ordinary Washingtonians to talk about love and relationships. One of the people she spoke to was a construction worker named Rabbit. He was just getting off work (underground, building Washington's subway system) and wanted to sit down somewhere and relax. Madeleine took him to a neighborhood bar and started her tape recorder.

Rabbit I walk the streets and I carry two suitcases. You can't see 'em. Nobody can see 'em. But I got two suitcases. I'm right-handed. In my right hand I carry a suitcase that's full of love, and it's always open. Anybody can come and grab what they want. The one I carry in my left hand is full of hate. I don't open that. I've been married seven times. Sure, it's a lot. One is a lot. But they were all beautiful marriages. I like getting married.

Lundberg Even if it doesn't last?

Rabbit My first one lasted for eighteen years. What lasts? Tell me, what does last? Nothing lasts.

Lundberg You mean you'd leave a woman when you don't love her any longer?

Rabbit Sure I'd leave her. I don't have time to dwell on things that are dead.

Lundberg Is happiness always with a woman?

Rabbit Most of the time. Do you like to be by yourself when it's snowing? I don't. Or when it's raining, when it's storming outside? I would like to have someone I love close to me. What else is there? I'm always looking for that one woman. Hey, I walk the streets, I fall in love a thousand times. A thousand times I fall in love in a day, in passing. And I love the woman I pass — I don't even know her name, but I love her.

Lundberg Doesn't it hurt you every time you leave a woman?

Rabbit Well, sure it hurts. This last old lady of mine hurt me so bad, a year and a half I never touched another woman. I couldn't. She was so buried in my head. And yet I loved her so much that, after I die, I'm going after her. I'm going to put out my hand, she's going to grab it, and we're going to leave. This woman's life, I'm going to take it. I'm gonna take her soul with me. I know people don't live on love, but that's all I have. I don't *own* anymore, I don't *want* anymore. I'm fifty years old. I have this jacket and another jacket, two pair of pants, three shirts, four pair of socks. That's all I got. But if, for a second, for one second, you are loved and loved for yourself only, then you are fortunate.

BLACK PASSOVER

In the spring of 1980, the celebration of the Jewish holiday Passover coincided with the twelfth anniversary of Martin Luther King, Jr.'s death.

Bob Ray Sanders, the manager of member station KERA, Dallas, discovered a connection between the struggles of Jews and blacks, at a time of tension between the two groups. He taped this essay:

> *Let me taste a bitter herb, lest I forget the bitter struggle of my people. Tell me once again of the exodus, lest I forget that my people were ever in slavery. Give me a sip of the blood-colored wine. Come, let us have a seder and remember the Passover.*

I am not Jewish, but I do commemorate the Passover. I must commemorate the Passover for I do understand slavery, and struggle, and hope for deliverance. My people have suffered as slaves and disadvantaged free men in this country for more than 300 years, and I cry, "What a shame." Then I consider that my Jewish brothers and sisters have struggled for more than 3,000 years, and I cry even louder, "What a shame." And I commemorate the Passover, for, when one man's a slave, we all are slaves. And as Martin Luther King, Jr., said from his Birmingham jail, "Injustice anywhere is a threat to justice everywhere. Struggle is struggle." And I commemorate the Passover, for it is symbolic of the experiences of all downtrodden, dispossessed, and desperate people. I hear the voices of four million slaves crying in Egypt as a hardhearted pharaoh turns his back, but I also remember the great peacemaker Ralph Bunche during the 1963 march to Montgomery. I hear him saying, as he stands in the shadow of the Alabama state capitol under a breeze-whipped Confederate battle flag, "I've come to tell Pharoah Wallace to let my people go." And I hear the moans in the wilderness as the people wandered two score years, and I hear moans still, in a world full of oases but also full of barren deserts for certain people, of certain colors, of certain races, of certain nationalities, and certain religions. And I can hear Moses and Martin saying, "I've been to the mountaintop and I've seen the Promised Land." I commemorate the Passover, for I never want to forget Babylon. And although Nebuchadnezzar's fiery furnace was to be feared, it was nothing compared to Hitler's chambers. And a lion's den, well, that was a picnic compared to the church bombings and lynchings and police dogs and fiery crosses and firehoses that confronted freedom-loving people in the South in the tragic, triumphant sixties. I commemorate the Passover, not because I'm Jewish, but because I'm a man who understands slavery and struggle and the hope for deliverance.

NO APRIL FOOL

A Commentary by Kim Williams

Kim Williams made her debut on _All Things Considered_ in 1976, and the program has not been quite the same since. Maybe it was something she made us eat. Kim is an expert on edible wild foods. A naturalist, she teaches courses on sprouts and mountain ashberries (which she pronounces _ash-BEAR-eees_) and strawberry-leaf tea at the University of Montana in Missoula. She has published a book on edible wild plants and leads nature-study enthusiasts on exuberant hikes in the Rocky Mountains. Member stations KUFM in Missoula told us about Kim when we asked around for suggestions of people who might freshen up our roster of regular commentators. Kim got to Montana via upper New York State, where she was born and raised, and Chile, where she lived for nineteen years with her husband, Mel, a mining engineer. Mel's the native Montanan.

Kim Williams has a sweetly bumpy voice, a confidential tone, and sounds like a cross between Edith Bunker, a twelve-year-old, and your favorite Norman Rockwell grandmother. She may serve one of her dishes on April Fool's Day, but she's not kidding—she means for you to eat it.

I have a pot boiling on my stove, but I don't know if I dare mention what's in it. I'm designing a new recipe for a contest. The main ingredient has to be . . . well . . . here it is. Earthworms! A company in California that raises earthworms is going to put out a recipe book using the worms. Last year the recipe that won first prize was called Applesauce Surprise Cake. You can imagine what the surprise was.

"Well," I said to my husband, Mel, "don't we eat shrimp and crawdads and frogs' legs?" In South America we once ate a dish of spaghetti and, when we looked closer, each piece of spaghetti had a little black eye. It was baby eels. Our South American friends were playing a joke on us. Well, it wasn't really a joke. They were eating the same dish. It was right on the menu—considered a delicacy. Delicious.

© P. OLLSWANG · '81

A baby eel is long and thin. So what's a worm? A worm is long and thin. And how about the French, who love to eat snails? I've eaten them, too. All you taste is butter and garlic, but you're eating the whole snail, stomach, small intestines, everything. When we eat oysters, do we eat the whole oyster, stomach and all? I'm sure we do. I've sat in an oyster bar and watched the counterman open up oysters and set them in front of you—one, two, three. He doesn't remove anything. Maybe a pearl, if he finds one.

Have you eaten baby octopus? Squid is another name. Sometimes Spanish restaurants serve them in the chicken and seafood dish called paella. Anyway, when I ate it there was a lot of rice and pieces of chicken, hot spicy sausages, green pepper, red pepper, clams, and then these odd little creatures with a great many legs. My Spanish-speaking friend said, "Oh, they're calamares." "Calamares?" I said. "Oh, well, that's fine." Sometimes a good motto is "When in doubt, don't ask. Just eat." So I ate these many-legged creatures and, after I ate them, my friend said, "Well, you just ate baby octopus."

If I did all that, I guess I can eat some nice little angleworms from our own backyard. We've got lots of them. In fact, when you mow the lawn, you have a very bumpy job because those worms are working night and day, digging holes and spewing out mounds of digested earth. I dug up a cup full of worms, washed them thoroughly, and now I'm boiling them. Then I'm going to sauté them in butter, just like those baby eels in South America. But I won't serve them on a plain white plate like spaghetti. Oh no, that recipe would never do! I'm going to dice up the worms

Kim Williams

and add them to a casserole that has spicy ingredients in it — lots of onion, diced green pepper, mushrooms, maybe some slices of Jerusalem artichokes.

Now, who will I invite over to try out these earthworm recipes? Hey, April 1 is coming up! Suppose I serve the casserole and that Applesauce Surprise Cake, and at the end of the meal I say, "Surprise!" No, I'd better not. Nobody would ever come to my house again. I'll try it out on my husband, Mel.

Bruce Marsden, still driving home, in Oakland, California.

AND ON THE FOURTH OF JULY, EAT YOUR CATTAILS

Another Commentary by Kim Williams

If you're lost in the wilderness, head for a cattail swamp. That's a bit of advice I give to the students in my edible wild foods class. It's good advice. There's no excuse for starving if you can find cattails. There is some part of the cattail plant that is edible all year round. Right now, in spring, the part that is most edible is the new shoot that comes from the perennial root. It's called Cossack Asparagus because, in the old days, in the Don area of Russia where the Cossacks were living, the people were so fond of cattails (or else they had nothing else to eat, maybe) that they used the new shoots of the cattails almost like we use asparagus.

Every year, I pick Cossack Asparagus from the cattails and take it to a Fourth of July picnic that my Montana relatives have. Now, they're not really my relatives, they're my husband Mel's relatives, because you can tell from my accent that I come from the East some place. But my husband and I stop on the way to the picnic, and we pick a whole armload of fresh shoots from the cattails. We get to the picnic and people say, "Oh, there's Kim Williams with her edible wilds again!" And I say, "You don't have to eat them, but I'll put them on the table." So I peel off the green outside and cut the central core, which is about eight or ten inches long. It's white just like asparagus. I put them on a platter with a little bit of mayonnaise at one end, and put the dish on the picnic table. First come the little children, then come the teenagers, and last come the adults. Of course, by that time there are no cattails left. And they say, "Well, Kim Williams, is that all you brought?" And I say, "Well, next year I'll bring some more."

If the season is a little bit earlier, I'll bring some corn on the cob. Cattail corn on the cob, that is. That is the part that is the new, green cattail. You all know the brown cattail in fall and winter. Well, in June and July there is a new, green cattail on the shoot. If you cut that off and cook it two or three minutes, it's like corn on the cob.

Well, not quite. . . .

A WINE FOR ALL SEASONS

A Commentary by Gerry Pratt

The dandelion wine would have been close to forty years old today, if we'd kept it. I haven't touched a drop since I was ten or twelve. It was the color of brandy—amber—and it stood still, potent in the glass, poured carefully so that none of the silt was stirred up from the bottom of the bottle. It was soft and warm to taste, harmless and friendly, until suddenly it stole away your sanity and left you in a euphoria of loose-lipped, foot-stumbling, finger-fumbling relaxation.

Our wine began high on the plains, where the yellow-headed dandelions covered the fields in a sea of golden yellow heads, through the first wet, warm days of spring. We would pluck the heads between our fingers until the pollen dusted deep into the skin of our hands, turning the fingers to paws. It was a stoop harvest, much like the row-crop workings of the migrants today, only we lacked the urgency of picking for food and livelihood. We always felt like amateur moonshiners, at play with the idea that wine making was against the moral principles of our neighbors on the block. And when we stuffed the heads into a sugar sack and set them to soaking in the crock behind the stove, Mama would hide the whole thing with a blanket if there was any outsider coming to call. But you couldn't hide it. The smell of that wine—with raisins and sugar and the pungent dandelion heads—all but thundered its presence through the house. It worked into our clothes and became part of the taste of everything that we ate for a time.

When the brewing was done and the bottles were filled, funneled, and ladled, the ambrosia dipped out in measured portions, we pushed the corks in, or screwed on the tops, and laid the thirty or so bottles in the batch across the shelves of preserves in the basement. Then the real days of expectation came, the bottles stored away in the quiet darkness of the basement, somewhere beyond the woodpiles. They were as secure and as safe there as they would have been in a vault, because to stand near the new wine was to stand in a dangerous place indeed. Regularly, in the midst of dinner, in the quiet of the night, or even through the noise of a family argument, you'd hear the rifle-shot explosion of a bursting wine bottle.

But by October it was safe again, and from day to day the magic medicine of the dandelion would be administered, providing physical and emotional health and happiness at winter's darkest moments. By the middle of March, our potion had been aged, the alcohol had grown robust, and the wine kicked some, over the tongue. It was then that Mama went to the last bottles and filled the waterglass to the brim. "Take this," she'd say. "It's springtime and you need it." And we'd line up with the magic of the booze in our eyes, the girls pinching their noses, swallowing it down.

Only when she discovered my brothers sipping and savoring did Mama begin to get apprehensive about the curative effects, and then she began to take notice of the loud voices and the sudden outbursts of laughter that followed the wine. But it was a tonic, marvelous to behold, and if we had kept it longer I'd take a glass today.

Commentator Gerry Pratt told us about his family's dandelion wine in June 1977, but the wet-season dandelion crop on Oregon's coast at Gearhart is a regular, annual celebration. He says his stint as chief executive officer of a savings and loan association seriously cribbed his wine making for a number of years.

KEEPING COOL IN SUMMER

A Contest

One spring we wondered aloud why April is the cruelest month. Some reasons arrived quickly from listeners: "Because T. S. Eliot said so." My favorite answer came from three-and-a-half-year-old Arthur Hart, in Eugene, Oregon. With some clerical assistance from his mother, Arthur wrote that April is the cruelest month because "some days are sunny, but my parents tell me it's still too cold to play in the green turtle wading pool." The prize for that contest was May.

By June and July, we're wishing we could still fit into wading pools (or our bikinis, for that matter). And we're in serious need of ideas for how to keep cool. In July 1977, we issued an appeal for help. Another contest. Tell us how to keep cool. But tell us how to keep cool the old-fashioned, energy-saving way. Like Grandma used to do. Well. Grandma might have approved of Pearl Anna Petras's suggestion, from San Francisco: "Put a wet hanky on your head, around your neck, or hide it in your bodice. Sit near a ceiling fan." But Grandma would have had very little truck with some of the other ideas from listeners.

> Clean house in the nude. Save the bathroom for last. Work up a sweat while you're cleaning. Then get into the tub or shower, and clean it and yourself at the same time.
>
> —Lynn Atkinson
> Schenectady, New York

> Take a lukewarm bath and don't dry yourself off. Wet a sheet and wring it dry. Aim a portable fan at your bed. Lie down. Put the wet sheet on top of you. At two in the morning, wake up shivering. Remove the wet sheet. Find a dry one. Whine, "I'm so cold." Sleep soundly, newly warmed.
>
> —Mrs. H. E. Perry
> Black River Falls, Wisconsin

Henny Youngman, How Hot Is It?

"It's so hot in Las Vegas, it was 130 degrees in the shade."

"That hot, eh?"

"Yeah. I'm no dope. I went out in the sun."

Mark Milam, David Llewellyn, Greg Hines, and Janet Delahanty listen on the evening shift at an in-patient adolescent psychiatric service in Indianapolis, Indiana.

One cool, old-fashioned, energy saving idea called for some organization ahead of time.

> Eat oatmeal cookie–watermelon sandwiches. Cut the watermelon into circles with a glass. Pick out the seeds. Chill two oatmeal cookies. Slap the slice of watermelon between two cookies. It's a filling, chilling, no spilling cooler.
>
> —Tom Louis
> Richmond, Virginia

A listener in Iowa sent in a long letter that sounded on the air like a tall glass of iced tea:

> In one of the hot summers in the early 1930s when our Ames, Iowa, neighborhood group hung around front porches and speculated about where the money could come from for an Eskimo Pie or a swim at Carr's pool, a neighbor's cousin came up from Tarkio, Missouri, with a cool new game. She quickly assumed the stature of a minor savior in my eyes. The game itself was stark in its simplicity, ideal for the hottest and poorest of children, but containing all the elements of risk, wit, and luck to make it a good game. The only equipment needed was a pan of cold water and a small container, such as a shot glass. We lined up on the porch railing, five or six sweating children, all facing "It" with her pan of cold water. We called the game Rainbow. The object was to guess the color "It" was thinking of. The prize was that cold insult of water in the face when we guessed right. There it was. Excitement without enervation—the cure for all the ills of boredom, heat, and pennilessness. It became a standard change from going under the hose, quietly reading a book, or just lolling around, moving as little as possible. There was a gentle aggressiveness about the game, and the guessing could become quite spirited. It was also impossible to know if "It" really had been thinking of puce or just liked the sound of the word. At any rate, the hidden object was to get as wet as possible and with luck one could catch a few stray splashes as well as one's legitimate prize. It had the attraction of being a game never played in school or Sunday school, although it had clear educational benefits. How many other nine- and ten-year-olds knew about chartreuse and magenta back in the days before television?
>
> —Alice Willis
> Des Moines, Iowa

HALLOWEEN, 1980 STYLE

A Commentary by Paul Hemphill

The first time I kissed a girl was on Halloween night in our neighborhood in Birmingham. Everybody wore costumes; the only light came from a candle jabbed inside a jack-o'-lantern; and we were playing spin the bottle. When the old Coca-Cola bottle pointed toward me, I simply reached over to the nearest female and did it! She and I blushed, and everybody else laughed. Then all of us twelve-year-olds of the block bobbed for apples and ate pumpkin pie and danced up and down the street playing trick or treat. Halloween, back then, was a jolly good time.

But then a mean streak began to develop in America. We started hearing stories about people poisoning the candy they dropped into the trick or treat bags when the happy little scamps came knocking at the door. And about people unleashing German Shepherds the minute the gaggle of children hit the porch. And then, one that I still can't believe: the story about people who carefully inserted razor blades in the Halloween apples they proffered. We've come a long way in these thirty years from innocently bobbing for clean apples and playing spin the bottle.

All of this came to mind the other day when the mayor of Atlanta announced a curfew, between eleven at night and six in the morning, for children under the age of fifteen. Mayor Maynard Jackson also asked that all parents keep their kids off the streets on Halloween night. Much of this was precipitated by the disappearance of fourteen Atlanta children. Most of the bodies have been found. Nobody knows who did the killing, or why. You simply have to figure it's a lone killer out there who's mad at the world, or his mama, or something. But I tell you, and I hope you'll do the same, that my Martha and my Molly are going to do their apple bobbing at home this Halloween.

Commentator Paul Hemphill says he is the son of an Alabama truck driver and looks it; the author of seven million words and five books and looks it; the father of four children and looks it. He lives in Atlanta.

CRANBERRIES FOR THANKSGIVING

NATIONAL PUBLIC RADIO'S

*"all
things
considered"*

Thanksgiving, 1979

Dear Listener:

Glad my annual description on the air intrigued you. My mother-in-law and I are delighted to share the recipe for Mama Stamberg's Cranberry Relish -- the relish that <u>sounds</u> terrible but tastes terrific.

        2 cups raw cranberries
        1 small onion
        ½ cup sugar
        3/4 cup sour cream
        2 tablespoons horseradish

Grind the onion and cranberries together. Add all the other ingredients and mix. Put in a plastic container and freeze. About an hour before serving, move the container from the freezer to the refrigerator compartment, to thaw. The relish will be thick, creamy, chunky, and shocking pink. Makes 1½ pints.

Hope your family enjoys it. Happy Thanksgiving.

Sincerely,

Susan Stamberg

National Public Radio, 2025 M St. NW, Washington D.C. 20036

npr

Congratulations a Mother Stanberg for her Cranberry Relish. It makes an old tired piece of ham a treat. It also clears the sinuses.

Many thanks from a former Ocean Sprayer —

Marion Critchlow
La Cañada, California

Glad you like the recipe — Give my regards to your sinuses.
Glad travels to working!
(you are a speedy cook!)

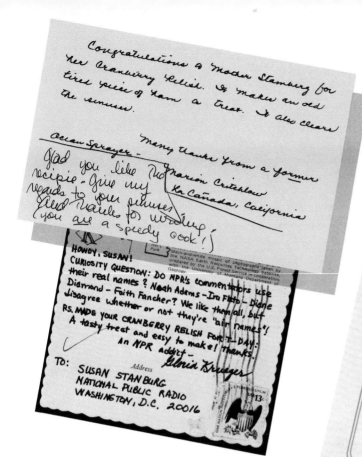

HOWDY, SUSAN!
CURIOSITY QUESTION: DO NPR's commentators use their real names? Noah Adams — Ira Flato — Diane Diamond — Faith Fancher? We like them all, but disagree whether or not they're "air names"!
P.S. MADE YOUR CRANBERRY RELISH FOR T-DAY. A tasty treat and easy to make! Thanks.
An NPR addict —
Gloria Krueger

Address
TO: SUSAN STANBURG
NATIONAL PUBLIC RADIO
WASHINGTON, D.C. 20016

Tuesday, November 18

Dear Mrs. Stanberg,
I am writing to you on behalf of my whole family. A few years ago you first gave your recipe for Mama Stanbergs cranberry relish. You said "it sounds awful but it tastes delicious." Well we tried it thinking you would never steer us wrong. Our reaction: YCHHHH! It sounds awful and tastes even worse! We think your radio program is wonderful(!) but frankly, your taste in relish doesn't compare.
sincerely
Emily (me), Rachel,
Herb & Althea Glick

Dear Susan Stanberg,
Thanks for Mama Stanberg's delicious cranberry relish recipe. Also — thanks for repeating it — the ingredients were so unusual I was sure I had written it down wrong the first time.
I had to tell you that my mother-in-law (a plain, old-fashioned Pennsylvania Dutch cook (round cranberry sauce school)), took seconds! I think Mama Stanberg's recipe will become one of our family traditions.

Robin Attwood Fiedler
Hanover, Pa.

Dearest Susan,
Your Cranberry Relish was not a big hit at our Thanksgiving dinner! In fact, it was just terrible..... yuk!!!!)
The following list of names is signed by those who tasted the relish and their comments — — — — — :

Laura Ball ..... extremely unpleasant! — — — — —
Harold Herzy — the old recipe "(4pt + PR claim) was much superior!
Mary Jean Royan — What a combination! Blah!
Joe Grimani — Has a combination of singular and astonishing qualities I've never tasted in another salad.
Daril Holt — Mercy ......
Ros Amberg — It just wasn't very good.
(inside)

G. Callaway — Being a person who likes the taste of raw onions, I could tolerate it.
Brenda Vance — I don't recommend this relish!
Bob Vance — You must be kidding
John Wilson — disgusting

Thanksgiving Day 1980

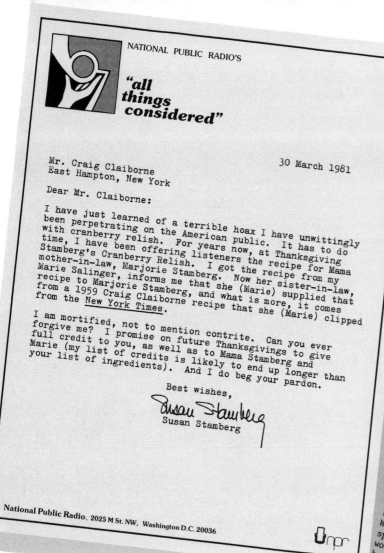

30 March 1981

Mr. Craig Claiborne
East Hampton, New York

Dear Mr. Claiborne:

I have just learned of a terrible hoax I have unwittingly
been perpetrating on the American public. It has to do
with cranberry relish. For years now, at Thanksgiving
time, I have been offering listeners the recipe for Mama
Stamberg's Cranberry Relish. I got the recipe from my
mother-in-law, Marjorie Stamberg. Now her sister-in-law,
Marie Salinger, informs me that she (Marie) supplied that
recipe to Marjorie Stamberg, and what is more, it comes
from a 1959 Craig Claiborne recipe that she (Marie) clipped
from the New York Times.

I am mortified, not to mention contrite. Can you ever
forgive me? I promise on future Thanksgivings to give
full credit to you, as well as to Mama Stamberg and
Marie (my list of credits is likely to end up longer than
your list of ingredients). And I do beg your pardon.

Best wishes,

Susan Stamberg
Susan Stamberg

National Public Radio, 2025 M St. NW., Washington D.C. 20036

npr

CRAIG CLAIBORNE

Susan Stamberg
National Public Radio
2025 M Street, N.W.
Washington, D.C. 20036

April 6, 1981

Dear Susan:

As a long time admirer, I am delighted to know that one of my
recipes has given you and yours pleasure. I promise you my
full-hearted permission to use the recipes in print or as you
please in return for the hours of pleasure you have given me.

As to the origin of that recipe, unless you have a very long
memory you will not recall that in 1959 there was a terrible
scare among cranberry users. The government had declared
that a certain weed-killer, deleterious to human health, had
been used on a small portion of that year's cranberry crop.
When it proved to be false or when the scare had passed we
spent a few hours contriving recipes in my own kitchen that
would lure home cooks back into using that year's cranberry
harvest. The cranberry relish that you have in mind was one
of three such recipes that appeared in one edition.

Fond regards,

In addition to the annual recitation of Mama Stamberg's Cranberry Relish, _All Things Considered_ offers a recipe for _traditional_ cranberry sauce from the family of NPR President Frank Mankiewicz. Mr. Mankiewicz himself presents the recipe on the air.

The Mankiewicz Family Recipe for Traditional Cranberry Sauce

1 Take one can Ocean Spray Cranberry Sauce.
2 Open can.
3 Hold can over a decorative dish.
4 Thump can until jellied sauce falls onto decorative dish.
5 Slice and serve.

CHOCOLATE FOR CHRISTMAS

Mama Stamberg's Cranberry Relish is meant for Thanksgiving. So is the Mankiewicz version. But no one would quibble if you served them at Christmastime too (except for Laura Ball, *et al*, in Marshall, North Carolina, back on page 133). Perla Meyers's recipe for chocolate truffles was offered as a Christmas gift idea but could do equal damage to your hips on Thanksgiving or Ground Hog Day.

Seasonal chef and *All Things Considered* commentator Perla Meyers is one of those rarities: a slim cook you can trust. Born in Vienna and raised in Spain, Switzerland, England, France, and Italy, she is author of *The Peasant Kitchen, The Seasonal Kitchen,* and *Perla Meyers's from Market to Kitchen Cookbook.*

What I like about Perla is that she's so authoritative. You rarely encounter such certainty in the news business. When a politician says he's going to cut taxes, you make a mental note to check on what he does after the election. He'll probably change his mind. But when Perla Meyers tells you that butter can only be cut into melted chocolate one tablespoon at a time, you can be absolutely sure she will stand by that statement long after the first Tuesday in November.

Meyers	Chocolate should be melted only in a double boiler.
Stamberg	Really? Can't you just put it in a pan over a piece of asbestos?
Meyers	No. Never. It will scorch the pan immediately and change the flavor of the chocolate.

Now, for years I have put chocolate in a pan over a piece of asbestos without scorching the pan or changing the flavor of the chocolate. But Perla is so definite in her instructions that asbestos-melted chocolate has never again tasted good in my household. Here's her set of no-fault chocolate-truffle instructions, given to *ATC* listeners in December 1978:

John Harper Reeves listens in Long Valley, New Jersey.

How Do You Make A Sugar Plum?
You use prunes. The bigger the prune, the prettier the sugar plum. Steam the prunes, let them cool, slit them open, and take out the seed. Stuff the steamed prune with icing, candied fruit, chopped nuts, marzipan, or whatever you like. Close the prune around that ball of stuffing, and roll the prune in sugar. You can dip one end in melted chocolate if you like. That's how you make a sugar plum. I researched them. They were first made in England, years ago.
—Georgianna Lundgren,
The Candy Factory,
Columbia, Missouri

Chocolate should be melted only in a double boiler. The double boiler melts the chocolate slowly and evenly. If you're using a semisweet commercial chocolate that's not top quality, add a good amount of fresh sweet butter to the chocolate, plus some instant coffee. That heightens the flavor of the chocolate. Never add vanilla to chocolate. Vanilla immediately gives it a fake flavor and is not very good. You can add sugar to unsweetened chocolate. And you can work in a good liqueur such as a brandy, a rum, or Grand Marnier—all of these liqueurs add flavor and zest to chocolate.

One of the nicest things to do around Christmastime is to make a chocolate truffle. It's called a truffle because, once it's made, it looks very much like the black truffle, that great delicacy found in the Perigord region of France and used in pâtés and terrines.

A chocolate truffle is done very simply by taking six ounces of very good bittersweet chocolate, melting it in a double boiler, and then whisking two egg yolks and two tablespoons of heavy cream into the nicely melted chocolate. Beat the chocolate mixture with a wooden spoon until it's cool enough so you can touch it with your finger. Add two tablespoons of brandy or Amaretto or rum, whatever you like. Then use a wooden spoon to beat half a stick of sweet butter into the chocolate, a tablespoon at a time. That's four tablespoons. The chocolate must not be too hot, or else the butter will liquefy. Chill this mixture a good long time, until it is almost set. Then, just like a little child, take a healthy pinch of chocolate and roll it into a ball between the palms of your hands. Keep dipping your hands into cold water, so the chocolate doesn't melt. Then roll the little balls in powdered unsweetened cocoa. (The best cocoa is, of course, Dutch cocoa.) Refrigerate or freeze the chocolate truffles. They can be frozen for two or three months and then given as Christmas gifts in pretty boxes. They are extremely rich and absolutely wonderful.

Put a piece of paper in the typewriter and type:

"Dear Mother,
I am having an awful time trying to begin a piece of writing.
It just won't work. It's wretched. It's dreadful. You see, it has to
do with a certain grizzly bear in northwest Alaska. I can't do it.
It's awful. This bear was standing on the hillside eating blue-
berries. . . ."

Keep on writing about the bear. Then keep going. Then go back and cut off the "Dear Mother" and all that garbage at the beginning, and everything that went after it. And there you are. You've gotten somewhere.

—John McPhee
January 1978

The only interview John McPhee has ever granted for broadcast was aired on *All Things Considered.* The *New Yorker* writer shies away from microphones. Noah Adams, a fan of McPhee, courted him for months, hoping to convince him to agree to an interview. When Noah visited member station WUHY in Philadelphia to help them with some fundraising broadcasts, someone on the staff arranged for William Howarth, McPhee's anthologizer, to join him on the air. In between pitching the audience for contributions, Noah and Howarth talked about John McPhee. Howarth made a tape of their conversation and played the tape for McPhee. Apparently McPhee was impressed with Noah's knowledge of his work. And the next time Noah asked for an interview, the writer agreed. The story is not uncommon, for writers often feel their best work is on the page, not in conversation.

Still, literary conversations on the air have become a standard part of "the book tour." That's when authors go to sixty cities in twenty days, appearing on all the talk shows, chatting up what they've written in hopes of convincing listeners to buy the book. Most writers say they hate the tours. I don't blame them. I can always tell when I am interviewer number fifty on the itinerary. The author comes in, eyes glazed, ready to deliver a three-minute wrap-up of the book, dead sure I haven't read it. I've lost count of the times writers have told us how amazed they are that we've actually read their books. I've never felt there was much choice. You can't *really* talk about a book without reading it.

There's a certain knack to interviewing writers. It's not like a news interview, where the emphasis is on facts and information. In literary interviews, ideas and personality are the real topics of conversation. I try to go in with a point of view about the author and his or her work, and a sense of what the focus of the conversation should be.

Then there's the matter of the questions themselves. Fancy questions don't work. In fact, sometimes the simple question, "Why?" will produce the most intriguing answer.

Often I ask how the writer was feeling—what was in his or her mind when the work was created. That approach also works well with painters and dancers. It gets to the heart of the creative process.

I'm intrigued by the mysteries of inspiration—what it is, where it comes from. A book may find its sources in religious feeling, social observation, private experience, or fascination with language. When authors reach to explain themselves or the characters they've created or the symbols they use, they think out loud. Listeners are able to sit in on that process and hear an interesting mind at work.

I'm curious about the details of the craft. I want to know how writers write. Do they use legal pads or typewriters? Do they sit at a desk or under a tree? Sometimes we get so wrapped up in these questions that we barely get around to the author's latest work.

For me, reading has always been one of the great pleasures. And speaking of writing on *All Things Considered* is my favorite kind of conversation.

THE ACT OF WRITING

> *Writing*
> *is the art of keeping still*
> *indoors for days at a time*
> *while others are out*
> *shuffling their papers.*
>
> — Richard Elman
> "Calliope Song"*

Writers listen to voices in their heads. Radio producers listen to voices in their headsets.

Wendy Blair, a freelance radio producer, created this exploration of the act and art of putting words on paper. Essentially, it's a piece about silence — "keeping still indoors for days at a time." To produce it, Wendy had to keep still, too. For days she sat listening to tapes in a tiny edit booth at the end of a dark corridor. Some were interviews I had recorded especially for the project: conversations with the young poet Katha Pollitt; science-fiction writer Isaac Asimov; editor-biographer Thomas Congdon; and a psychiatrist who helps creative patients work through writer's block. Other tapes came from the NPR archives: interviews with Saul Bellow, Joan Didion, and Henry Miller, collected and broadcast by various reporters.

Wendy picked excerpts (some as brief as ten seconds) in which the writers spoke with special excitement or humor or conviction. Then she intercut the voices — going quickly from Susan Sontag to John McPhee to Katha Pollitt to give a sprightly pace to the tape. Wendy kept her own writing — the scripted words I would speak as linking narrative — to a minimum. The result, aired in April 1979, was a seventeen-minute piece. But it was seventeen straight minutes of talk. Would voices alone hold listeners' attention for that long, or should she add other sounds . . . music, background noises? We talked about it.

Since the piece was basically about writing — an act of silence — I felt it would be a contradiction to use music. But I agreed that there should be some break between the words, something to spice up the tape and also signal a change of subject or new idea. Finally I suggested we include the one sound that is often part of the writer's otherwise silent environment: the typewriter.

(Rapid typing/ringing of carriage return/more typing/fade and hold under)

Stamberg   Saul Bellow has won three National Book Awards. This is what he said after he was awarded the Nobel Prize for Literature in 1976.

Bellow   I long to get back to a quiet room where I can do what I've done for most of my life: sit there writing. As a rule, when I'm at work at something I get up quite early. I begin to get pre-conscious intimations of what the work is going to be like, even before I

---

* *Homage to Fats Navarro*, New Rivers Press.

awaken. I see faces and scenes, floors, walls, landscapes. I hear lines of dialogue. And then I get up. If the fates are kind, I'm in a state of some excitement. I have a cup of coffee and sit down immediately to work. I generally stop by about noon. By then I'm streaming sweat. One would think that I'd been shoveling coal instead of writing words in a notebook.

Stamberg The act of writing involves labor—and a state of grace.

John McPhee It's not a case of laying down a sentence that looks sort of mediocre and ordinary and then doctoring it until it is unique. If you do that, you're going to create something exaggerated and lifeless. I think that's why so much time is spent doing nothing. I spend my days staring out the window. I'm thinking all day long about what it is I'm trying to write. And then finally, about five or six o'clock, I start to write. I don't know where it comes from.

Stamberg Writers also say that the muse is susceptible to some manipulation. Here's Ivan Doig. His book about the West, *This House of Sky,* was nominated for a National Book Award.

Doig Occasionally, when I'm going really well, I will quit in the middle of a sentence or a paragraph or whatever so that I will have something to pick up with very readily the next morning. But primarily, I simply glue myself down in front of the typewriter and something eventually comes. It doesn't matter terribly much how good what comes really is, as long as something comes up on that typewriter.

(Typing, sporadic, then speeding up)

Stamberg More about the working writer's state of mind from Susan Sontag.

Sontag The wonderful thing about writing fiction is that there are surprises. You have this material. It begins to develop. The people start to talk. You know who the people are, you know what the situation is, the material, the theme, the anguish. And then it can become quite different from what you thought it was going to be.

Stamberg But John McPhee says that the process of discovering the unknown can be frightening, and the pressure on a writer can be inhibiting.

McPhee Joan Didion calls it "the low dread." Every day she feels the low dread of going into that room (which she calls "there; in there") and doing her writing. Those words ring very true to me. She puts it just the way it is.

(Typewriter sounds/paper ripped from machine and crumpled angrily)

Stamberg The writers' overwhelming fear is that they will not be able to write. Psychiatrist Gregory Rochlin has worked with people suffering from so-called writer's block.

John Gardner Tells What a Book Has to Do to Engage Him

It has to start a dream in my mind. I read the first three pages and I fall through the print on the page and I'm in Russia watching a train go across a field. I never wake up in *Gulliver's Travels,* either. I just start and I'm in the dream all the way through. The same thing with Shakespeare and Chaucer.

Rochlin   Writers don't have special psychological characteristics that separate them from the rest of humanity. Their motives are diverse; their neuroses are not unique; they suffer from the same inhibitions or anxieties and obsessions that the rest of us have. But writers have an occupational hazard. Their unresolved conflicts may inhibit their writing. Also, the writers I know who have had difficulty writing are people who feel they want to write an immortal work. Well, if Abraham Lincoln had been told that on the back of an envelope he was supposed to scribble a Gettysburg Address that would be immortal, I think he would have been paralyzed.

Henry Miller   At the age of sixteen or seventeen I was already irreligious. But I remember praying to God in bed at night: "God, please make me a writer—but a GREAT writer." Then came a period in which I couldn't do anything. I didn't even try.

Once I was sitting at the kitchen table with a woman I was going with, and I suddenly said, "Have you got a piece of paper or a pad? I think I can write something." She gave me a little pencil—that's what I always remember, that size, you know, about two inches long. And I wrote a few lines—say three or four lines—and I suddenly stopped and threw the pencil away. I had run out of my idea already. And I said to her, "No, I don't think I'll ever be able to do it."

Stamberg   Here is the poet, Katha Pollitt.

Pollitt   George Orwell said that writing a book is a horrible, exhausting struggle, like a bout of some painful illness. And I certainly have found that to be true with friends who have written books. One of them said that, if people saw what he did while he was writing, they would just think he was totally mad and cart him away.

Stamberg   It's the rare writer who does not struggle. Isaac Asimov published his two hundredth book this year.

Fluorescent painter Stephen Hannock listens in Northampton, Massachusetts.

(Typing/carriage return/steady typing)
What, Mr. Asimov? No blocks? No anxiety? You seem much too straightforward a writer.

Asimov Writing is the only thing I'm interested in doing. I enjoy it. It's fun. It's relaxation. It's a vacation. Coming here, in order to talk to you, that's work.

(Typing/carriage return/more typing)

Stamberg To sustain them in their daily work, writers sometimes use magic. They speak of the importance of certain ways of doing things: writers' rituals.

Sontag I always write in long hand for the first draft. Then I start typing.

Pollitt I find that places get used up. After I've sat at my desk for a couple of weeks, I like to move into the other room and write at another table for a bit.

Stamberg Thomas Congdon is a book publisher and a biographer of Maxwell Perkins, the famous editor of F. Scott Fitzgerald, Ernest Hemingway, and Thomas Wolfe.

Congdon The hardest thing for a writer to do is to establish constants. In a madly variable situation, writers attempt to establish constants. I always sit on the same cushion of the same sofa in the same room, and arrange the pillow and the lights so that all distractions, all the variables that I can possibly control, are controlled. It's an attempt to regularize what is essentially a chaotic situation.

Asimov Rituals? Ridiculous! My only ritual is to sit close enough to the typewriter so that my fingers touch the keys.

Stamberg What do you do the day the typewriter breaks?

Asimov Well, that's why I've got four typewriters.

Stamberg You have four typewriters?

Asimov Right.

Stamberg I'd call that a ritual, Mr. Asimov!

(Asimov laughs.)

Isaac Asimov may not admit to having any rituals, but he does observe certain rules about writing.

Asimov I don't like to talk about any book that's in progress. If you talk about it, you bleed off some of the internal pressure. In fact, if you talk about something enough, you never write it.

Stamberg Joan Didion says, "If I could tell you my story, I wouldn't have to write it."

Didion I write entirely to find out what is on my mind, what I'm thinking, what I'm looking at, what I'm seeing, and what it means. What I want and what I'm afraid of. I'm talking about finding out what's going on in the pictures in my mind. If you lie low enough and stay quiet enough and if you don't talk to very many people and you keep your central nervous system from shorting out, these pictures come to you and then you try to find out what they mean.

Congdon There are people who write, and there are people who talk about writing. It's one thing to talk with an editor about a plot problem. But it's not nearly as desirable for the writer to sit down and tell the editor the whole story. It's bad for the editor because, when he or she finally does read it, it's not as fresh as it would have been. But it's also bad for the writer, because that storyteller's urge, that storytelling passion, is diffused.

(Typing slow/then speeding up/typing stops/silence)

Stamberg Successful writers are courted by the public: broadcasters want to interview them; readers want to meet them. But they must be isolated while the actual work is going on.

Sontag It isn't that the desire to be alone is the motivation of the work. It's that you have to be alone in order to do the work, in order to go further in the work. You have to not answer the telephone. You have to refuse invitations to go out. You have to just sit alone eight, ten, twelve, fifteen hours at a stretch.

Didion For me this is one of the great advantages of being a writer. I like to be alone.

Bellow It is terribly difficult. It is hard to see the Chicago streets go bare as people make their way to their jobs, leaving me in this extraordinary position—connected with nothing except my own imagination. It takes some strength of will.

Sontag It is an ascetic occupation, being a writer. But obviously it's one that one chooses. Nobody makes you be a writer, or a painter, or any of those things that you can only do alone. It's what you want to do, and you do it in a state of obsession. I'm much more motivated by obsessions than I am by my "iron discipline." My discipline is far from being iron.

Miller I would sometimes become so obsessed that I would sort of hit my head with my fist and say, "Stop it up there, turn it off, turn it off. I can't stand it!" It was going too strong, you know. I couldn't eat. I couldn't sleep. I would always be urged to go and pour out more words.

Bellow I think it is probably the hardest course of all, this self-imposed course.

Stamberg Writing. A brave act. An act of love.

(Silence/then typing/carriage return/more slow typing/silence again/then barely audible voice, picking out the letters T-H-E-E-N-D/sound of paper being pulled out of machine)

Writers are very dull people. So we don't really associate with each other. We seek out people who are not writers because that's where the lively life is. Writers are only interested in themselves and their own work. They're not interested in you or anybody else. They're very selfish people. They're good people to avoid.
—Erskine Caldwell, November 1976

JOHN IRVING

In April 1979, John Irving traded the solitude of his work room for the hubbub of radio and television stations. He was on "the book tour," and his route included *All Things Considered*. The buzzing in our halls increased. *The World According to Garp* was the book we were talking about during coffee breaks, and we were all curious to see its author.

I prepared very carefully for the interview. I read all of Irving's earlier books, and had lines and scenes from *Garp* practically committed to memory. But the interview was nearly a disaster.

Partly, it was a problem of time. John Irving arrived on a very busy day, and the studio was only available for fifteen minutes. Also, I took a risk at the beginning of the interview that almost put the kibosh on it. I started this way:

"Mr. Irving, on the basis of your brilliant writing, and your photograph on the dust jacket of *Garp,* most of the women on our staff have told me they'd like to run away with you."

Total silence. I plunged on.

"But I said to them, 'Why would you want to run away with a man who is totally obsessed by children and bears?' "

Not a blink. Not a smile.

Drowning, with one minute of the precious fifteen already shot, I kept going, backing off from a tack that was clearly wrong (too brazen, or aggressive, or intimate to engage him), searching for an area that was more neutral and comfortable.

I finally found it.

> **Stamberg** It took John Irving five years to write *The World According to Garp*. He says he could have produced his best-selling novel in two and a half or three years, but he couldn't afford to. He had to teach and give readings to earn money while he was writing. The success of *Garp* means that John Irving can stop teaching and stop reading aloud, for money anyway.
>
> **Irving** I've given fewer readings this year than I ever have, and probably will give fewer still next year. It's nice to have those options. It's not that I don't want to do readings — when you've been working well for a few weeks it's nice to get out and try some new things on an audience. But they shouldn't interfere with the main stuff: writing.
>
> **Stamberg** Do you revise as a result of the readings?
>
> **Irving** I revise as a result of everything. I revise right up to the galleys, and frequently there, too. I revise all the time. I never read to an audience something that to my knowledge is finished. If it's a larger, formal reading, I may tend to read something that's more finished, but it will always be from a work in progress. I don't read from things once they're books.
>
> **Stamberg** Why?

Irving   Well, what's in it for me? Then you really are wasting your time. You do get a certain fee when you give a reading, but the larger benefit is that you get to see which lines will make some people get up and walk out. You can sense the restlessness and the attention of an audience. You can sense the sympathy, the willingness to extend themselves, or go along, and you can see when you've lost a group. Sustaining a pace on the page is something that matters to me very much in my fiction, because my novels are very consciously narrative. There is an "and then, and then, and then" quality about them. Those are qualities I like to test: Can I really stretch this scene? Can I really sustain this comedy or this sadness over eight pages? What about fifteen pages? When do I sense somebody's tiring of it?

Stamberg   Why do bears reappear in all your books? Not just in *Garp,* but in *Setting Free the Bears, The 158-Pound Marriage,* and in the novel you're working on now, *The Hotel New Hampshire?*

Irving   Oh, I don't know what I mean by those bears. I think that bears are like human beings: not altogether predictable; lovable, frequently more lovable from a distance than they are in reality. They seem to me to be animals particularly befuddled and lost in the modern world. They have abilities that aren't often recognized, or they're not allowed to indulge in them in the world as we've made it today. Remember, I only write about bears in an unnatural situation. I only write about bears in captivity or bears in zoos, trained bears, domesticated bears. It seems to me that there is some kind of human parallel there. Many of us are people whose instincts for living may be profound, but the terms of modern society make it difficult for our instincts to be appreciated. What we have to do instead is find a job, be useful, function, and many of the things we have to do just in order to live take us a long way from what instinctually we might do well.

Stamberg   So the bear is natural man? Man in his natural state?

Irving   Yes, but I wouldn't want to—

Stamberg   Is that too fancy for you?

Irving   It's too worked out for me. I don't work things out that way. The reason that I write about bears is that it seems right. The instinct seems right.

Stamberg   But aren't you a little obsessive about the bears? You write about them all the time. Of course, you also always write about marriage, children, sins, violence, sex. . . .

Irving   Well, these days many of our best writers seem to me to be writing about very little. That is, they're not taking on potentially dangerous and risky themes. I would say that if you tell a novel, a whole novel, and you don't run the risk of being sentimental, exploitative, excessively violent, excessively sexual — excessively *something* — if you don't run the risk of telling a story that we've heard a hundred times, then it's quite possible that you're not writing about anything important.

Stamberg Because you are a facile writer (I mean that in the best way) and a glittering writer (I mean *that* in the best way, too), do you have to control that a bit? Stop dancing so much on the tightrope?

Irving I think I dance less on the typewriter than I did, but you're quite right.

Stamberg I said "tightrope." You heard "typewriter."

Irving Oh, typewriter! Well, you see, it's the same thing. *(Laughter by both.)* There's a sort of "look at me, look at me, look at me write" quality to any writer who loves prose, and you can easily love your own language to excess, as you can love anything to excess. I hope I indulge that vice a little less than I used to. But it strikes me most of the time that, whatever your virtue is as a writer, it probably also is your vice. Whatever you do well, you will tend to do to excess. If terseness, sparseness, irony is your bag, you can kill a novel that way, too. I think what I do best as a fiction writer is sustain a scene that could have been (or should have been) finished ten pages ago. Obviously, I take some pleasure and find some challenge in sustaining something in that sort of breathless "and then, and then, and then" way. I think it's like knowing that the best joke is going to alienate some people. The

Lynn Moser listens in Rochester, N.Y. Her message on the heart reads "Everyday 5 PM on the press with NPR *All Things Considered* XX Lynn Moser".

joke that everybody laughs at is not the best one. The best joke is the one that the best people laugh the hardest at. And that may drive three other people right up the wall.

I'm speaking aesthetically in favor of a kind of extremism. The writers I tend to like to read are people who did things to extreme. Not always the same extreme. People like this have as strong enemies as they have friends, and that says something good about them to me. It says that they have insisted on the world according to them. They've been powerfully effective, or powerfully resisted, but they haven't been polite; they haven't been like politicians, trying to touch every base, trying to warm every heart. You can't write things that are genuinely sad without being gross to some people, and you can't write things that are really comic, ambitiously comic, without offending some people or causing others to groan. In other words, to be extreme in your art, you have to be very good at it.

As you can see, none of my initial floundering got on the air, but even so I feel this interview didn't quite work. It has no logical order, no real beginning, middle, and end. Irving speaks wonderfully about extremes in art, and the best people laughing at the best jokes, and he gives insights into the act of writing. But the interview *as* an interview seems to ramble, to stroll from one point to another. No real exchange of ideas takes place, which would have made it a conversation, rather than just an interview (question-answer-question-answer). I don't stop John Irving enough, to ask him to analyze or develop any of his rich ideas.

Irving talks about sustaining the pace of his narratives (see p. 146). What he says is fascinating, but, instead of pursuing it, I switch the subject to bears. A mistake. I should have followed up on the business of pacing and asked why he lets a live audience dictate whether he shortens or lengthens a scene. Isn't the experience of reading silently very different from the experience of hearing something read? (Hindsight, as always, is terrific. I rarely walk away from an interview without thinking, "Why didn't I ask *that*?") I didn't ask Irving those questions, possibly because I didn't think quickly enough, but probably because I wasn't listening carefully enough. To me, that's always the secret of good interviewing: listening.

I must have done 7,000 interviews in the first ten years of *All Things Considered*. And my best interviews are the ones in which I listen most carefully: for new ideas, new perspectives, but also for slips of the tongue, slips of logic; for contradictions, enthusiasm, tension; for what's not being said; for silences, too, and what they reveal. "Manic-depressive listening," a reporter once called it. I'm not sure I know precisely what that means. But it sounds right.

JOAN DIDION

A Book of Common Prayer was the novel Joan Didion was taking to radio and television stations in the spring of 1977. Before our interview, I read all her earlier fiction and journalism, as well as everything I could find that had been written about her—reviews, profiles, critiques.

I admired Didion's writing, especially her essays: models of sharp, compressed observation and insight. In re-reading her novels, though, I discovered I was less enthusiastic about her fiction. The parched landscape of her literary world, the emptiness of her characters' lives disturbed me. Thinking about my reaction, I decided to make that the subject of our conversation. Her point of view in the novels seemed to be that aridity is part of life, a reality to be dealt with. My point of view was that aridity is a nightmare, to be avoided. Perhaps the difference would give us a focal point when we sat down to speak. But I wondered how to bring it up.

The sitting down itself took some thought. I was excited about the interview. And worried. Worried because Joan Didion seemed, in her writing, like a rubber band stretched taut, ready to snap. How could I create an atmosphere in which she would feel relaxed? A radio interview is always a potentially strained situation: It's not just talking to someone across a table; it's talking so that several million people can listen. There's nothing natural about two people speaking into electronic equipment in a glass-enclosed room. Knowing there's an audience, we choose our words more carefully, more self-consciously than we would in ordinary conversation. For both of us, it's an exercise in self-editing. I work against that self-consciousness, trying to create the illusion of naturalness. But it is work. And it is an illusion. As we're talking, I have to pay attention to the pace of conversation. I have to take mental notes on where the tape we're making should be edited, and, out of the corner of my eye, I've got to watch the clock and keep track of the limited studio time. With so much to concentrate on, it's very rare, during an interview, to forget that a tape is being made. When that does happen, it means something exciting is going on.

I considered inviting Didion for a cup of coffee at a restaurant across the street, where I could use a portable tape recorder. But I've found that people get even more unnerved when you keep shoving a microphone under their nose, and I didn't want to risk that with a writer whose fragility concerned me. I decided to take my chances on the studio.

When Joan Didion arrived, I ushered her to her chair. Engineers took levels on our voices, and we began recording. Facing Didion across the table, I found myself still worrying about her response. My distractedness got on the tape. For the first fifteen minutes of our hour together I stopped, started, paused to look at my notes, began a question, decided it wasn't coming out properly, said so, started again. Miraculously, after a quarter of an hour of this, something clicked, and we began to talk together so effortlessly that at times I actually *did* forget we were making a tape. Maybe in this case the initial fumbling helped put us both at ease.

All of that awkwardness was ultimately cut, a contribution to the edit-booth floor. Here is the conversation as it was edited and aired in April 1977.

Stamberg You've said there are no terrific stories. There are only terrific ways of writing them down. Is that really true? Aren't there some terrific stories that are terribly written but still fascinate the reader?

Didion Well, yes, there are. But most stories are banal stories. *Anna Karenina* is a banal story. It could be called a soap opera. *Madame Bovary* is a banal story. It is the way they are written down.

Stamberg But what about mystery stories, where the story—the twists of the plot—become much more important than the language the author uses?

Didion I don't know. Do you ever read Ross MacDonald? The film *Harper* was based on one of his mystery novels. For years he's been writing the same book. The detective, Lew Archer, goes out on a case and always finds that the solution lies several generations back. But Ross MacDonald has been writing closer and closer and closer until his books are all plot, almost like geometric exercises. They're very exciting. If he wrote that story down any other way I'm not sure it would have such tension. His books are very, very peculiar and frightening.

Stamberg I find *your* books very frightening, especially *Play It As It Lays* and *A Book of Common Prayer*. The tension is distasteful.

Didion *A Book of Common Prayer* is not as ugly as *Play It As It Lays,* though. It's not a great deal more *cheerful,* but I think it's not as ugly.

Writing *A Book of Common Prayer* aged me a great deal. I don't mean physically. I mean that in adopting Grace's (the narrator's) point of view, I felt much sharper, harsher. I adopted a lot of the mannerisms and attitudes of an impatient, sixty-year-old dying woman. I would cut people off in the middle of conversations. I fell into Grace because I was having to maintain her tone.

It's a very odd thing with novels. You don't know where they come from. They don't exactly come from you, and while you're writing them they seem to influence your mood more than your mood influences them. You begin by trying quite consciously to maintain the mood simply because you don't want to break the tone of the novel.

Stamberg John Gardner says that, when he reads, he gets inside the dream of the book and doesn't wake up until the book ends. Is that what happens to you in the course of the actual *writing?* Does the world you are writing about become more real than reality?

Didion Yes. More real. And I really resent any intrusion. I didn't answer mail for a long time while I was writing this book, and I didn't

"My name is Grace Strasser-Mendana, *née* Tabor, and I have been for fifty of my sixty years a student of delusion, a prudent traveler from Denver, Colorado. My mother died of influenza one morning when I was eight. My father died of gunshot wounds, not self-inflicted, one afternoon when I was ten. From that afternoon until my sixteenth birthday I lived alone in our suite at the Brown Palace Hotel. I have lived in equatorial America since 1935 and only twice had fever."
—from *A Book of Common Prayer*

	talk on the telephone very much, and if I had a certain amount of business that had to be conducted during the morning before I started work I resented it, because it was easiest to move from being asleep directly into this dream without waking up entirely.
Stamberg	But in your fiction you are in the middle of a dream that is consistently a nightmare. It's on the edge of horror all of the time. You write about people who are not connecting, who have no real relationships and very little happiness or fulfillment in their lives.
Didion	I've always thought of my novels as stories I tell to myself. They are cautionary tales. Stories I don't want to happen to me. *A Book of Common Prayer* to some extent has to do with my own daughter's growing up. My child is not anywhere near the age of Marin, the girl in the novel, but she's no longer a baby. I think that part of this book came out of the apprehension that we are going to both be adults pretty soon.
Stamberg	Marin is the daughter of a very wealthy family who turns her back on all of those family connections.
Didion	And has been misperceived by her mother most of her life.
Stamberg	"Cautionary tales" you don't want to happen to yourself, you said. Do you really mean it that personally? Or do you mean it as cautionary to all of us, to every one of your readers—
Didion	*(Interrupting)* No, no, no. They are just cautionary tales for me.
Stamberg	Why do you jump to say that?
Didion	What I work out in a book isn't what the book is about. I mean, this book isn't about mothers and daughters. That's part of what it was for me, but I don't think it's what it is for a reader.
Stamberg	Alfred Kazin called you a "professional moralist." I thought maybe that's what you were getting at here. Cautioning us to pay attention to certain grim possibilities.
Didion	I am a moralist, but I grew up in such a strong West Coast ethic that I tend not to impose my own sense of what is wrong and what is right on other people. If I do impose it, I feel very guilty about it, because it is entirely against the ethic in which I was brought up, which was strictly *laissez-faire*. But I myself tend to perceive things as right or wrong, in a very rigid way. And I don't necessarily perceive the same things as wrong that large numbers of people perceive as wrong.
Stamberg	I think I want you to be telling me, through all of these books, that these women and their life-styles are wrong. I want you to tell me that, because I find them so distasteful. I find them to be people I must read about (because you're that good a writer), but people I would never want to know or be near. It's okay for me to enter their nightmare for awhile as a reader, but I want to be

very sure that you know—sitting there with your pen or your typewriter—that it's wrong.

Didion You see, there I can't make a judgment because they are other people. They are not me. I just want to tell you the story. I can't make a judgment on it.

Stamberg What about the judgments in your essays about Haight-Ashbury, in *Slouching Towards Bethlehem?* When did you do those?

Didion Spring of '67. Just before the "summer of love."

Stamberg You went to that section of San Francisco, tooled around, made connections with people who were living there, and gave us bare snapshots—quick glimpses—of some of their lives.

Didion That was an extremely frustrating piece to do research on, simply because you couldn't make appointments. To begin with, nobody was up before noon or one o'clock, so you lost the morning. Then, it was a very suspect thing to make appointments.

Stamberg You might have been a Fed, or you were too old—over thirty—and they didn't want to talk to you?

Didion Right. You just had to hang around.

Stamberg Your tone is as cool in these sketches as it is in the pieces of fiction, until you get to the end. It's been sheer description, a catalogue of what you saw, who said what, until the end. There, it seemed to me, the moralist came out, the right-and-wrong lady. At the end you told about the three-year-old child.

Didion Yes. I had spent a lot of time hanging around a place called the Warehouse, a place where a lot of people lived. It wasn't actually a warehouse; it was the basement of an abandoned hotel, and there were a great many people living there on a fluid basis. One of the long-term people living there had a child who was three. It was very dark in this place. There were no windows, or the windows were walled up. It was a very theatrical place with colored spotlights all over. The child was rocking, always, on a rocking horse in a blue spotlight. That was where its rocking horse was. But, one day I was over there and the child had somehow started a fire and burned his arm. I was terribly worried, because my child was almost that age. His mother was yelling at him in a kind of a desultory way. There had been a floorboard damaged in the fire, and some hash had dropped down through it, and everybody else was trying to fish around and get this hash back. I wanted to take the child out, but I had no business doing that.

Stamberg That's where you lost your coolness. The child was badly burned. Nobody had grabbed him in time, or knew that he had to be rushed to the hospital. That's where it all broke down for you. You could be a reporter just that far, and then you really had to

The center was not holding. It was a country of bankruptcy notices and public-auction announcements and commonplace reports of casual killings and misplaced children and abandoned homes and vandals who misspelled even the four-letter words they scrawled. It was a country in which families routinely disappeared, trailing bad checks and repossession papers. Adolescents drifted from city to torn city, sloughing off both the past and the future as snakes shed their skins, children who were never taught and would never now learn the games that had held the society together. People were missing. Children were missing. Parents were missing. Those left behind filed desultory missing-persons reports, then moved on themselves.
—from *Slouching Towards Bethlehem*

make a judgment. And, in making a moral judgment, you gave a context to the whole experience.

The essay "Slouching Towards Bethlehem" became the definitive portrait of Haight-Ashbury in the 1960s and the title piece of that collection of your journalism. In the introduction you write:

My only advantage as a reporter is that I am so physically small, so temperamentally unobtrusive and so neurotically inarticulate that people tend to forget that my presence runs counter to their best interests. And it always does. That is one last thing to remember: Writers are always selling somebody out.

This past November I went to a journalism convention in New York, and at three separate sessions that same passage was quoted. Incidentally, none of the people who read it aloud was in any way unobtrusive or inarticulate!

Didion It's very odd to have written things that people quote (*laughs*). Especially that introduction. I had written it late one night and hadn't thought much about it. Usually I spend a great deal of time finding a tone that is not my own, and then adopting the tone and getting it right. But with this, I just typed it out, very fast, and rather in my own voice. Normally I have difficulty "expressing myself" in any natural way. I'm not that open. Anyway, I had just written it out as a rough draft. John read it in the morning—

Stamberg This is your husband, John Gregory Dunne.

Didion Yes. And he said, "This is fine, don't change it."

But to get back to that passage, the statement "writers are always selling somebody out" means that it is impossible to describe anybody—a friend or somebody you know very well—and *please* them, because your image of them, no matter how flattering, never corresponds with their self-image.

Stamberg But I hear it in a very different way for my work. I hear it right now, sitting here wanting to talk to you about the things that most concern you in your life, and feeling that I could never do that because there is no reason why I should rip off your emotions and your privacy to make my living. That's how I hear that line, now.

Didion Really?

Stamberg Yes. I'm thinking, give me my great story, give me my great radio tape. And knowing I could never dare, never dare to ask, because it simply would invade a kind of privacy that's nobody's damn business.

Didion Yes. It's not what I meant in that passage, but I know what you mean. I can never ask people even simple questions that all reporters know how to ask—like, "How much money do you make?" I don't like sitting in all those Best Western motel rooms trying to make the first telephone call to the district attorney. Many reporters have mentioned to me that they feel the same way. David Halberstam, who seems to me a very aggressive reporter, very confident, said that he hates to make that first phone call, and just sits on the edge of the bed for a while first.

Maybe that's why we chose this work of writing. So we could disappear, in a way. I'm not sure that people who write had much sense of themselves as the center of the room when they were children. I think the way people work often comes out of their weaknesses, out of their failings. In my case, I wasn't a very good reporter. If I got into a town where a story was and I found a *Life* team there, I'd go home. So I had somehow to come out of every story having *interpreted* it, because I wasn't going to get it from anybody else.

Stamberg You found a way around something that other people can do straight on?

Didion Right. If you can't talk to the mayor, then maybe if you sit around the gas station long enough you can figure out what it's all about. In a lot of situations — particularly when you're dealing with people who are interviewed frequently, like politicians or anybody who is in the middle of a breaking story — they tend pretty much to have an answer to every question you're going to ask them. I mostly use interviews, when I do them in that kind of a situation, as just a way of insinuating myself into the person's day. The actual answers aren't ever very significant.

I'm never happier than if I go on a story and I find myself with the person and they are doing whatever they do — say it's a

Ralph Ian Rabin listens in Verona, Wisconsin.

movie set—and it turns out that they are too busy to give me twenty minutes. Then I am there without having to go through the interview (*laughter*).

Stamberg What about all this business of fragility? "Joan Didion is so fragile, so delicate." I notice, talking with you, that you have a thin, almost whispery voice. You speak very softly but with great firmness.

Didion I think my physical size is deceptive.

Stamberg You are very small.

Didion I am not only small, I am too thin, I am pale, I do not look like a California person. It generally makes people think that I must be frail. I'm not actually very frail. I'm very healthy. I eat a lot. I don't cry a lot.

Stamberg But do they say that about you because of your physical size, or—getting back to the people and things that you write about—is it because the fragility of your characters and the kind of perceptions you have make people think you must be emotionally fragile? When I read the essays in *Slouching Towards Bethlehem*, I thought of you as someone who was just trembling with antennae that were constantly vibrating, picking up on things that other people simply weren't sensitive to.

That desolate landscape that you create, and those characters who move through it in their parched ways—it seems to me that you'd never get a Nobel Prize for Literature. Not because of any lack of *skill*, mind you, but because that prize is given for optimistic and positive views of life.

Didion I think that's probably true. I am more attracted to the underside of the tapestry. I tend to always look for the wrong side, the bleak side. I have since I was a child. I have no idea why. Talk about unexamined lives. . . .

I'm rather a slow study, and I came late to the apprehension that there was a void at the center of experience. A lot of people realize this when they're fifteen or sixteen, but I didn't realize until I was much older that it was possible that the dark night of the soul was . . . it had not occurred to me that it was dryness . . . that it was aridity. I had thought that it was something much riper and more sinful. One of the books that made the strongest impression on me when I was in college was *The Portrait of a Lady*. Henry James's heroine, Isabel Archer, was the prototypic romantic idealist. It trapped her, and she ended up a prisoner of her own ideal. I think a lot of us do. My adult life has been a succession of expectations, misperceptions. I dealt only with an idea I had of the world, not with the world as it was. The reality *does*

intervene eventually. I think my early novels were ways of dealing with the revelation that experience is largely meaningless.
(Long pause)

Stamberg   You've spoken in the past about the picture that's in your mind before you do a book, and said the act of writing is to find out what's going on in the picture. For *Play It As It Lays,* you imagined a blonde girl in a white halter dress being paged at one o'clock in the morning at a Las Vegas casino. For *A Book of Common Prayer,* the picture was of the Panama City airport, at six A.M., heat steaming up from the Tarmac. Do you have a picture in your mind, now, of something else that you're going to have to be working on?

Didion   Yes. My next novel is going to take place in Hawaii. I can't describe the picture, except that it is very pink and it smells like flowers, and I'm afraid to describe it out loud because if I describe it out loud I won't write it down.

THOMAS MERTON, A PROFILE

> *(Monks chanting slowly/oboe continues melody/oboe under and hold)*

Noah Adams December. A cold drizzly afternoon at the edge of the forest. Some cabins mark the beginning of the Abbey of Our Lady of Gethsemani, a Trappist monastery in the rolling hills of Kentucky, about fifty miles south of Louisville.

There's a wooden cross inside the church where Thomas Merton used to pray. The interior has Gothic arches and false ceilings. The plaster is all gone now—it's been torn away—and the inside as well as the outside of the church is plain brick, painted white. It looks contemporary: clean lines, dark beams, simple stained-glass windows. The nave, where the monks chant, is narrow and three stories high. Part of the floor is carpeted in gray. The other part is pebbly stone. The monks stand or kneel before wooden stalls made of oak. After the services in the evening, the lights are turned out, a few candles burn. Some stay behind to pray alone, their white robes ghostly in the dark, as the quiet returns to Gethsemani.

Noah Adams is describing the world of one of America's most prolific, influential, yet elusive authors. Thomas Merton—religious writer and poet, monk, hermit, and social activist—spent half his life in the monastery at Gethsemani. He took vows of silence but spoke to the world through nearly a hundred books and countless articles. Merton's first book, *The Seven Storey Mountain*, an account of his religious awakening and early years at Gethsemani, was published in 1948, and quickly became a best-seller. His subsequent writings explored the troubling issues of our time: war, peace, civil rights, social responsibility.

In 1979, as the eleventh anniversary of Merton's death approached, *All Things Considered* introduced listeners to the life and ideas of this writer of social conscience and religious conviction. Noah Adams traveled to Gethsemani to interview Trappists who had known Merton, and to record the sounds of monks chanting, footsteps echoing in the church, bells tolling. Back in Washington, he taped conversations with other sources. An actor was hired to read passages from Merton's writings. A musician came to the studio to improvise on the recorded chants—his saxophone, flute, and oboe weaving variations on their theme. Noah Adams's piece was a search for the man behind the written words.

> *(Music/jazzy saxophone playing melody of monks' chant/fade and hold under)*

Adams Thomas Merton spent seven years in New York in the 1930s. He joined a fraternity at Columbia College, drank in nightclubs, played jazz piano, saw movies, had girlfriends, belonged to the Communist Party for a short while. He was writing a lot. His master's thesis was on the poetry of William Blake. Merton tried novels, kept a journal, reviewed books, and found plenty of time to read. On impulse, one Sunday, Merton went to a Catholic church. His mother was a Quaker, his father a Protestant. Merton had never been to a mass before and was intrigued.

He learned about mysticism in Aldous Huxley's book *Ends and Means;* studied the Jesuit sermons in Joyce's *A Portrait of the Artist as a Young Man;* and read a biography of Gerard Manley Hopkins, poet, convert, and Catholic priest. One day, he left the apartment, walked to the Church of Corpus Christi, and told the priest, "Father, I want to become a Catholic."

After he joined the church, he thought about training for the priesthood. He did volunteer work at a mission in Harlem, taught for a time at a Franciscan college. And then, during Easter of 1941, he went on a retreat at the Trappist monastery Gethsemani, in Kentucky. Later, in December, a few days after Pearl Harbor, Thomas Merton took the train back to Kentucky to become a postulant at the Abbey of Gethsemani. He was almost twenty-seven, halfway through his life.

(Music/monks chanting)

Adams *(Voice echoing in church)* What do you think he would have been, had he not become a Catholic?

Father Matthew Kelty God knows. I think the monastic life was a great grace for him, because when you have all this inner power, as he did, and you control it, you've got something very beautiful. And if you don't . . . well . . . that's why so many artistic and gifted people lead lives that are not always particularly happy. They get hung up with many problems and in the end they may be ruined. Not because they're wicked or evil people but simply because the intensity of the fire that they have is so hard to control.

(Monks chanting/hold under)

Adams Trappist life was at first very difficult for Merton. The monks woke up at two in the morning to go to chapel. Breakfast was at seven. Bread and coffee. Only bread and coffee for supper, too. Perhaps some fruit. Lunch was the big meal—cooked vegetables and bread. They worked during the day: farming, cutting wood, making cheese that was sold by mail order. They communicated with one another only by sign language and tried to get to sleep by seven, on straw pallets in cold dormitories. The world outside the walls was left behind. The news came three months late that atomic bombs had been dropped on Japan.

Tom Merton thought he would not be permitted to write after he had taken the Trappist vows of poverty and silence. But he found himself wanting to continue his journal and to write poetry.

He confessed to this one day, expecting an order to stop. Instead, he was encouraged, and went on to write more than ninety books and hundreds of articles: history, theology, verse, literary criticism, essays, translations of poetry from Latin and Portuguese. His first book, *The Seven Storey Mountain,* described his life through the first two years in the monastery. He sent the manuscript to an old friend in New York, Naomi Burton Stone, a literary agent, who took it to a publisher.

Naomi Burton Stone got special permission several times to visit Tom at Gethsemani (ordinarily, the monks could not have visitors). She recalls the first trip, taking a taxicab from Louisville to visit Brother Louis, as Merton was now called.

Stone I thought he would be very different from the kid I had known. It had been about seven years since I'd seen him, and I thought he'd have a halo and downcast eyes. Well, this cheerful, jovial soul burst into the room and said, "Hi, wonderful to see you! I hear you came in a yellow cab!" I thought to myself, *this is a place where they don't speak. How could he have heard about the cab?* We talked for a while about this and that; I was at ease immediately. He was a very funny guy, a very warm personality. As we were talking, the abbot knocked on the door and, instead of saying "come in," Tom knocked on his desk in reply. The abbot came in and said, "I'm so glad to see you. I hear you came in a yellow cab." The news really must have spread through the silent monastery. I don't know what the sign is for yellow cab, but, boy, they knew it!

Adams Ron Seitz, now a professor at Bellarmine College, in Louisville, met Merton in the late 1950s. Merton once came to Louisville to see a doctor and had the abbot's permission to stay overnight. In his journal, Seitz wrote a kind of open letter to Merton about that evening.

Seitz
(reading)
"We went to a jazz place on Washington Street, downtown by the river. By then several photographs of you had begun to appear in magazines and the newspapers from time to time, and you were afraid of being recognized because of this kind of embarrassing exposure and unsought publicity. So you wore this almost Groucho Marx disguise of beret and dark glasses, *sans* cigar. Anyway, once everyone was settled, you left the table to move down closer to the musicians. I remember watching you completely swept away and borne off with the sound. Gone with it. Crouched with your face and eyes raised to the sight of it, nodding your head yes and yes, and coming back to the table, you saying, 'Now that's praying. That's some kind of prayer.'"

Adams
Did you know that he was a very special person at that time? Or was it a normal relationship, based on shared interests and values?

Seitz
Well, I was intimidated for too many years and felt uncomfortable. I felt always like a novice with a teacher. He was always ten or so years ahead of me in what was going on artistically — new movements. After he died I thought, *my god, all the things I want to talk about, now it's too late. When you were there, I wasn't. Now I'm gettin' there and you're gone.*

(Flute playing softly/hold under)

Adams
In the late 1950s and through the 1960s, Thomas Merton was writing about war and about peace and about civil rights. His parents had been pacifists. His brother, John Paul, was killed in World War II. Merton's call for a ban on nuclear weapons and for peace demonstrations was controversial within the Catholic Church. For two years he was forbidden by his abbot to write about these matters. That was before the new spirit of Vatican II, and before the war in Vietnam. Many in the anti-war movement of the late 1960s and early 1970s had been influenced a decade earlier by what Thomas Merton was writing. Many of them went to Gethsemani to talk with him.

Jesuit priests Daniel and Philip Berrigan were two such travelers. Philip Berrigan has called Merton "the Church's most eloquent spokesman for human rights." I asked Berrigan whether those who shared Merton's anti-war feelings had hoped he would leave the monastery to join their protest.

Berrigan
I must say that it was rather a naive hope on our part, yes. We perhaps even said things to him during the course of these visits

Adams regarding leaving. I'm sure that things were clumsy and they were ill-timed and pretty gratuitous on our part. I don't think we understood the kind of work that he was doing and all of its value.

Adams Sister Elena Malits, author of *The Solitary Explorer: Thomas Merton's Transforming Journey*, confirms Berrigan's intuitions.

Sister Elena I don't think he would have left. From his published writings and a few of the letters I've read, I'm sure Merton had a profound conviction that his vocation was to offer what he called a "critical perspective from another point of view." He felt that he would have betrayed the particular gift he had if he had gotten in the front lines. It was a great personal struggle for him, a truly painful thing to be sitting home at Gethsemani when his friends went off to march. But I think that finally Merton could not have gone off without betraying himself.

Adams Didn't he call one of his books *Conjectures of a Guilty Bystander?*

Sister Elena Right. That's a very consciously chosen metaphor. I think you have to appreciate Merton's ironic sense of humor to get the full implication. He was guilty, not because he was standing on the sidelines, but guilty in the sense that we are all accomplices to what is happening in our society. He came to terms with his guilt by working out the sources of evil in his own soul. That's his contribution to the anti-war movement as he saw it: to come to terms with the roots of evil in himself, the kind of violence that is unconsciously present in all of us. And to the extent that he came to terms with that, he had a gift to give to the world.

Adams Father Flavian Burns, who had come to Gethsemani in 1951 after reading *The Seven Storey Mountain*, speaks of Merton's wholehearted commitment.

Father Flavian Part of the monastic tradition involves a breakthrough of some sort. If you don't break through into this core of meaning, then the life can make you into some sort of freak. You're taking a chance, entering the monastic life wholeheartedly. I think Merton is one of the few people I know who broke through and got to the heart of the matter.

(Flute up again/fade to monks chanting)

Adams Merton loved the woods around Gethsemani, and he asked for, and finally received, permission to become a hermit. For the last three years of his life, he lived in a small house about a ten-minute walk back in the woods from the monastery. There was no plumbing; a fireplace was the only source of heat. Merton would go to the monastery occasionally for a good meal. By this time, however, he had become very well known and many people wanted to meet him, coming almost as pilgrims. Some would even go back in the woods to find him, disrupting the solitude.

(Monks continue to chant in background)

In 1968 an invitation came for Merton to travel to Thailand to attend a series of conferences and to meet the Dalai Lama. He'd long been interested in Eastern religions and had written extensively about them. He saw the trip as a chance to learn more. He also thought he might be able to find a place in the East, or in Europe, to establish a true hermitage. It would be his first real trip away from the monastery. This first journey, however, would be Merton's last.

(Monks continue chant)

In Bangkok, Thailand, on December 10, 1968, twenty-seven years to the day after which he had entered the Trappist monastery in Kentucky, Thomas Merton went to his room after talking at a meeting. He wanted to sleep for a while, so he took a shower and went to the sleeping mat, his feet still wet. It was hot. There was an electric fan. He wanted to adjust the direction of the air. The fan had faulty wiring. When he touched it he was electrocuted.

(Soft chanting/up full, fade and hold under)

Actor
(reading from Merton's **The Seven Storey Mountain***)*

I hear You saying to me:

"Do not ask when it will be or where it will be or how it will be: On a mountain or in a prison, in a desert or in a concentration camp or in a hospital or at Gethsemani. It does not matter. So do not ask me. . . . You will not know until you are in it.

"But you shall taste the true solitude of my anguish and my poverty and I shall lead you into the high places of my joy and you shall die in Me and find all things in My mercy which has created you for this end and brought you from Prades to Bermuda to St. Antonin to Oakham to London to Cambridge to Rome to New York to Columbia to Corpus Christi to St. Bonaventure to the Cistercian abbey of the poor men who labor in Gethsemani:

"That you may become the brother of God. . . ."

(Soft chanting/cross-fade to flute/chanting out/flute up full to end)

Thomas Merton lies buried in the cemetery next to the quiet church at Gethsemani.

THE MAN WHO ~~LOVED~~ *Liked* SWINBURNE

In June 1978, writer Paul Theroux, satirist Fran Liebowitz, poet Donald Hall, and historian Walter Jackson Bate helped put together a list of summer reading for _ATC_. What a jumble! It included *The Oranging of America; The Family, Sex and Marriage: England, 1500–1800;* and *King Solomon's Mines.* We offered the list, free of charge, to listeners, and had fun thinking about those titles sharing a beach bag with Coppertone.

We also have been known to ask *listeners* what they read. In March 1981, Dr. Gordon Sabine described his "books that make a difference" project at the Library of Congress Center for the Book. Sabine asked people two simple questions:

> 1 What book made the greatest difference in your life?
> 2 What difference did it make?

When we put those questions to _All Things Considered_ listeners, they cited the Bible again and again, and then went on to list titles from every conceivable bookshelf. In Monona, Wisconsin, Fred Petillo said *The Spirit of St. Louis* by Charles Lindbergh taught him logistics, leadership, and courage against the odds. In Lexington, Kentucky, Mark W. Lusk said Jack Kerouac's *On the Road* gave him new ideas about freedom in America. And Harold Orlandini, in Benton, Illinois, named *Beano, Circus Dog* by Helen Orr Watson. "It's the first book I read all the way through without moving my lips."

We got advice on books *not* to read, from Robert Reynolds, a listener in Washington, D.C.

> 1 Books with the author's name in larger type than the book's title.
> 2 Books about anyone who died the week before. Most were written in ten minutes to cash in on the publicity.
> 3 Books you see next to day-old bread or ground beef at $1.59 a pound.
> 4 Books everyone else is reading.

One of the most priceless (or expensive?) conversations about books was co-host Sandy Ungar's chat, in April 1980, with John Mayfield. Mr. Mayfield has a passion for collecting rare books. Sandy thought the hobby would interest listeners. People with passions are always wonderful to hear, as much for their single-mindedness as for the volumes of information they have to share.

Ungar The Georgetown University Library recently opened an unusual exhibit of 101 volumes from the rare-book collection of Edith and John Mayfield. What makes it unusual is that all 101 volumes are of the same book, the first edition of *Atalanta in Calydon* by Algernon Charles Swinburne, published in 1865. Bibliographers had always assumed that only 100 copies of that first edition were ever published. Then along came Mr. Mayfield.

Mayfield I've collected Swinburne since 1929, and I was determined to get a copy of the first edition of *Atalanta in Calydon.* From 1929 to

Stamberg
Know what I'm reading this summer?
Edwards
No, what?
Stamberg
The menu.

1943, I solicited book dealers in this country and in England, Canada, and elsewhere for copies of the first edition. But not until 1943 did I get a copy. Now, the first thing a collector does is to compare his rare book with the standard authority in bibliography, just to check to see if it is the genuine article. When I did this, I noticed several differences in my copy that had not been noted in any bibliographies. There were printer's errors corrected by hand, for instance. The first thing a collector wants to know is what the error was, because he will then know that the copy with the error uncorrected is a prior state of the first edition. So, we have to go for the second copy. The second copy, unfortunately, is just the same as the first copy. So you go for the third copy, and the fourth, and the fifth, and not until about the nineteenth copy (*laughter*) do you find a copy of the book with the errors uncorrected. That is the "black tulip" of a first edition . . . the best type of copy you can get of a rare book.

Ungar Is it exciting to keep tracking it down that way?

Mayfield Yes, it is. Every time you receive a copy, it's like Christmas morning. By the time I had around 50 copies I started to wonder about the limitation. All the bibliographers had said, "A hundred copies, no more than 100 copies." I knew it was an impossible task, but I decided to strike for 100. It took a long time.

Editorial cartoonist Tony Auth listens in Philadelphia, Pennsylvania.

Ungar	How long? When did you get your hundredth copy?
Mayfield	1977. The hundredth copy came to me from a dealer in New York City who knew that I had 99. He also knew that I had to have 100, and, of course, he priced it accordingly.
Ungar	How much was it?
Mayfield	It was my right arm.
Ungar	You don't want to tell us how much your right arm is worth?
Mayfield	Well, it might discourage some other collectors. But anyway, Mrs. Mayfield said, "We've got to have it, so you go ahead and get it." And she bailed me out.
	Word got out to San Francisco that I had gotten 100. I was visiting a friend of mine, a dealer out there. He said, "I understand you got 100. But if you could get 101 copies, then you could really bust the legend of limitation of 100 copies." I said, "I am not going to buy any more copies of *Atalanta in Calydon.*"
Ungar	I can't stand the suspense. Where did the 101st copy come from?
Mayfield	One of the librarians in the rare-book room over at Georgetown University (may his name be engraved forever in my heart), Mr. Nicholas Scheetz, showed up at my house one day and said, "Here is copy number 101." It took me several days to get over it.
Ungar	Why have you gone to all this trouble to collect so many copies of *Atalanta in Calydon?*
Mayfield	I collect them because I like them.
Ungar	You didn't say you love them.
Mayfield	Well, the word bibliophile has been described by appropriate authorities as a "lover of books." I don't agree with the word "lover" because that belongs to an entirely different category. How can you be a lover of books? You can't love something that cannot return that love . . . although some rare books do return a great deal of love.

EPILOGUE

Noah Adams	Do you have any curiosity about your readers? Let's say you were in a bookstore and saw a person buying your book, and then went to a café and saw that same person reading the book. It's a perfect chance to have an encounter with a stranger. Would you be curious enough to introduce yourself and try to find out something more?
John McPhee	I'd never do that. I'd be pleased to see somebody buying my book.
Adams	But you wouldn't have the curiosity to find out why they bought it?
McPhee	I'd be too shy to do that, period. I just wouldn't do it. Once I found a copy of one of my books in a store in Bermuda. This is a perfect symbol of ego inflation and deflation all in one capsule. The mere thought that a book of mine would be for sale in Bermuda just quickened my pulse. I felt marvelous at the sight of this thing. I went over and opened it up, and the price was written in just inside the cover. It said three pounds ten shillings. Bermuda's currency has changed, so that figure was crossed out, and the book was selling for $6.00 Then the $6.00 had been crossed out, and it was $5.00, and the $5.00 had been crossed out, and it was $4.50, $4.50 had been crossed out, $4.00, $3.80, $3.60, $3.40, $3.20, an absolute ladder of figures all the way down, crossed out at one time or another, until way down at the bottom it said FIVE CENTS. I went over and plunked down my nickel and bought that book. I still have it at home.

Curiosity did the cat no good, but we thrive on it. Information of any kind finds a home on *All Things Considered*. We tell you whom the president saw at the summit conference, what influenced the Senate vote, and when African leaders will meet in Addis Ababa. We also tell you what to do in a tornado, how the brain functions, and what happened to shopping-center parking spaces in 1979 (they shrank by half an inch because cars got smaller). It's this mix of serious and foolish information that gives *All Things Considered* its spirit.

Listeners get hooked on the mix. They write us all the time, confessing that they're information addicts. Those letters go up on the bulletin board for the staff to enjoy. The staff is addicted to fan mail almost as much as it is to information.

A curiosity-ridden bunch, we lug around vast assortments of odd facts. State Department correspondent Bill Buzenberg knows the history of the Somoza regime in Nicaragua and is an equally reliable source on the best backpacking trails in Colorado. Music producer Fred Calland says Marion Anderson sang Ulrica in Verdi's *A Masked Ball* at her debut at the Met and, without missing a beat, displays the quilt he's making. Reporter Margot Adler, in the NPR New York bureau, is an expert on warlocks and witches. And director Jo Miglino has the lyrics of at least 400 rock-and-roll classics committed to memory (she even sings them, and got raves for her interpretation of the words "Do WAH, Do WAH" when she starred as lead singer in *ATC*'s disco version of "The Chicago White Sox Song").

If *All Things Considered* didn't exist, this staff would have to invent it.

Some of what we find out has practical application. When coffee prices got too high, Neville Cartwright from the University of Wisconsin told us how to recycle the grounds:

> Start with fresh coffee and save the grounds. When you make a second batch, put one spoonful of fresh coffee in a new filter, put a spoon of old grounds on top of that, then another spoonful of new coffee, then more old coffee. You get a new-and-old-coffee sandwich. You can use this technique for every other batch of coffee you make.

The arrival of asparagus in supermarkets made us wonder how to cook it perfectly. Associate producer Katharine Ferguson converted her curiosity into a radio feature. On *All Things Considered* three European master chefs disagreed over whether or not to peel the stalks, and then food commentator Nika Hazelton described her favorite spring meal: Asparagus. Nothing but asparagus. With three sauces. Plus cake for dessert.

Consumer commentator David Klein of Michigan State University told us what to do when the car repair place won't give back your keys until you pay for the work they have (or haven't) done:

> I'm not sure you can do this in large cities, but in smaller places what I do regularly is pay by check, drive the car out, and if I

> find they haven't done the work properly, I stop payment on the check.

Then, we'll tell you things that have no practical use whatsoever. You could find out, for example, that every year, elevators carry 50 billion people a distance of 600 million miles, at speeds of sometimes more than 1,800 feet per minute.

People turn to the program for these snippets of information—things they always wanted to know that *All Things Considered* wasn't afraid to ask. I have to qualify that. Co-host Sandy Ungar was afraid to ask the wife of Israel's prime minister how old she was. But Mrs. Menachem Begin didn't mind telling Sandy what she worried about at her age: "At my age there are three problems: the daughter-in-law, the servant, and health."

When we don't know the answers, or can't find them, *All Things Considered* just might spin them out of thin air. We call that playful invention. (Please don't tell me what you call it. We're careful to label our spoofs.) Say someone wonders who invented dry cleaning . . . or, better yet, whether salmon talk?

On April 1, 1979, NPR's Scott Simon introduced listeners to the (now) legendary Talking Coho Salmon of Wisconsin. Scott learned that these fish not only talked—they could sing. Scott asked one to sing "Anything Goes." But the scientist in charge of the salmon protested. "That's ridiculous. This salmon has been living at the bottom of the river all of its life. How would it know a Cole Porter tune?" Scott gave in, and asked the salmon to just go ahead and sing whatever it pleased. The salmon sang "Strangers in the Night."

Sometimes *All Things Considered* sounds like "Ripley's Believe It or Not." Sometimes it's like the reference desk at your local library. And sometimes it sounds like school. Except school was never this much fun. And in school you never got fan mail.

FINDING OUT BUSINESS SECRETS

Business fascinates NPR's Robert Krulwich. Lucky, since he's our correspondent for business and economics. Krulwich romps through the puzzlements of the business world the way toddlers on the block attack pots of fingerpaints. The results are colorful, original, and very funny. When Krulwich started reporting, economics stopped being a dismal science. He finds stories everywhere. In the showroom of a very large East Coast bed-linens company, he unearthed one of those great industrial truths the public ordinarily never hears about.

Woman There are some things that just don't look right on a bed. You get to know that, after being in the sheet business for several years.

Krulwich Give me an example of something that doesn't look right on a bed.

Woman Gee, I can't think of anything right off hand.

Krulwich Pictures of spikes, perhaps?

Woman Well, for one thing, I can tell you that green on sheets does not sell. If you go in a store, you'll see very few green sheets.

Krulwich This is learned from experience, mainly?

Woman Yes. Many mills have tried to come out with a green pattern or a green color. It doesn't sell well. Consumers may ask for it, but when it comes right down to buying, they just don't buy green.

Leaping from sheets to beds, Krulwich also found a story in the hotel industry.

Man People talk jokingly about 110 percent occupancy rate. There are hotels in the city that have as many as 10 or 15 percent of their rooms set aside for such a purpose.

Krulwich The purpose is romance. The concept is "noonies." Noonies is the phrase the hotel industry uses for the group of people who come to the hotel after 11 A.M. and before 1 P.M. At noon. For brief encounters. Some hotels even set their checkout time early, to accommodate them. They arrange for overnight guests to leave the hotel by eleven. They set the check-*in* time at two. This opens up three hours in the middle of the day when the rooms can be filled by a completely separate category of paying guests. I learned this from a number of hotel people who said they didn't do it in *their* hotel, but they'd all heard of "noonies."

Krulwich finds stories when he chats with the heads of huge companies. Here's what Seymour Flug, president of Diner's Club, told him in 1979:

Flug There are six countries in the world today where you cannot use your Diner's Club card.

Krulwich Let me see if I can guess. China?

Flug Correct.

Krulwich Ah, let's see. Russia?

Flug No, you can use your card in Russia.

How to Get a Hotel Room
I arrived at the hotel in Montreal, with a reservation in hand, and was told by the hotel clerk, "I'm terribly sorry, sir. We just don't have any more rooms." And I said to him, "I'm even sorrier than you are, because I've just come off a long flight. If you don't get me a room within three minutes, I'm going to take my clothes off and put on my pajamas and go to sleep on the sofa right over there in the lobby." I got my room in less than three minutes.
—David Klein, consumer commentator, Michigan State University, East Lansing, Michigan

Krulwich	Cuba?
Flug	Cuba is the second one, and we're working on that.
Krulwich	Rumania, East Germany, Czechoslovakia, and Poland?
Flug	No. *(Laughter.)* The other countries in which you can't use your Diner's Club card are North Vietnam, North Korea, Albania, and Burma.
Krulwich	The day you get Albania is the day we'll probably elect you president of the United States.
Flug	Or the president of Albania.

Krulwich finds these stories because his genuine, natural curiosity makes people want to tell him things. He also finds them because he wonders about things the rest of us tend to overlook. For instance, Krulwich wondered how they get those perfect glasses of beer in the beer ads.

Krulwich	This is the story of one photograph for a beer ad. For the food preparer, Amanda Kayser, the challenge was to get two glasses of beer foaming simultaneously, with perfect heads. This photogenic miracle was to be accomplished at a photographer's studio in New York City. The company clearly was willing to spend a great deal of money on the project. Amanda Kayser was told that the beer mugs had been custom-designed for this photo session, which would show two hearty men clinking mugs of beer. Amanda's first task, as food preparer, was to "dress" the mugs. This is a technical term. Once the beer is poured into the glass, the photographer has just seconds to shoot. The longer the head lasts, the better. It turns out that warm beer produces a longer-

Photographers listening in their darkrooms: Ray Fisher, Miami, Florida; Jack Spratt, Wickford, Rhode Island; Alan Mickelson, Largo, Maryland; Shutterfingers Smithfall, Bala-Cynwyd, Pennsylvania; Don Albrecht, Bayfield, Wisconsin; Sam Wang, Clemson, South Carolina; George Braslaw, New Orleans, Louisiana; Bob Campagna, Mt. Vernon, Iowa.

	lasting head. On the other hand, frosty beer is much nicer to look at. A dilemma. How do you get warm beer to look frosty?
Kayser	You coat the glass with a spray that graphic artists use, and then spritz it with a combination of Karo syrup and water. That way you make beads that adhere to the glass. See? They don't roll down. They stay just where the photographer wants them to stay, so the glass looks frosty.
Krulwich	And it's still okay with truth in advertising if the beads of frost are really kerosene, or whatever you just said?
Kayser	I think so. Karo syrup.
Krulwich	When the mugs are properly dressed, they are brought over to the models. These models may have perfectly ugly faces, legs, and torsos, but their *hands* are gorgeous. In the trade they are called hand models, or—for short—hands.
Kayser	The hands talk, chat—you know: "How ya doin'?" and, "Well, last weekend I went here or there." They know each other very well. They've been doing this work for years.
Krulwich	How much do the hands cost?
Kayser	The hands are $100 an hour apiece.
Krulwich	Oh.
Kayser	So the hand models are in position, the glasses are given to them, the photographer or his assistant fills up the glasses at just the right moment, and they shoot the picture.
Krulwich	The trick, of course, is to snap the photo just as the heads in both glasses reach a simultaneous peak. That rarely happens. So the glasses have to keep being emptied and then re-filled. Emptying the glasses is delicate.
Kayser	If you get any moisture on the front of the glasses, it ruins the Karo syrup and water dots. You have to scrub down the bare crystal again, which takes about twenty minutes.
Krulwich	Since you don't want to drip real moisture on top of the false moisture, after each shot the glasses are placed on a table and Amanda has to remove the beer without tipping the glasses.
Kayser	I siphoned the beer out with a rubber hose. I was very drunk by the end of the day.
Krulwich	How many times did you have to siphon out the beer?
Kayser	Oh, probably several hundred times.
Krulwich	Sounds as if this client was willing to wait forever, if necessary, to get things perfect.
Kayser	Perfect. Perfect. I mean unbelievably perfect! You wouldn't believe the attention to detail.
Krulwich	I asked Amanda whether this incredible attention to detail really makes a difference to the public. She believes it does.

Kayser   Because you end up with perfect beer in the picture. That's what the ad is selling. It has to be more real than life. I mean, life is cloudy ice cubes and crumbs on the plate. But for an ad, it has to be more real. There cannot be anything wrong.

Krulwich   This single photograph took more than five hours to shoot. The hands cost over $1,000. Amanda Kayser says, when you add in the cost of the photographer, the beer mugs, the beer, and Amanda, the final price was between $4,000 and $5,000. Just for one picture. But that picture, in the end, was perfect! I'm Robert Krulwich.

Which leads us to another business secret. Ice cubes.

Krulwich   According to two industry insiders, every time you see ice cubes in a newspaper or a magazine ad for a glass of cola or whiskey, the cubes shining there in the glass are phonies.

Ice cube lady   I don't think anybody ever uses real ice cubes, because they just don't look right. They always use plastic cubes. Those look very real, because they're molded individually by hand. They cost $25 each, and photographers keep them in boxes like you would keep your jewelry in.

Krulwich   Why doesn't regular ice look right?

Ice cube lady   No one wants to see regular ice. They want to see perfect ice. People think of ice cubes as being clear and luscious and cool, and that's what you have to show them. Regular ice cubes are cloudy.

Krulwich   But that's life!

Ice cube lady   Yes, that *is* life. But, when you're doing a perfect photograph, you need a perfect ice cube, and there's no such thing as a perfect ice cube except if it's plastic.

Sounds like perfect egg in your beer to me. If the Unidentified Ice Cube Lady read strangely like Amanda Kayser to you, you're half right. The Unidentified Ice Cube Lady is a friend of Amanda Kayser—and also a food preparer—who was at Amanda's house when Robert taped the beer interview. The friend chimed in on ice cubes, but Robert couldn't find a way to include perfect ice cubes in his perfect-beer story. Nor could he find a way to throw out the wonderful ice secret. He held on to the tape for a year. By then, he'd accumulated so many other taped bits and pieces of curious information that he was able to stir the ice cubes up with green sheets, noonies, and the Diner's Club president, to present a quick review of business secrets that only *All Things Considered* would tell.

EINSTEIN'S THEORY OF RELATIVITY

On *All Things Considered* we perform feats you wouldn't think could work on the radio:

- Playing pick-up sticks for a Christmas feature on children's toys.
- Practicing how-to-flatten-your-nose exercises, with the author of a book by the same name.
- Brewing the perfect cup of coffee.
- Dancing. Disco lessons, when the beat got popular. "Shuffle Off to Buffalo" routines so Robert Krulwich could put quick bits of business news into a vaudeville setting.

In fact, they worked wonderfully. The sounds were so unexpected on the air, that they made people sit up and listen more closely.

But there *are* some things that continue to challenge the properties of this marvelous medium. Which doesn't mean we won't try them. The example that leaps to mind: a brief, straightforward, definitive, scientifically accurate explanation of Einstein's theory of relativity; an explanation that would be accessible to listeners without sounding textbook-dull.

Science correspondent Ira Flatow decided to tackle it on March 14, 1979, the one hundredth anniversary of Albert Einstein's birth. Ira used sound effects and standard science-class examples from daily life in his narration. Ready for Ira's explanation? Don't bother taking notes, by the way. There'll be no test at the end.

(Train chugging noises in distance)
Consider an observer standing on a railroad platform. Two bolts of lightning strike the tracks—one at the east end of the platform, the other on the west.
(Train/thunder)
The observer on the platform sees them strike the tracks simultaneously but, just as the bolts hit, a train goes by.
(Train sound, closer)
A passenger on the train also sees the flashes of lightning. But he does not see the lightning bolts strike simultaneously because he is moving toward the bolt in the west. The light from the western bolt reaches him sooner. The flash from the other bolt, having a greater distance to travel, reaches him later. So, what the observer on the platform sees as two bolts striking simultaneously, the train passenger sees as two separate flashes of lightning striking at different times. Which observer is correct, then? Did the lightning bolts actually strike at the same time or at different times? The answer, said Einstein, is that both are right. Time is not absolute. Measurement of time depends upon your reference point. The time that elapses between two events depends on where you are when the events occur.

So far so good. Next, Ira tried to help us understand gravity by suggesting an experiment anyone can conduct

To study the effects of gravity on an object, step inside an elevator. As the elevator accelerates upward, the first thing you notice is that you experience extra weight. It's that common, shrinking feeling. To most people, the occurrence is not worth a second's thought. But to Einstein, it was a key issue. Einstein said the force of acceleration that pushes you to the floor of the elevator is very much like the force of gravity holding objects to the ground on earth.

If you drop an object in an accelerating elevator, it crashes to the floor as it would if you were outside the elevator, on the ground. Dribble a ball in the elevator and it bounces, as expected. Gravity works inside this accelerating elevator as it does outside. But shine a flashlight on an elevator wall, and something very strange and unexpected occurs. Instead of appearing to travel in a straight line, the light beam bends toward the floor. In the time it takes the light to travel across the elevator, the elevator itself has moved upward, making the light strike a lower place on the wall. The light appears to curve downward.

Still with us? Or have you run to the nearest elevator to see whether your flashlight still works? Perhaps you would prefer to read one of the exercises on how to flatten your nose? Never mind. The indefatigable Flatow continues.

- -

Sculptor Frank Fleming puts up preserves as he listens in Birmingham, Alabama.

Einstein concluded that objects that move with accelerated motion (rocketships, for instance) behave the same as objects under the influence of gravity.

Imagine a rocketship accelerating through space, far distant from the gravitational pull of any planet. Drop a ball in that spaceship and it will fall to the floor. The fall is *not* due to gravity, since there is no gravity in the spaceship. The *acceleration* of the spaceship affects the object the same way gravity would affect it on earth. This example illustrates Einstein's theory that you cannot tell the difference between acceleration and gravity.

Thank you, Dr. Science. To comfort any bewildered listeners, Ira ended his piece in the streets.

Flatow	Do you know what the theory of relativity is?
First man	How long do we have?
Woman	I know it's a chemical, scientific theory of the relationship between elements within a substance.
Second man	Ha-ha-ha-ha-ha.
Third man	Oh-h-h-h, I know it's great in mathematical-type things.

OF TIME AND THE RADIO: LIFE'S LITTLE MYSTERIES

Beauty and truth come first. After that, the broadcaster's most basic obligation is to make the program end on time. Bob Edwards says he wants his tombstone to read HE GOT OFF ON TIME. Getting off on time isn't that easy. In fact, it's never easy. Time, in radio, is precise and perverse.

Only in broadcasting and psychoanalysis does an hour not equal sixty minutes. Nor are there thirty minutes in a half hour. In broadcasting, a half hour actually lasts twenty-nine minutes and thirty seconds. The additional thirty seconds are for station breaks—the FCC requires that stations periodically identify themselves. To make the half hour run for precisely twenty-nine minutes and thirty seconds, each element is carefully pre-timed, and once we're on the air the director adds dabs of music, or asks us to speak more slowly or more quickly—whatever it takes to get off on time.

But accidents do happen, and sometimes more than a dab is necessary. Like the time our studio turned into a ballroom on a half-second's notice. That day, despite everyone's best efforts, the program was running two minutes short. That's a *big* gap. Director Rich Firestone grabbed a record and began to fill out the time with music. Mike Waters, my first co-host, thought it was too much music, told me to follow his lead, and called for our microphones to be opened. "Come here often?" he said. "Well, yes, actually. I'm here pretty much every night from five to six-thirty." And we were off, ad-libbing the kinds of things people say to one another at a dance. Every now and then I would grunt, pretending he'd stepped on my feet. Mike apologized, kept chatting, the music played, finally he offered to get me a soft drink. The music ended. So did our dance and that night's program.

Usually, though, by late afternoon, the director and producer have a pretty good sense of the timing for each half hour. They know whether music will bring the program to time, or whether more radical steps must be taken: bumping pieces completely or finding new pieces to fill big gaps.

Bumping means removing a story that can wait until the next day (the producer courts enmity from the reporter for this decision, but enmity-courting is in the producer's job description). Finding an additional piece to put in at the last minute is considerably more difficult.

One afternoon, shortly before air time, producer Neal Conan discovered a one-and-a-half-minute hole in the second half hour of *All Things Considered*. All the items in that segment had run short. Nothing in the ever-handy stack of shelf tapes would quite fit the slot. What to do?

Solutions to *All Things Considered*'s problems often come while staring into space. Or standing in supermarket lines. Or taking showers when the water is precisely the correct degree of hot and the bar of soap creates the perfect volume of suds. Solutions emerge from sheer desperation. Too late for a shower, Neal sat staring at the road map of that night's program. Staring into a one-and-a-half-minute space. The last item in the half hour was a conversation with seasonal chef Perla Meyers . . . about figs. Neal tried free association. Figs. Figs. Dates? Figs. Fig . . . Newtons! As in cookies. But why are they called Fig *Newtons?* Neal figured the answer must be worth a minute and a half. He asked me to phone a spokeswoman from Nabisco, who explained that the cookie is named after Newton, Massachusetts. The National Biscuit Company was based in Boston when that cookie was invented, and the organization wanted to honor its environs (Newton is a suburb of Boston). The minute-and-a-half hole was filled with a single phone call. And a mystery was solved.

The minute-and-a-half Newton solution was such a hit that a few days later it dawned on us that life was full of small mysteries, just begging for ninety-second explanations. In fact, we could probably *make up* answers that sounded just as plausible as what the Nabisco lady had told us in all seriousness. Our fictional answers might amuse listeners even more than the truth. So we created a contest — Life's Little Mysteries. This time we asked for questions, not answers. And we grandly promised to provide "creative" solutions to mysteries that had always puzzled listeners. Mysteries like: Why can't you tickle yourself? What do you call the tips of shoelaces? Why do mattresses have those little tags on them that say DO NOT REMOVE UNDER PENALTY OF LAW? NPR's senior editor Robert "The Wag" Siegel could sit down at a typewriter and bat out totally believable, 100 percent false answers to such questions in a matter of minutes.

Why Do Mattresses Have Those Little Tags on Them That Say
DO NOT REMOVE UNDER PENALTY OF LAW?

by Robert Siegel

It goes back to one of the most interesting cases in all of American furniture law, a case cited in any discussion of mattresses in the courts. In the summer of 1927, the city of Pittsfield, Massachusetts, was the scene of a bizarre kidnapping. A nineteen-year-old boy named Godfrey McMee was found buried under eight feet of earth inside a large cardboard box, a box that had contained a mattress. The youth was still alive but so stunned that he was unable to provide any information about his abductor. The only clue was a number on the mattress box. Number XL3M897506. If the actual mattress could be found, it might be the best clue to uncovering Godfrey McMee's kidnappers, and perhaps those guilty of an entire string of cardboard-box crimes farther west.

In one of the first applications of the so-called Lindbergh Law, named after the Lindbergh kidnapping, the FBI claimed jurisdiction. A national order proclaimed that no mattress tag could be removed, and any mattress could be inspected upon request by federal agents. When the American Civil Liberties Union protested, the U.S. Circuit Court in Boston settled the case with an unusual compromise. The court ruled that a man's mattress is his castle. As such, it is covered by the search and seizure provisions.

Federal agents cannot walk into your home and inspect your mattress. But people can be enjoined from removing what may be criminal evidence from their homes, even if that evidence is not available to the police without a warrant.

So, since the ruling of July 1928, the removal of the tag from a mattress has meant the destruction of potential evidence in a criminal case. Applications of the law have varied over the years and, in some jurisdictions, no longer apply. Mattresses do remain subject to inspection in cases involving condominium conversion.

Who Invented Dry Cleaning?

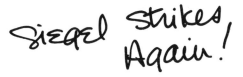

The birthplace of dry cleaning is Frankfurt, Germany. That's where, in December of 1889, Ludwig Drei was born. The itinerant saxophone tuner who lent his name to the most common method of cleansing fabric has all but vanished from recorded history, like a grease spot in carbon tetrachloride. But in the twilight of imperial Germany, the name of Ludwig Drei was as much a household word as *Weltanschaung* or *Anschluss*.

To understand Drei's achievement, you have first to appreciate the state of the cleansing art before March 1912. In those days a soiled coat was routinely stuffed and made into a wing chair. Dirty sweaters were unraveled and used for fishing lines. Ludwig Drei saw the waste in the old system, and he invented a new one, using materials that had been around for decades. In the front of his shop he placed a large picture window. Inside the window, a tailor behind a sewing machine. Behind the tailor he designed a special counter with tickets that could be torn in half. Each half bore the same number, with one piece going to the

customer, the other kept by Drei. Behind the counter were hundreds of hangers and a vast supply of plastic bags.

The use of picture windows, perforated receipts, and plastic bags to clean clothes revolutionized the industry. It's all told in Ludwig Drei's memoirs, *My Life: I'll Have It for You Tomorrow.*

During the hysteria of World War I, Ludwig Drei's American imitators changed the spelling of his name from the German D-r-e-i to the English D-r-y, giving rise to much confusion and to the spurious notion that clothes can be cleaned dry, meaning without water. That, as everybody knows, is preposterous.

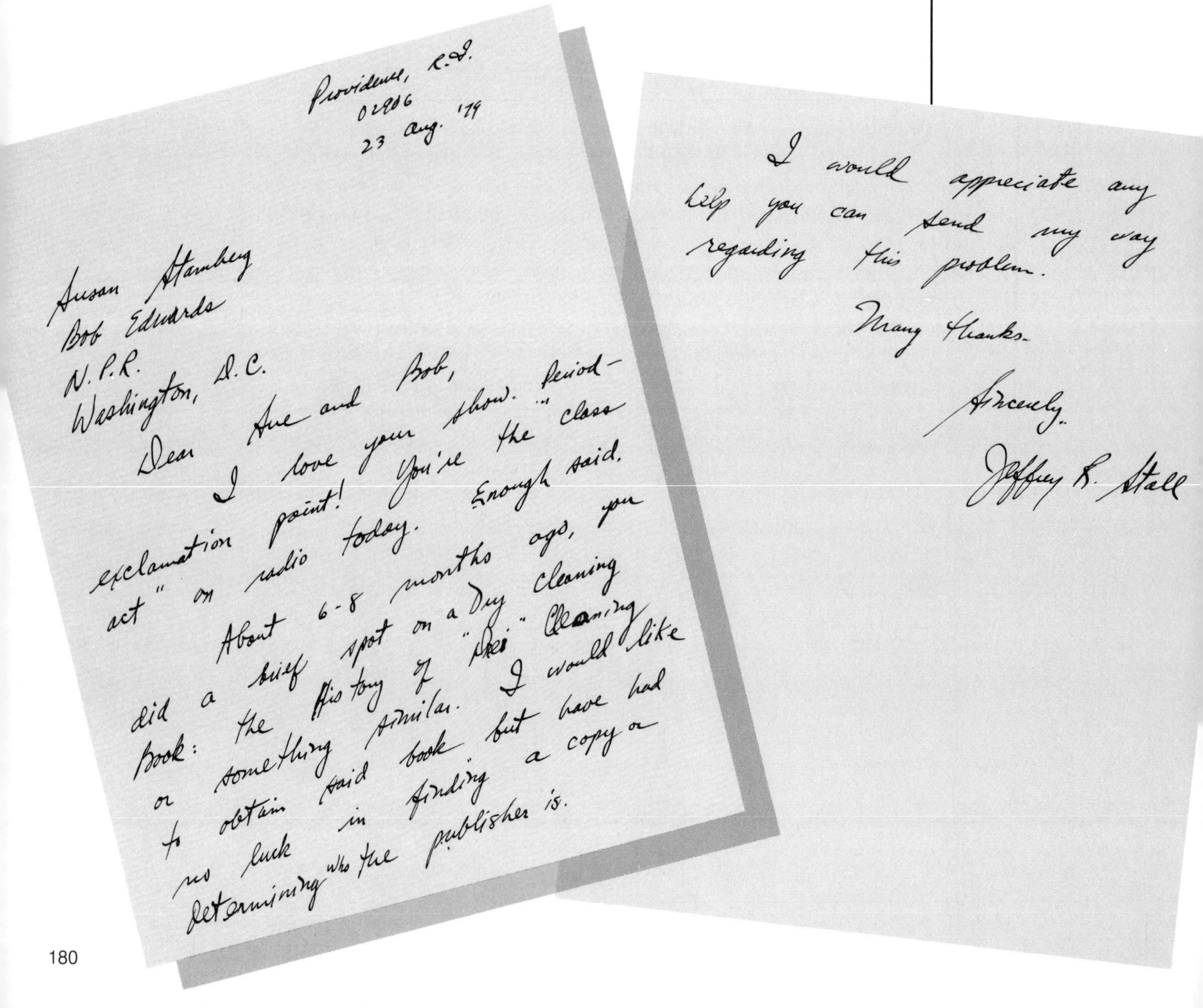

Providence, R.I.
02906
23 Aug. '79

Susan Stamberg
Bob Edwards
N.P.R.
Washington, D.C.

Dear Sue and Bob,

I love your show. Period — exclamation point! You're the "class act" on radio today. Enough said.

About 6-8 months ago, you did a brief spot on a Dry Cleaning Book: the History of "Drei" Cleaning or something similar. I would like to obtain said book but have had no luck in finding a copy or determining who the publisher is.

I would appreciate any help you can send my way regarding this problem.

Many thanks.

Sincerely,

Jeffrey R. Stall

Bob Edwards
All Things Considered
N.P.R.
Wash. D.C.

Dear Bob,

Thanks for your note of 8/30 explaining why I have had no luck in finding The History of Dry Cleaning. Its rare that I get spoofed so badly, however in retrospect, the whole bit does seem to be too ridiculous to be true and thus fun has been had by all.

However you might point out to Robert Siegel that there probably is a need for a true history of the Dry Cleaning Industry and that when he is done with satire, he might find that some non-fiction, truly historical writing on this subject is as funny as is his satire on this subject, and you never know - it may sell too!; all things considered ....!

Thanks for your card.
Keep 'em laughin'-

Jeff Hall

WHAT'S WRONG WITH THE MARYLAND STATE SONG?

Plenty, in the ears of some Marylanders. The song consists of the poem "Maryland! My Maryland!" set to the music of "O, Tannenbaum, O, Tannenbaum." The poem was written in 1861 as a call to Marylanders to join the Confederacy. Maryland reluctantly stayed in the Union, but the state held on to the song and made it the official state anthem in 1939. In 1980, state legislators debated a plan to get rid of the song. The problem occurs in some of the later stanzas, which advocate the overthrow of the government, refer to Abraham Lincoln as a despot, and call Yankees "Northern scum." Read for yourself.

3. Thou wilt not cower in the dust,
      Maryland!
   Thy beaming sword shall never rust,
      Maryland!
   Remember Carroll's sacred trust,
   Remember Howard's warlike thrust,
   And all thy slumberers with the just,
      Maryland! My Maryland!

4. Come! 'tis the red dawn of the day,
      Maryland!
   Come with thy panoplied array,
      Maryland!
   With Ringgold's spirit for the fray,
   With Watson's blood at Monterey,
   With fearless Lowe and dashing May,
      Maryland! My Maryland!

5. Dear Mother! burst thy tyrant's chain,
      Maryland!
   Virginia should not call in vain,
      Maryland!
   She meets her sisters on the plain,
   "Sic semper," 'tis the proud refrain
   That baffles minions back amain,
      Maryland!
   Arise in majesty again,
      Maryland! My Maryland!

6. Come! for thy shield is bright and strong,
      Maryland!
   Come! for thy dalliance does thee wrong,
      Maryland!
   Come to thine own heroic throng,
   That stalks with liberty along,
   And give a new KEY to thy song,
      Maryland! My Maryland!

7. I see the blush upon thy cheek,
      Maryland!
   But thou wast ever bravely meek,
      Maryland!
   But lo! there surges forth a shriek
   From hill to hill, from creek to creek
   Potomac calls to Chesapeake,
      Maryland! My Maryland!

8. Thou wilt not yield the Vandal toll,
      Maryland!
   Thou wilt not crook to his control,
      Maryland!
   Better the fire upon thee roll,
   Better the shot, the blade, the bowl,
   Than crucifixion of the soul,
      Maryland, My Maryland!

9. I hear the distant thunder-hum,
      Maryland!
   The Old Line's bugle, fife and drum,
      Maryland!
   She is not dead, nor deaf, nor dumb—
   Huzza! she spurns the Northern scum!
   She breathes—she burns! she'll come! she'll come!
      Maryland! My Maryland!

Always willing to help out a state, *All Things Considered* offered a solution to Maryland's problem. Musician Larry Massett composed new verses for the state song. Verses that would offend absolutely no one.

1

We've got some hills, we've got some trees.
We sing in four-part harmonies.
There's shopping malls and city halls
And cats and dogs and ponds with frogs.

But none of us has ever meant
To overthrow the government.
From Baltimore to Hagerstown,
Just take your car and drive around.

2

We touch four states and several bays,
The highways mostly run two ways.
We hope you come and say hello
And maybe stop and spend some dough.

We're near the nation's capital
But we are not stuck up at all.
So take a stand and shake the hand
Of every crab in Maryland.

3

I had a dog whose name was Jack.
I threw a stick, he brought it back.
My sister had a cat, I think.
My mother had a kitchen sink.

My father was a decent man
And we all lived in Maryland.
O Maryland!   O Maryland!
O Maryland!   OMaryland!

4

Our nights are dark, our days are fair,
We're right next door to Delaware.
Our song before was full of gore,
But then the Union won the war.

We're sorry if we made you mad.
It was the only song we had.
O Maryland!   O Maryland!
O Maryland!   O Maryland!

Well, it remained the only song they had. The Maryland senate decided to keep it official. Still, Larry Massett's lyrics live on in the hearts of many a Maryland crab.

Bruce Marsden, arriving home in Oakland, California.

FINDING OUT RADIO SECRETS

Question: What do Noah Adams, Jonathan Baer, Bill Barber, Wendy Blair, Mary Beth Bowen, Gary Covino, Lorne Cress, John Dimsdale, Todd Easton, Neenah Ellis, Rich Firestone, Ira Flatow, Liane Hansen, Richard Harris, Carol Kadushin, JoAnn Kawell, Paulette Kernis, Dave Lerner, John Morello, Kris Mortenson, Joe Oleksiewicz, Cathy Primus, Barbara Reinhardt, Betty Rogers, Jeff Rosenberg, Paula Schiller, Art Silverman, Lynn Smiles, Al Smith, Susan Stamberg, John Weber, Dee Clarke Welles, Linda Wertheimer, and Bob Wisdom have in common?

Answer: Each of them, at one time or another, has been a tape editor on *All Things Considered*. Young (well, some of us were, when we started), with premature circles under their eyes, editors prepare each day's tapes for broadcast. The work is demanding, often thankless, and takes a strong temperament. One fellow who was a substitute tape editor for just two days said the job was like experiments designed to drive laboratory rats insane. Nothing happens for hours, then comes an impossible crunch, and the editors scurry to cut the tapes.

In November 1979, our senior tape editor moved on to another job at NPR. The essay I wrote and broadcast on his departure described the task of editing *All Things Considered*.

> **Stamberg**   We have a farewell to say tonight, to a young man who's been with *All Things Considered* for the past six years. Jonathan Baer — our Smokey — is leaving Washington to join NPR's Chicago bureau. This program will sound different because he's leaving, and, in the course of explaining why it will sound different, we'll explain something about ourselves and the way we operate.
>
> Jon Baer edits audio tape. He has a fancier title — assistant producer. The title both obfuscates and illuminates his contribution to *All Things Considered*. Jon Baer edits tape the way no one else here can edit it. All the other tape cutters agree: Smokey is our Picasso, our Casals. He edits tape more quickly, more slyly, more lyrically, more skillfully than anyone on the staff. He's the "dean of the razor blade."
>
> That's his basic tool. The blade. Plus a grease pencil and a roll of sticky white tape. His real tool, of course, is his steady knowledge of how radio should sound.
>
> Here's an example. One day we received a tape of an interview with singer Bo Diddley. Every now and then, in the middle of the taped conversation, Bo Diddley would break into song. Smokey liked the tape but thought he could enhance it by adding some band accompaniment from one of Bo Diddley's records. Sounds simple: Get the record and sneak it in under the taped interview. But it wasn't that simple. Smokey discovered that Bo

Diddley was singing *faster* on the tape than he sang on the record, and when he first tried to mix the two sounds together they didn't fit:

On the tape, Bo Diddley sang: dun-duh-duh-DUN-duh-duh-dun-duh-dun.

On the record, Bo Diddley sang: dun . . . duh . . . duh-DUN-duh-duh-dun-duh-dun.

To make them fit, Smokey decided to slow down the rhythm of the taped Bo Diddley. Meticulously, surgically, he slipped silences in between Bo Diddley's syllables—as many short silences as he needed to make the tape mesh with the record. Here's Bo Diddley on tape:

I wrote me a tune that has the same feel, that I could do my lyrics to. Chuka-chuka-chuka-chuka-HAMBONE-chuka-chuka-chuka-chuka, you know, something like this (begins singing): *Dun . . . duh . . . duh-DUN-duh-duh-dun-duh-dun.* (Record sneaks in.) *Dun . . . duh . . . duh-DUN-duh-duh-dun-duh-dun.* (Record up full to end of song.)

By adding silence, Smokey retained what was there to begin with, but made it better . . . something exciting to hear.

Our tape editors improve on life.

Everything you hear on *All Things Considered* passes through their editing machines. The cutting ratio is about five to one. Of a fifteen-minute recorded interview, three minutes may get on the air. They're the best three—focused, with a beginning, middle, and end spliced into place by that razor blade and sticky tape.

Some of the editing is easy—snip out the *ums* and *ahs* and *unh-h-hs* and the sloppy thinking in the question or answer. It's like getting rid of all the capital letters in this sentence:

OH, GEE, UH-H-H-H-H-H we ER-R-R-R AH-H-H-H-H robbed the OH, I REALLY SHOULD . . . bank . . . IT'S JUST ON THE TIP OF MY TONGUE, I'LL THINK on . . . OF IT IN A . . . Friday!

But most of the editing is hard: You have to find the right order, re-arrange sentences, words, even syllables, without destroying the original intention of the speakers or distorting their meaning.

Tape editors are the nets over which we fly. They save us from mistakes. Like this one:

Tagory wanted the goat to stay inside the hotel with him. He wanted to drink the goat's milk. But that was a bit much, even for

the imperturbable Swedes, and officials of the Nobel committee were summoned to deal with this problem. They offered to keep Tagory's goat outside the hotel, along with some nice Swedish goats. Tagory said no. The goat stayed.

When that tape came in, someone realized the reporter was pronouncing the name wrong. The Indian poet is Rabindranath Tagor*e* (silent "e"). The reporter said Tagor*y*. What to do? We were pushing our five-o'clock deadline. There was no way to get the reporter to file the story again. Smokey wielded his razor blade and excised the offending *y* sound—cutting out a piece of tape the size of a hangnail. If too much tape was removed, he'd end up with Tag—— or Tago——. If not enough tape was cut, you'd hear an annoying, abrupt glitch (and any edit you can hear is a bad edit). Smokey removed just the right amount of tape:

Tagore wanted the goat to stay inside the hotel with him. . . .

Tape editors know more about us than our spouses do. They know all our wrinkles, the places where we're flabby or unattractive or bad-tempered or downright wrong—and they make us sound right.

Day after day, deadline after deadline, under tremendous pressure, Smokey never let us down. When a tape arrived ten minutes before air time and was scheduled to run ten minutes after we went on the air, there was never any question about what to do. Give it to Smokey. The tape was broadcast on time, even if Smokey had to throw the reel across the control room to get it to the tape machine. We've lost track of how many times he's had to do that. We always knew it was happening, but *you* never knew it.

And that's the main thing about Smokey and his editing colleagues. When they do their best work, you can never hear it. You don't hear the edits or the re-arrangements or the pressure or the impossible problems solved. What you hear is a smooth radio broadcast.

As dean of our tape editors, Smokey Baer has trained (and been a model to) all the rest of us. The training has stuck, so that we are also able to make the sound seem flawless. But never quite the way Smokey would do it. Which is why this program will sound different after he leaves today. It will sound different to you, if you listen very closely . . . and, especially, it will sound different to us, his fellow workers and greatest fans.

As of this writing, Smokey loves Chicago, and we in Washington still miss him.

HOW TO MAKE THINGS WORK

A Commentary by Gordon Baxter

First engineer Gaffey had a madman's look. In dungarees and black watch cap, his white singlet shirt soaked to his gaunt frame in the engine room's heat, he stood there, foot braced on the oil-slippery steel floor as he bashed at the feedwater pump with a long pipe wrench. I was seventeen years old and this was my first trip on a tanker, and I wasn't sure if I was seeing a madman or whether this was just part of how you run a steam engine. Well, he drew back again, mightily full-armed, like Babe Ruth at bat, and swung that Stillson wrench at the cast-iron body of that feedwater pump. *Kabam-m-m!* I watched from a respectful distance. The duplex reciprocating pump jerked fitfully; its pistons convulsed and stopped again. *Kabam-m-m!* There didn't seem to be any anger between him and the cast-iron steam pump. The two of them seemed to be at work on some kind of understanding. *Kabam-m-m!!!!!* He hit it again. Pouring a rhythm of flowing sea curses over this piece of ancient machinery. And suddenly the pump found itself, and it began to pump in its orderly two-legged stride, and Gaffey turned and, after that long wrench, not a word; but the satisfied gleam in those socketed eyes said, "See?"

That was my first experience in the unwritten scientific procedure that I called Justifiable Equipment Slapping. I've used this technique ever since, and I've sometimes observed other craftsmen and mechanics do so, too. But because the blow looks so much like temper or despair, few people are willing to talk about it. The secret to Justifiable Equipment Slapping is, of course, that it must never be done in anger. In my later years, after a transition into aviation, I observed professional airline pilots using a refined variation of this same physical contact—mental domination over their instrument panel. A vital instrument goes astray at a critical moment in flight. And the old captain leans forward with a fixed stare and taps the offending gauge with a very stiff index finger. The needle nearly always swings right back to where it belongs.

I was pretty sure that the advanced technology of solid-circuitry jet aircraft would be just about the limits of Justifiable Equipment Slapping, until my wife got involved with computers at her office. Now, you know that computers can think back, and talk back, and do so in a very insulting manner. And you know computers have no simple plumbing. Their brains and organs are made up of mysterious silicone chips with inner circuitry too fine for the human eye to see. Therefore, I was really surprised when Diane came home from work one evening with this story. The computer was speaking gibberish again. Nothing would help. She called the data-bank home office and got the expert on the phone. After a fruitless "try this, try that" conference over the long distance phone, the chief technician told her to lift that computer keyboard about two inches up off the desk, perfectly level, then drop it. And you know, that thing cleared up right away?

It's encouraging for me to report to you that Justifiable Equipment Slapping, which I think actually began with men and mules, has survived the age of steam, internal combustion, and transistors, and is still useful in the computer age. Although the technique has never been formally acknowledged or printed in any operational manual, I would like to pass it along to you here as legitimate human folklore.

Commentator Gordon Baxter, who contributed this piece of timely folklore to *ATC* in April 1980, tells stories with happy endings. He's a broadcaster and freelance writer whose books include *Village Creek* and *Bax Seat: Log of a Pasture Pilot.* Baxter lives in a cabin he built on Village Creek in Silsbee, Texas.

Love Makes Things Work
Some people think I'm queer when I leave at night and say, "Good night, little typewriters." But I feel very kindly disposed toward them. My whole life is made up of living with typewriters. It's the only thing I know and the only thing I love. I have an affection for them that you may not be able to fathom.
—Martin Tytell, typewriter expert, New York City

Jody Rickard, Patti Kato, and Marge Catterson listen while running proof machines at the First National Bank of Oregon. in Eugene.

189

FINDING ANTARCTICA: A REPORTER'S NOTEBOOK

Over the years, science correspondent Ira Flatow has had me slosh my arm around in a fish tank filled with oil and water, to demonstrate that they don't mix. He's taken me into a dark closet to see whether Wint-o-Green Life Savers really do make sparks when you chew them. (They do. Just for fun we ended the program in the closet and had to read the closing credits by match light. It was one of the most popular items ever broadcast on *All Things Considered.* Sales of Wint-o-Green Life Savers must have tripled that night.) But the day he posted a guard outside the Ladies Room so we could go inside and record the toilet flushing was a high-water mark in Ira's scientific reportage.

> **Flatow** And you'll notice, Susan—here, move over this way so you can really see it—when I flush the toilet, the water goes down clockwise.
>
> **Stamberg** Are you sure Walter Cronkite started this way?
>
> **Flatow** But in Antarctica the water flushes counterclockwise. At least, that's what I hear. I'll let you know when I get back.

This was part of his meticulous preparation for a trip he was about to take to a place most of us aren't sure how to pronounce. Here are his travel notes.

Ant - ärk′ - tə - kə

by Ira Flatow

The South Pole was always at the top of my list of places in the world I thought I'd never visit. I've had to revise the list.

For two weeks in November 1979, I was one of a small group of reporters who took part in an expedition to the bottom of the Earth—the continent of Antarctica. We flew to the South Pole from McMurdo Station, the main American base in Antarctica. As we take off, a voice greets us over the plane's scratchy public-address system:

> Welcome aboard the Antarctic Queen Six over the South Pole. Flight time will be about three hours.

The Hercules LC-130 four-engine turbo prop is uniquely equipped for the mission: a pair of skis juts out underneath the tires to handle the runways made of ice. My stomach knots as I record last-minute instructions coming over the public-address system.

> If an emergency occurs while we are in flight, when we get into a ditching situation you will be notified by three short rings. At this time, remove all sharp objects from your pockets. Remove your eyeglasses. Put everything underneath the seats. I will direct you to the exits.

These are not the first sobering words we've heard today. Earlier, at five in the morning, I was awakened by Jack Reinirie, public-information officer for the National Science Foundation, a veteran of more than a dozen trips to Antarctica.

Think about taking a toothbrush. We are planning to stay only for the day but the weather may suddenly turn bad. One military officer who came for the day stayed for ten. The main thing you have to worry about is if the airplane goes down some place and it takes a while for them to get in to us; so pack extra warm clothing. It's not that you'll need it at the Pole but, if the airplane goes down, you'll be awful happy you have extra stuff with you.

I packed two hats (one wool, one with a beak and earflaps), three pairs of gloves, two pairs of mittens, one pair of longjohns, T-shirts, heavy woolen shirts, an insulated vest, two pairs of woolen knee socks, two pairs of thermal booties, mukluks, woolen pants, insulated pants, giant gloves that run up the elbows, and sunglasses.

Military airplanes have none of the "frills" of commercial liners: no sound-proofing, padded seating, toilets, or hot food. Even though the plane is "heated," my pocket thermometer reads five degrees below zero at floor level. It's a three-and-a-half-hour flight. Just before landing, the captain gives final instructions:

> The aircraft will stop immediately in front of the station. We will not be shutting down the engines. We don't want them to freeze. You will be de-planing through the forward door, so we request that you use extreme caution until you get clear of the aircraft. Please make a right turn out the door and stay away from the propellers. We hope this has been an enjoyable flight, and we also hope that you'll have a nice stay at Pole Station. Thank you.

I jot down notes of what I will say in the first "stand up" I plan to tape as soon as I'm outside the plane. My tape recorder has been carefully prepared for cold weather. I've had its battery pack specially designed so I can keep the batteries warm inside my shirt pocket. A cable runs from the pocket to the outside of my parka and into the cassette recorder.

Finally, with a blast of cold air, the door opens, the engines roar a greeting, and we climb out. I wander a few feet, trying to untangle my cable, and juggle my duffel bag, tape recorder, pencil (a pen would freeze), sunglasses, and parka. Needing an extra hand, I shove my reporter's notebook into my mouth. Bad move. The metal rings freeze instantly to my lips, and for a fleeting moment I fear the notebook will never come off. With a strong yank, away it comes, skin and all.

No time to worry. Must record my "stand up" before I freeze to death. Oops. Never mind fooling with my notebook. Have to ad-lib.

(Plane noises in background)

Flatow   Well, as we get off the plane, the temperature is minus forty-six degrees Fahrenheit, and the sky is clear . . . blue . . . sunny. *(Gasp.)* As we walk toward the sign that says WELCOME TO THE SOUTH POLE, I can already feel my mustache freezing over. The base itself is made of a big silver geodesic dome with silvery tube-like huts branching from two ends. Flags of the Antarctic treaty nations flutter outside. *(Walking sounds.)* If I *(gasp)* sound out of breath, that's because I am!

Back inside, Steven Glenn, medical doctor at the Pole, checks us for altitude sickness. The South Pole Station sits on a sheet of flat ice nearly two miles thick. You have the illusion that you are at sea level. In fact, you're above some of the highest mountains on the continent. (So *that's* why I was so out of breath!) Glen tells us how to check for frostbite and has one further bit of advice: Never go outside alone.

Geologist Bruce Gaylord, a seasoned Antarctic explorer, accompanies me on my first stroll at the Pole. It's as exciting as walking on the moon. I tape our conversation.

> **Flatow** This is absolutely amazing out here. As far as the eye can see, there's nothing but blue sky and white snow. *(Crunching of snow underfoot.)* And the sun just hangs overhead.
>
> **Gaylord** It just circles around over the top of you. You don't know what time of the day it is. You lose track of it. You become an insomniac.
>
> **Flatow** It doesn't set in the west; it doesn't rise in the east.
>
> **Gaylord** No. It just circles right overhead, gradually getting higher and higher, until December 21, when she'll start her decline again.
>
> **Flatow** And it's so clear out here. Absolutely crystal clear. And the horizon is deceptive since there is nothing to compare it to, no buildings on the horizon. . . . I can see how you would think you were falling off the earth.

I feel like a child at the circus, trying to see everything and experience it all. I begin to take off my gloves to adjust my parka and hood, but Gaylord advises against exposing my skin.

> **Gaylord** If you've got any moisture on your hands they're going to stick to your metal zipper. People learn bitter lessons here: Don't put nails in your mouth if you're a carpenter; don't drink a can of soda, it will freeze to your lips. That happened to one of the guys last year.

Our afternoon is filled with interviews and briefings about some of the scientific work being carried out at the Pole: monitoring air pollution coming from the other side of the world; studying the sun's activity during the twenty-four-hour Antarctic summer daylight. Veterans tell us what it's like to live at the Pole in the winter, when the sun sets for six months, temperatures drop to a hundred degrees below zero, and the only link with the outside world is by shortwave radio.

How to Keep Your Car Locks Unfrozen Squirt windshield de-icer into the locks. Use a match or a cigarette lighter to heat up your key.
—Richard Hiebert, American Automobile Association

Another Way to Keep Your Car Locks Unfrozen Try preventive medicine. To keep moisture and cold out, put a piece of masking tape or electrical tape on the door lock.
—Richard Hiebert, American Automobile Association

Otto Knauth of the *Des Moines Register* ventures outside with me again for a picture-taking session. By now the wind has whipped up and the horizon is beginning to disappear under a veil of blowing snow. It doesn't snow on the Pole. It just blows. Visibility is getting worse. Otto and I finish taking pictures of one another's ice-covered faces. I decide to tape one more "stand up" outside. As I record the crunching of snow beneath my feet, I tell myself it would be a sin to leave the South Pole without walking over to the bamboo stick planted in the ice that marks the site of the true, geographic South Pole.

Making sure Otto has me in sight, I turn my back on him for the last recording I will make at the bottom of the Earth.

(Crunching snow)

Flatow   What people come to the Pole to see, of course, is really *the* South Pole. What does it look like? Does it look like the barbershop pole we *(out of breath)* think of? Everyone wants to go to the exact location of the Pole *(heavy breathing)*. Well, the exact location is out here *(gasp)*, a long . . . walk from the hut, a few hundred . . . yards. Unless you know where to look, you could be misled *(gasp)*. There are no fancy markings on it, no gimmicks, nothing to give it away as *the* South Pole. Just a twenty-foot wooden stick with green . . . and red flags at the top. *(Crunch.)* In fact, there are markings around the bottom of it and you could walk 360 degrees, like this, walk . . . around in a circle and claim that just by circling the Pole, you have . . . walked

Rose Schuyler listens in Rego Park, New York.

Now Richard Hiebert Tells How Not to Unfreeze Your Car Locks, and I Ask Two Foolish Questions

"Pouring hot water on the lock is a bad idea. If it doesn't work right away, the water can freeze."

"How about a hair dryer running out of the house on a long extension cord?"

"Sure."

"Heavy breathing?"

"Heavy breathing will do it."

totally around the world. *(Heavy breathing.)* This is Ira Flatow, at the South Pole.

It takes three attempts to record the walk around the world successfully. The weather is deteriorating quickly, and my hands are now very cold, almost numb. Otto, who watches the entire production, tells me it's not so bad out. Sometimes it gets this cold in Minnesota. That warms my heart, but little else. The walk back to the dome seems frighteningly long. Exhausted, we climb back aboard the plane for the flight to McMurdo. Our day at the South Pole has ended.

Ira spent eight more days in Antarctica, visiting penguins, taking a shower (water is rationed, and only one shower permitted every seven days). He went ice fishing, became the first person since Admiral Richard Byrd to file a shortwave news report to the United States, and got lessons in Antarctic geography.

And in his capacity as NPR science correspondent, Ira Flatow performed the much heralded "on site toilet experiment." Very disappointing. He discovered that water flushes clockwise in Antarctica, just as it does in Washington.

SEVEN THINGS WE FOUND OUT

Why Are the Letters on Typewriter Keyboards Arranged So Oddly?

The basic format of nearly every typewriter keyboard was developed in 1873. It's called the Universal Typewriter Keyboard or, QWERTYUIOP. QWERTYUIOP is the word spelled out by the top row of letters. The QWERTYUIOP keyboard was designed to be inefficient. The creators of the first Remington figured typing too quickly would jam their machine. So they intentionally made speedy typing difficult.

> —Martin Tytell, typewriter expert
> New York City

What Good Is Fidgeting?

Very good. Fidgeting makes you smarter. It increases the circulation of blood to your brain. People taking tests get better scores if they fidget. If you express tension in motion, it helps you to deal better with the tension. The best kind of chair to sit in for fidgeting is a big, flat chair. Bucket or contour seats restrict movement.

> —Laurence Morehouse, psychologist
> UCLA

What's the Secret to Quitting Smoking?

The main problem, when you try to quit smoking, is to break down all those conditioned reflexes, like lighting a match or a cigarette lighter. I quit by analyzing what was happening to me when I got a strong urge to smoke, and then satisfying part of the urge without actually smoking. Take something out of your pocket—a pen, even a cigarette—put it in your mouth, and then proceed *not* to light it. Go ahead and obey all of the impulses without actually smoking. By obeying some of the habits, you eliminate at least some of the discomfort of quitting.

> —Jim Cook
> Nashville, Tennessee

How Do You Get a First-Class Meal on a Plane?

Call the airline ahead of time and order a low-sodium diet meal. They're much better than the regular meals. You get filet mignon instead of an unidentifiable gray mass hidden under gravy. You get fresh fruit instead of the usual soggy cake.

> —David Klein, consumer commentator

Which Side of Your Face Cries?

Researchers at the University of Pennsylvania took photographs of six people, and made twelve composites of left faces and right faces. The left side shows much more emotion. Happiness, surprise, anger, fear, disgust, and sadness all show up more intensely on the left side of the face. The hemispheres of the brain create the differences. People tend to look at the right side of faces, which is the wrong side for perceiving intense emotions.

— Ira Flatow
NPR science correspondent

What Makes People Happy?

It's not money, and it's not sex. People are happy when they think they are achieving what they should be achieving in life. Married people are happier than non-married people. Happiest of all are the young married people without children. Young married people *with* children tend to be less happy, because they have more financial problems.

— Phillip Shaver, psychologist

How Do You Prepare to Quit a Job You Hate?

Live off half your income for five years. Put the rest in savings. With the savings, buy a sailboat and go to the Caribbean.

— David Molpus, NPR correspondent
Reporting on a job-quitting class

SO YOU WANT TO RUN A RESTAURANT?

Ever fantasized about how marvelous it would be to own a restaurant? Ralph and Carole Cavalier acted out that fantasy. They had no experience in the restaurant business—Ralph is a doctor, Carole a housewife and mother. But for a long time, Ralph had toyed with the idea of running a little restaurant and bar in their hometown, Atlantic City, New Jersey:

Ralph It was always in the back of my mind, *Gee, wouldn't it be nice. . . .*

Carole I thought he was crazy.

After months of planning, the Cavaliers were ready to open their restaurant in June 1980. NPR's Robert Krulwich spent the week before opening day telling their story. He called the series, for reasons that will become increasingly obscure, "Twenty-One Things You Should Know About Opening Your Own Restaurant."

Krulwich **Tip Number One** *Get oriented.* Start with a simple little project that doesn't cost a lot of money. Like choosing a name.

Ralph Hellzapoppin?

Carole Too funky.

Ralph Giggles?

Carole Too cute.

Ralph Happy Place?

Carole Too trite.

Krulwich The Cavaliers finally decided to use their street address for the name: 12 South. Carole liked the way it looked in script.
Tip Number Two *Do not spend big money without professional advice.* The Cavaliers got professional advice from a restaurant designer named John Maurer. The restaurant designer felt they were too inexperienced and had romantic, rather than solid, reasons for wanting to get into the restaurant business.

Maurer My advice to them was to stay away from it.

Derek Mansell and his goat, Star, listen in Andover, New Hampshire.

Krulwich	**Tip Number Three** *Do not follow all advice.* Do not be embarrassed if your real reasons for wanting to open a restaurant are basically romantic.
Ralph	I remember a 1940s movie with Dick Powell—or Cary Grant—in a restaurant, and it had some sort of a lounge. I guess I always pictured myself sitting in the corner.
Krulwich	**Tip Number Four** *Ask not what you love to cook. Ask instead what your customers want to eat.* The Cavaliers wanted to attract locals to 12 South—the people who work at the big Atlantic City casinos. To find out how much these people were willing to spend for a meal, they brought in Howard Gevertz, a restaurant consultant from New York.
Gevertz	We knew what the dealers were being paid; we knew what they made in tips; we knew what the pit bosses were getting. So we developed a price range that would average out to an $8 check. That's what the local people will pay.

But what do they like to eat? We checked out menus of local restaurants. Based on that survey, we designed a menu that featured ribs, combination salads, and hamburgers. Every item fell within the $8 price range. The plain hamburger, for instance, would cost $3.25.

Krulwich	**Tip Number Five** *Know thy expenses.* Account for every item, every ingredient you serve. In a hamburger, you need to know how much the patty will cost, how much the roll will cost, the lettuce, the pickle. . . . From that you determine the percentage cost that you will charge your customer. Typically, the cost of food and labor is about 70 percent of the average menu price. So if you sit down to a $10 steak, it should have cost the restaurant about $7 to buy it, cook it, and serve it. With the extra $3 the restaurant pays its rent, its electricity bill, and makes its profits. With beverages, basic costs are lower, mark-ups higher. That's why restaurants always love you to drink it up.

Tip Number Six *Menus suggest moods.* If the menu is written in French, you know you're in a formal restaurant and you should sit up straight. If the menu has silly expressions like "m-m-m-m what a treat!!!" or "your tummy will thank you for this one!!!" you know you can relax and slump a little. The menu at 12 South says, "Our ribs will tickle yours."

Carole	That was Ralph's. Mine was "our burgers—naked or with coverups." That was my entrepreneurial contribution.
Krulwich	**Tip Number Seven** *Design the restaurant for your customers.* The Cavaliers' designer, John Maurer (he went to work for them, even though he'd advised them to stay away from the restaurant

Some of Carole's

Ralph's

12 SOUTH'S ANYTIME DELIGHTS
MIX AND MATCH & PICK AND CHOOSE

CREATION
In the beginning...

A Bowl of Fresh Soup: Homemade, hot and tasty, ask what we have today $

Broiled Grapefruit Half: With two brandies and brown sugar—Unique! $

EMBELLISHMENTS

Vegetable Tempura: Fresh vegetables, dipped in our own seasoned tempura batter and lightly fried. You select mushrooms, egg-plant, zucchini, broccoli, peppers, cauliflower or carrots—any vegetable each $ Any three vegetables $

Golden Brown French Fried Potatoes $

Crisp Onion Strings: Thin, crispy and a 12 South marvel $

MUNCHIES
Substantial Starters or Significant Snacks

Chili, a Bowl: Made on premises, a tangy delicious blend of beef, tomatoes, beans and spices $

Two Tacos: Meaty, cheesey, spicy and a little messy $

The Big Dippers and the Little Dips: Three dips and two dippers for you to choose from. Choose one of each:

Dips:

Spicy Avocado: Our brand of North-of-the-Border guacamole, thick with avocados, onions, tomatoes and piquant spices

Tangy Onion and Sherry: The standard old favorite, updated for adults. Nostalgia modernized.

Spinach and Garlic: It's different, it's tasty, it's worth the hint of garlic, a dynamite taste treat

Big Dippers:

Crudite Colossal: A basket full of fresh crisp vegetables—at least five kinds—prepared for dipping $

Marvelous Munchies: The same type of basket, but full of chips, bread sticks and a variety of crackers—dip to your heart's delight $

EGGCITEMENT EGGZACTLY

Our Egg dishes are made with the highest quality eggs, combined with fillings and toppings to please almost everyone. All are served with our own neat accompaniment. French fries and fresh bread.

Huevos Rancheros: Fried Eggs Tex-Mex style with chili, peppers, Monterey Jack cheese on a tortilla—Wow, it's a treat! $

Italian Pasta Frittata: Very interesting—open omelette Italian style, with pasta, tomato sauce, mushrooms, spinach and two types of cheese—Delicioso! $

Omelette Gourmet: Connoisseur's blend of mushrooms, green peppers, onions and Canadian style bacon. Discriminatingly tasteful $

Cheese Omelette: You choose Monterey Jack or Cheddar or both. We provide three eggs, butter and cooking skills to make a great omelette $

BOUNTEOUS BURGERS & SUPER SANDWICHES

One half pound of fresh ground sirloin, hand-packed the old-fashioned way for unbeatable flavor. Served with our neat accompaniment.

Naked $ **or with your choice of any one of the following cover-ups:** Monterey Jack cheese, Cheddar cheese or sauteed onions $

Chili: With extra green chili strips $

Extraordinary style: Canadian style bacon, onions, mushrooms and green peppers $

Super Sandwich #1: Roast beef, roasted on premises, fresh with our bar-b-que sauce if you want it $

Super Sandwich #2: Roast turkey, white meat, real turkey, roasted fresh, with tomato, lettuce and a great dressing $

Super Sandwich #3: 12 South's Chef's own Daily Creation: We had to leave him something to create! Please ask $

SPECIALTIES 12 SOUTH
Our own favorite items. No better anywhere—couldn't be! All served with hot, crisp French fries

Baby Back Ribs: Our ribs will tickle yours. You get a slab bar-b-qued 12 South's special way and the best bar-b-que sauce North of the Carolinas $

It takes a tough man to make a tender chicken.... Frank Perdue's own one-half chicken, bar-b-qued and bursting with flavor $

Ribs and Chicken: Can't make up your mind? Don't! $

Turkey or Roast Beef Hash: A hearty lunch or a light dinner, made with meats roasted at 12 South and onions, potatoes and seasonings, then sauteed and served with a poached egg and our own special sauce $

The Kabob Connection: Your choice, char-broiled mix or match. You get three kabobs—they each taste terrific! $

☐ **Scallop** ☐ **Shrimp** ☐ **Chicken** ☐ **Filet of Fresh Fish**

SALADS
Each the famous one-dish "Meal in a Bowl"!

Fresh Spinach Salad: Crisp chilled raw spinach, topped with hard-boiled egg slices, crumbled bacon, toasted almonds, fresh mushrooms, seasoned croutons and our house dressing $

Freshest Fruits Salad: A base of greens topped with a variety of fresh fruits and either cottage cheese or yogurt and a honey-lime dressing $

12 South's Chef's Salad: Greens, hard-boiled egg slices, two types of cheese, turkey, roast beef, ham and some of our fresh raw vegetables, everything delicious and Good For You $

Other Delights (Drinks & Desserts) On the Other Side

business), says, if you run a bar in a train or bus station where people are just ducking in and out for a quick drink, your customers are embarrassed to be seen. Therefore, you don't put any mirrors in the interior. That way people don't worry about being watched. But if you've got a singles bar, mirrors become a service to the customers.

Maurer also says people in different cities have different feelings about space. In New York City they jam the tables very tightly together. But in the same size room in Miami, you can put only two-thirds the number of seats. Miamians won't sit that close to one another.

Tip Number Eight *The height of your tables affects the mood of the room.* The standard restaurant table is twenty-nine inches high. The Cavaliers ordered tables one inch lower. Their consultant, Howard Gevertz, told them the closer you are to the floor (this is one of those restaurant rules), the more relaxed and intimate the feeling.

Gevertz Just that little inch tends to make a little bit more of a feeling of warmth, a little bit more of a social feeling. It brings people closer together.

Krulwich **Tip Number Nine** *What's true for tables is also true for table settings.* Some restaurants feature long-stemmed roses in tall vases, and napkins fancily folded into tall wine glasses. Tall is elegant. The Cavaliers wanted a relaxed atmosphere, so their napkins lie flat and the accessories are short, like their tables.

Tip Number Ten *Restaurants pay more than you'd think for tables, chairs, plates, and accessories.* They pay retail prices. And they don't buy tables. There is no such thing as a table in the restaurant business. Tops are sold separately from bottoms. Table tops run about $60 each. Bottoms cost $30; chairs average $40. On the tables:

one lamp – $12	wineglass – $1.25
ashtray – $.50	liquor glass – $1.75
sugar bowl – $5	flatware – $5.00
bread basket – $2	salt and pepper
mug – $2.25	shakers – $7
water glass – $1	

When two people sit down to dine at the Cavaliers' restaurant, they will be using $225 worth of merchandise. That's $112.50 per person.

Tip Number Eleven *In some restaurants, furniture is designed to make you uncomfortable.* John Maurer also designs fast-food

	places, where he's paid to produce uncomfortable chairs.
Maurer	You must make them small and hard. When you're working for a client in the fast-food business, they want to turn over a chair three or four times at lunch. If you give a comfortable chair to a fast-food client, she'll stay all week. You know why, in some places, chairs are cup-shaped? Because when you lean back, they stick you in the back and push you forward again. Eat that food!
Krulwich	**Tip Number Twelve** *In some restaurants, colors are designed to make you uncomfortable.* Bright lights, bright colors—red and yellow—make people nervous. Nothing is dim in a fast-food place. They want to get you in and out. In a fancy restaurant, you use gray or blue—pastel colors that encourage people to sit and eat the expensive foods and drink the expensive wines.
	Tip Number Thirteen *There's more to a napkin than meets the lap.*
Ralph	Napkins don't knock your socks off when you walk into a restaurant. I mean, there it is. As long as it is big enough to cover your lap, and as long as you can wipe your mouth and hands with it, you're satisfied.
Krulwich	But Carole disagreed. She wanted pretty, flowered napkins. They needed advice. Consultant Howard Gevertz is, among other things, a napkin authority. He outlined the options, starting with the basic variety in paper napkins (one-ply, two-ply, three-ply, four-ply), the different sizes, the different colors.
Gevertz	Do you want permanent press? There are napkins treated to make them water repellent. They stand and fold beautifully and never have a wrinkle. Unfortunately, they don't absorb anything! You need to know how many servings make up a napkin's lifetime. As it happens, the napkin's survival rate is quite discouraging. We figured each napkin would be good for about fifty uses before it disappeared, faded, or fell apart from washing. So we needed 3,600 napkins. When all the decisions were made, we figured that at 12 South your napkin would add about six cents to your bill—that's the purchase price averaged over its lifetime plus the regular laundry cost.
Krulwich	**Tip Number Fourteen** *When you hire a staff, give them entrance exams.* Put an ad in the paper and, when applicants show up, ask tough questions.
Carole	One of the questions we asked the managerial candidates was this: On Saturday evening at ten-thirty you have a restaurant full of people and your waiters and waitresses come to you and say they are quitting. How do you handle it?
	A good manager should say, "It will never happen to me,

because I'm on top of things and wouldn't let myself be surprised like that." A good manager doesn't have crises, because he plans ahead.

We also asked questions about food: What's the season for strawberries? What are the six types of apples? When they said, "Red, green, yellow . . . " we knew right off the bat they wouldn't be able to handle the food end of our business.

Krulwich **Tip Number Fifteen** *Plan to hold a full-scale dress rehearsal on Opening Night Eve.*

Carole Half of our staff will serve the other half. And then the other half will serve the first half. So not only will they get an opportunity to taste the food on the menu and criticize the service, they'll also get an opportunity to taste the drinks.

Ralph There's gonna be a lot of well-fed drunks wandering around our establishment, I'll tell you that.

Krulwich **Tip Number Sixteen** *We have no more tips.*

Tip Number Seventeen: Don't hold us to twenty-one tips just because we promised them at the beginning:

Krulwich ran out of tips, but *All Things Considered* followed up on what happened to 12 South. The day before they were supposed to open, the Cavaliers were scrambling to find a hinge. An Atlantic City building inspector had informed them their front door opened too far out onto the sidewalk. Front doors of restaurants in Atlantic City should open only one foot. The front door of 12 South opened two feet.

On opening day, a Friday, the Cavaliers were setting back their front door. I phoned to ask Carole why she didn't get a great big stone and stick it outside, so the door would only open one foot. Carole said she tried to get a great big stone, but not to stick outside. Here's what else she said:

Carole We're going to open the doors at six-thirty, and the phone has been ringing off the hook all day. I've had people calling to ask what our soup is.

Stamberg What is the soup?

Carole We have no soup today.

Stamberg I'm glad I called.

But they were not able to open at six-thirty that Friday. A final inspector never showed up. City workers are not permitted to work overtime in Atlantic City, so the newly set-back doors of 12 South remained shut until Monday morning, when the three-and-a-half-minute inspection was performed. Moments after the inspector left, 12 South officially opened for lunch.

Everything went smoothly. The only problem was that they'd polished the bar so much while they were waiting for that last inspector that the bar developed yellow waxy build-up. They had to strip it and repolish.

That first summer, 12 South exceeded the Cavaliers' expectations and served hordes of *All Things Considered* listeners as well as locals. Telegrams came in from listeners all over the country wishing them well. And letters arrived from people who planned to re-route their summer travel plans so they could see this restaurant they had learned so much about on the radio.

SIX MORE THINGS WE FOUND OUT

How Can You Stop People from Coughing at Concerts?

I called the Luden's Cough Drop Company. They sent me 28,000 cough drops. I had the cough drops passed out to the audience before the concerts. It worked.

—Joseph Leavitt, general manager
Baltimore Symphony Orchestra

What's the Secret of the Fiver?

There's a secret number in the bushes in the picture on the back side of the five-dollar bill. The picture shows the Lincoln Memorial. There's a hedge on the left side of the staircase in front of the Memorial. In the shadows of the bushes, just where the light hits them, is the number 172. At least, that's the number I see. The picture was drawn in 1927 by four government employees. I couldn't track them down in 1977. So I went right to the top. To James Conlon, then director of the Bureau of Engraving and Printing, in Washington, D.C. Conlon said that, as far as he knew, there had been no attempt to conceal numbers or a code in the bushes. People had been seeing numbers in the bushes on the five-dollar bill for years. Conlon, himself, saw the number 1392.

—Robert Krulwich, NPR reporter

What's the Difference Between a Curd and a Whey?

In the cheese-making process, the solid part of milk is separated from the liquid part. The protein coagulates into globs, which are the curds. What remains—a thin, whitish liquid—is the whey.

—Unidentified *ATC* listener

But what about a muffet & a tuffet?

Jim Conway listens in
La Crescent, Minnesota

Where Were Martinis Invented?

In Martinis, California. Martinis was a stopping place for thirsty gold miners on their way from their diggings to San Francisco. One day one of the miners couldn't come up with the twenty-five cents it took to buy a bottle of booze back then. This was in 1850. So he paid for it with a nugget of gold from his pouch. As he was leaving he said, "That's a pretty big price for a little bottle. Don't I get something extra?" The saloon keeper mixed him up a concoction of gin and white wine, threw in an olive, and handed it over. When the miner got to San Francisco, he told a bartender there about the terrific drink he'd had in Martinis. The San Francisco bartender mixed it up for him, and that was how it started.

— Jim Rich, local historian
Martinis, California

How Do You Ripen Pears?

Don't put them in plastic bags in the refrigerator. Pears will ripen beautifully unrefrigerated in a brown paper bag. But don't let them touch one another, or you'll get blemished pears. The trick is to put a ripened apple into the bag, along with the pears. The apple will speed up the pears' ripening process. After three or four days at room temperature, the brown-bagged pears will be ready to eat.

— Perla Meyers, food commentator

What Is the Meaning of Life?

The meaning of life? Well. The meaning of life as I have found it is: Try to help others the best you can; don't be selfish; just live every day the best you can. Don't look back. Be honest.

— Mal Sharpe's mother
Sarasota, Florida

Another Use For Paper Bags
A lunch box costs $4.88 with a "Battle Star Galactica" thermos and decorations. I didn't buy it. Paper bags are cheaper. The lunch box has good points. You can use it over and over again. But it will get dents. The paper bag can't get dents. It's possible, in a paper bag, for your lunch to get stepped on, of course. And with a lunch box you'd probably just break the lunch box and not the lunch itself. But in general, bags are better.
—James Tokunaga, age nine, Washington, D.C.

WHAT DO YOU KNOW AFTER ALL THESE YEARS?

In March 1979, Michael Myers, an art teacher in Kansas City, Missouri, asked people of different ages to sit down in a quiet place with a blank piece of paper and a pencil, and answer a simple question: What do you know? What, after all these years, do you know? Myers's only requirement was that they use the phrase "I know" at the beginning of every sentence. Michael Myers taped some of the answers. On *All Things Considered,* he described the project and played some of his tapes.

First woman I know that I change my mind every day.
I know I'm doing the right thing.
I know I'll always feel insecure.
I know I'll always long to be somewhere else.
I know I'm growing more and more to look like my mother.

Myers It started as a school project. I teach at the Kansas City Art Institute, and I was working with a series of college students on a kind of autobiographical art project. For me, this form is very similar to starting a picture. You don't always know where it's going. You make a few marks, and then you respond to those marks, and eventually those marks begin to become something personal, the picture takes shape out of itself.

Second woman I know the closer I get to honesty, the less room there is to breathe.
I know how to carry anybody's party card.
I know how to use a dictionary.
I know her husband is away.
I know the Bible means well.
I know that it's hard to help yourself.
I know not to eat cat.

Myers I didn't know what I was going to get. When they all came in and read their lists, I think everybody was overwhelmed with how smart everybody was.

Stamberg Did anyone choose to give you the dates for King Henry VIII?

Myers No. The only facts they wrote were personal facts, like the size of their clothes. Generally, what they wrote was much more remarkable. It struck me that if they got into the proper frame of mind when they were writing, which basically meant that they approached a piece of paper blank and then began to let one line refer to the next line, then the writing would flow in a very easy kind of way. What people were writing was like first-draft poetry.

Third woman I know I'll never write my mother regularly and
I know she'll never understand.
But I know she knows I still care.

I know I'll never find a million dollars someone must have buried for me long ago.

I know I'll always find new friends.

I know I'll never know how to handle rude customers.

But then I know I'll never know how to accept a compliment without being embarrassed.

I know wealthy people make me nervous and so do dentists, insurance salesmen, cosmetic-counter clerks, and cocktail parties.

First man   I know I don't like putting my foot into chuck holes while jogging.

I know I don't like my mother cleaning my room.

Nor do I like the fact that my entire wardrobe looks the same.

Myers   What I like about some of the lists are the jumps that people make. Sometimes the jumps occur when people find out that they are arriving at something that's a little too personal. At that point they tend to shift into a kind of abstraction, and then let the abstraction dissolve back to something personal again.

Stamberg   That's why I asked you about the dates for Henry VIII. Facts are always so manageable. You can spew them out on a moment's notice. But what you're doing is asking one of the most deeply personal questions that you can put to anyone.

Myers   It's very difficult. Some people wanted to look good, so they gave incredibly guarded answers. But it seems to be almost impossible to cover up who you are.

Second man   I know the following about the external world: Asparagus makes one's urine smell. Babe Ruth hit 714 home runs. Hank Aaron hit more. And truck stops have better parking than food.

I know that conditioning need not dictate my future behavior.

I know that conditioning dictates my behavior.

I know that my use of certain drugs has given me perceptions that I would not have reached at the time without the drugs.

Fourth woman   I know love comes in envelopes.

I know my father died in the morning.

I know there's something I want to give you.

I know my tonsils need to come out.

I know there is a pile of cardboard on the roof outside.

Young girl   I know that when you want to say hello to somebody it is very quick, but when you want to say good-bye, it takes forever.

I know that when you've taken all the hurt that you can—like when somebody just says things—after a while, you either sit down and just kind of quit, or you strike back, you yell at him, you hit him or something.

Stamberg   Professor Myers, what is your own list? What do you know? What, after all these years, do you know?

Myers   I knew you would ask me. Here it is:

I know that when I was inducted into the army I discovered that I was shorter than I thought I was.

I know that being five feet eleven and a half inches tall takes too long to say.

I know the contents of my dresser.

I know that the woman who works at the laundromat has an uncanny ability to remember names.

I know two poets who are not suicidal.

I know that in the house I used to live in I could sit undetected on the front porch, shielded by a row of blue spruce trees, and watch the neighborhood bully circle the block on his bicycle.

I know that my feet resemble my father's feet.

I know that after trips to famous places such as Pikes Peak or the Eiffel Tower the memories of those places are similar to the postcard images seen before the trip.

I know that in a prison in Glasgow, Scotland, all the windows are well above eye level and rimmed with barbed wire.

I know that it is easy to get romantic about prisoners.

I know that it is easy and effortless to fall in love with women sitting in other cars while you are waiting for the light to change.

Professor Michael Myers calls his project at the Kansas City Art Institute an "Audio Encyclopaedia of Personal Knowledge." It is an ongoing project.